THE BOOK THAT TAKES THE MYSTERY OUT OF COMPUTER PROGRAMMING— AND PUTS THE MASTERY IN

You don't have to be a magician to be master of your personal computer. You simply have to understand the problem or task that you want your computer to handle, and be able to translate your understanding into a series of instructions in a language your computer can follow.

That language is BASIC—and BEGINNING WITH BASIC is the one book that talks to you about BASIC in a language *you* can follow.

Complete with a section on how to easily convert the form of BASIC featured in this book—the Microsoft version, which ranks first in popularity around the world—to other BASICs you may encounter, BEGINNING WITH BASIC is the best beginning a new computer owner can make today.

BEGINNING WITH BASIC

KENT PORTER's background includes work for U.S. Army Intelligence, the Bell System, and the data processing section of a large bank, before he became a full-time writer and lecturer on computer-related topics. His widely acclaimed books include *Computers Made Really Simple* and *The New American Computer Dictionary* (available in a Signet edition).

BOOKS BY KENT PORTER

Computers Made Really Simple (1976)

Building Model Ships from Scratch (1977)

New American Computer Dictionary (NAL/Signet, 1983)

Mastering Sight and Sound on the Commodore® 64™
(NAL/Plume, forthcoming)

Practical Programming in Pascal (NAL/Plume, forthcoming)

Porter's Programs for the Commodore® 64™
(NAL/Signet Special, forthcoming)

Porter's Programs for the IBM® PC jr.
(NAL/Signet Special, forthcoming)

Mastering the Colecovision® Adam™
(NAL/Plume, forthcoming)

BEGINNING WITH BASIC
An Introduction to Computer Programming

by Kent Porter

A PLUME BOOK
NEW AMERICAN LIBRARY
NEW YORK AND SCARBOROUGH, ONTARIO

NAL BOOKS ARE AVAILABLE AT QUANTITY DISCOUNTS WHEN USED TO PROMOTE PRODUCTS OR SERVICES. FOR INFORMATION PLEASE WRITE TO PREMIUM MARKETING DIVISION, NEW AMERICAN LIBRARY, 1633 BROADWAY, NEW YORK, NEW YORK 10019.

SIGNET, SIGNET CLASSIC, MENTOR, PLUME, MERIDIAN AND NAL BOOKS are published *in the United States* by New American Library, 1633 Broadway, New York, New York 10019, *in Canada* by The New American Library of Canada Limited, 81 Mack Avenue, Scarborough, Ontario M1L 1M8

Library of Congress Cataloging in Publication Data

Porter, Kent.
Beginning with BASIC.

Includes index.
1. Basic (Computer program language) I. Title.
QA76.73.B3P67 1984 001.64′2 83-22030
ISBN 0-452-25491-4

First Printing, April, 1984

1 2 3 4 5 6 7 8 9

PRINTED IN THE UNITED STATES OF AMERICA

ACKNOWLEDGMENTS

Microsoft, Inc., assisted in the preparation of this book by furnishing a copy of the Microsoft BASIC-80 interpreter to the author, for which he is grateful, and that assistance is hereby acknowledged. Microsoft did not, however, underwrite or in any other way materially contribute to the writing of this book except by furnishing the MBASIC product, and any opinions, interpretations, or instructions pertaining to the use of the product are strictly those of the author.

The author also wishes to express appreciation to Trumbull Rogers for his consistently superb, meticulous copy editing.

TABLE OF CONTENTS

BEGINNING WITH BASIC
An Introduction to Computer Programming

CHAPTER 1

THIS BOOK, COMPUTERS IN GENERAL, BASIC IN PARTICULAR

This book. Computers in general. BASIC in particular. Implementations of BASIC.

This Book

This book is about how to program computers in BASIC, the most widely used programming language in the world and one of the easiest to learn. I expect the reason you are reading it is that you want to learn BASIC or to improve your skills because you have access to a personal computer. That computer might be at work, or maybe you shelled out some of your hard-earned shekels for one at home. In either case, you want to make it do things for you.

I assume that you have a nodding acquaintanceship with what a computer is for, and that you understand something about its external anatomy and components. There are hundreds of varieties of personal computers, and I cannot possibly endeavor to explain each one. If the whole machine is an intimidating mystery to you, read the operations manual that came with it and then rejoin me. At any rate, I presume you have an elementary grasp of the purposes of the display screen, keyboard, printer, and disk drives, and that you know how to power up.

I do *not* assume that you give a hoot about the inner workings of CPUs and registers and other "technicalia" beyond what is necessary to write decent programs. If, in fact, that stuff turns you on, you need to learn assembly language. BASIC is a high-level programming language, meaning that it worries about machine-level details and leaves you free to concentrate on solving problems using the computer as a tool. That, no matter how you slice it, is the ultimate purpose of any computer, and the goal of all high-level programming languages is to help you achieve it.

That doesn't mean programming is easy. It's not. On the other hand, it's not magic either. When you program you have to understand the problem you are working on and plan a step-by-step method for solving it. When you have worked out the steps (programmers call this plan an *algorithm*), you have to translate it into the statements of the BASIC language to make it understandable to the computer. Most people find this discipline fairly easy to learn. There are also programming practices that help to direct your thought processes. These methods will be described as we go along.

This book deals primarily with Microsoft BASIC-80, which works under Digital Research's CP/M operating system. There are reasons for these choices. First, CP/M is available on most microcomputers, (micros), but even if you don't have it on yours, don't despair, because BASIC is pretty much the same under other operating systems. Second, Microsoft BASIC is also available for most micros. It is commercially the most successful and widely used BASIC, and it is used in this book to serve the widest audience. For those who don't have Microsoft, Chapter 13 deals with other popular BASICs.

Computers in general

Although not essential, it is helpful for a programmer to understand a little about how computers work. This section briefly opens the cover of that impassive box.

Our point of departure is a general proposition: *all computers, regardless of size, work the same.* Obviously an Apple II and the giant IBM 3Ø81 differ, but in only three respects:

- Speed of execution.
- Complexity of the software they can handle.
- Numbers and kinds of external devices they support.

The last two are really functions of the first and most telling difference, speed. If an Apple could do 26 million things a second, it would be a 3Ø81, because internally they operate in the same general fashion.

The heart—brain, if you wish—of any computer is a bunch of electronic circuitry collectively known as the *central processing unit*, or CPU. Everything that happens in a computer happens under the CPU's control. All data-altering and mathematical operations occur in the CPU; all information moved into, within, and out of the computer passes through the CPU; all programs are interpreted and transformed into action by the CPU. It runs the show, and even the smallest CPU in the dinkiest computer runs it at a speed the human mind cannot comprehend.

The CPU is so dependent on the *memory*, another major component of the computer, that you can consider them a single unit. Memory is the place where the CPU keeps information about what it's working on. That includes raw data, the results of processing, and the program of instructions that directs the CPU.

Memory is organized into a number of "boxes," each holding one byte (character) of information. These boxes are sequentially numbered, starting at Ø. The box and its number, which are synonymous in computerese, are known as *addresses*.

The speed at which computers operate makes it necessary for the memory to hold a substantial amount of information at any one time. Memory addresses are numbered using the binary system, which is based on 2s rather than on 1Øs, as in conventional decimal numbering. You do not have to understand binary to write BASIC programs, but it is useful to know that 1024 is the nearest round number in binary to 1000. Because people tend to think of large numbers in terms of thousands, the notation used to represent the binary approximation of 1000 is *K*, which stands for 1024. Thus memory size is expressed in K. A memory of 64K has 64 × 1024 = 65,536 addresses, the equivalent of about 23 pages of this book.

The CPU uses memory for everything. When it wants to add two numbers it calls out the address for the first number. That address responds by sending the value it contains to the CPU, where it's placed into a special little memory called a *register*. The CPU then calls out the address of the second number. As that value arrives the CPU adds it to the number waiting in the register, thus making a sum. The CPU then calls out another memory address and sends the sum there to be saved.

This is a typical sequence of events in any computer. Data constantly fly back and forth between memory and the CPU registers. The part of the CPU that performs addition, subtraction, comparisons, and so forth is called the arithmetic/logic unit (ALU). The ALU (computerese is a form of alphabet soup) consists of a group of these registers, tiny memories supported by circuits that turn on and off to accomplish various operations on data. An ALU has several registers and so can hold several values at once. The Intel 8Ø8Ø, for instance, has seven. The capacity of each register in the CPU determines the computer's *word length*. This is usually expressed in bits; a character consists of eight bits, so if you have an 8-bit machine, your CPU works on one character at a time; if a 16-bit machine, on two at a time; etc.

The CPU knows the addresses of information and what to do with their contents because a program tells it these things. Like data, the program occupies memory, usually in one group of sequential addresses. And like data, the CPU reads the program by calling out addresses to fetch individual instructions.

This activity occurs in the CPU's control section. Its job is to translate instructions into action: read a number, read another and add them, store the results at a certain address, and so on. As the programmer, you are the general who issues overall strategic orders, and the CPU control section is the company commander who carries them out. How your instructions are transformed into action is described in the last part of this chapter.

A computer can stay busy all day doing astonishing things at blinding speed, but it serves no useful purpose if it cannot communicate. In fact, much of a computer's activity has to do not with computing, but with receiving information and reporting what it has done with it. In data processing a computer's communications with the outside world are referred to as input/output, or more commonly as—you guessed it—I/O.

The movement of information in and out of a computer differs little from the movement of data within the machine. Every computer has "doorways" to the world called *ports*. The CPU reads and writes ports by means of addresses, just as it does memory.

There is an important difference between ports and memory addresses; the port has an external gadget hooked to it, such as a printer or a keyboard, so it has to be smart enough to handle details of communicating with the device it services.

To send a character out, the CPU first fetches it from memory and puts it into a register. Next it calls out the address of the appropriate port. Upon hearing its address the port asks the external unit if it is ready to receive. When the unit says yes, the port sends an all-clear signal to the CPU, which then passes it the character from the register. In BASIC this process is triggered by the PRINT instruction.

In the reverse (input) process, the CPU asks the port for a character and the port prompts the external device. When a character arrives the port sends it to a CPU register, and the CPU then writes it into a predetermined memory address. This happens in BASIC in response to an INPUT instruction.

The overwhelming majority of BASIC programs deal with three kinds of I/O: interaction with a keyboard/display terminal, output to a printer, and the reading and writing of files. As it happens, those are also the three kinds of I/O devices nearly all computers have, and so in this book that's what we'll deal with. Other kinds of I/O—data communications via modems, output to plotters, remote telemetry, voice recognition, computer music, and so on ad nauseam—are not very different in their particulars from ordinary I/O. Learn to program the common I/Os in BASIC, and from there it is easy to branch into exotica.

As a BASIC programmer you do not have to worry about the assignment and utilization of CPU registers, the allocation of memory, or what the control section is up to. All those things are implicit in the statements of your BASIC programs, and BASIC itself takes care of them for you. Likewise you do not have to concern yourself with the port addresses and communications details of I/O. The operating system of the computer looks after those tediums. BASIC is a problem-solving language, not a system control language, so all you have to do is write a program that leads to the solution of an information problem.

BASIC in particular

BASIC is an acronym for Beginner's All-purpose Symbolic Instruction Code. It was originally developed at Dartmouth College in the 1960s as a tool for teaching principles of computer programming. Because it is quite easy to learn and oriented toward problem-solving without much concern for machine details, it quickly spread beyond the academe as a language especially suited for nonprofessional programmers and casual computer users. It became popular in commercial time-sharing and has spread rapidly with the proliferation of personal computers.

As initially conceived, BASIC was a simplified FORTRAN (in fact, almost a subset of it). It's still possible to write a simple BASIC program that will also work as a simple FORTRAN program. Over the years, however, BASIC has undergone many revisions, until it has become an extremely powerful language in its own right.

BASIC, a nonprofessional language, can today do virtually anything COBOL and FORTRAN, stalwarts of the professionals, can, and it can do almost everything Pascal can do, too. In most cases it "does it easier" because the language is less complex than other popular languages. You don't have to know much about computers to write BASIC.

That is not to say that BASIC is the perfect programming language. If it were, the pros would long ago have abandoned their beloved COBOLs and FORTRANs, Niklaus Wirth would never have invented Pascal, and there wouldn't be a dozen other languages in everyday use. BASIC has flaws, some of them quite serious.

For one thing, it is inefficient. There is always a price for convenience, and BASIC sends a steep bill in machine costs. Calculations and text manipulation in BASIC take typically ten to a hundred times longer than similar operations in the classier languages, making it unsuitable for high-volume commercial data processing. In personal computing, long running times don't matter as much as being able to throw together a program without a lot of planning and expertise, and that is where BASIC shines and why it has never been taken seriously for the heavyweight stuff.

Another drawback is that there is no "standard" BASIC, perhaps because it is not taken seriously. In the absence of any significant corporate investment in BASIC programs, the tendency has been to let competing market forces in the software industry guide the growth of BASIC. This is very different from the professional languages, where industry standards are carefully developed and vigorously enforced. The consequence is a mishmash of BASIC dialects that might or might not be compatible with each other. The closest thing to a standard in microcomputing (and the reason for its selection for this book) is Microsoft BASIC-80, also called MBASIC and repackaged under several computer makers' names. It's by no means the only BASIC for personal computers.

Lest you grow discouraged by this news if you don't have Microsoft BASIC, I hasten to point out that the main differences in BASICs involve statements for reading and writing files and using certain special (and thus seldom used) features to do "slick stuff" beyond the scope of normal programming. This subject—dialects and important features of other popular BASICs—is the sole topic of a later chapter (Chapter 13).

The main problem with a lack of standardization is that programs are not portable from one BASIC to another. A CBASIC program just won't work if you try to run it under Microsoft, and vice versa. The only solution is to rewrite parts of it, which means that the rewriter has to know both dialects.

Other weaknesses of BASIC are less broad, but no less annoying. One is the dogged line-number orientation of most dialects, in which every statement has a line number and the only way to refer to sections of the program is by the number of the first statement. In Pascal, COBOL, PL/I, and many other languages, a section that, say, figures the interest rate on a balance can be called COMPUTE.INTEREST, and that name can then be used as if it were a program instruction. In BASIC you have to code GOSUB 1500 (if 1500 is the first line number of the section), which is not at all self-explanatory. Another weakness of some dialects is the difficult names given to variables; I3 is harder to remember and less obvious than INTEREST. Other languages (and some BASICs, including Microsoft) let you use long variable names.

In my opinion, BASIC is wrongly criticized by some—notably Pascal enthusiasts—for being hard to read. It is true that many programs are. Some of the programs published in microcomputing magazines, for example, are absolute gobbledygook. But just because unreadable programs *can* be written in BASIC is not grounds for dismissal of the language. One sees plenty of incoherent Pascal programs, too. The point here and for the rest of this book is that BASIC programs can and ought to be readable, and that the programmer who creates an illegible program in BASIC (or any language) is guilty of irresponsible, shabby workmanship.

Its defects and weaknesses notwithstanding, BASIC is an excellent tool for personal computing. To date, despite numerous attempts, no one has come up with anything better. It won't do for big league data processing, but people don't play big leagues on TRS-80s anyway. Aside from that, its shortcomings are tolerable and it will do just about anything you want.

Implementations of BASIC

In data processing the term *implementation* means "the way something works in a particular situation." This section discusses the two fundamentally different implementations of BASIC in microcomputers. First, though, we need to talk a little about language translation.

When you write a program in any language, you are expressing your desires and issuing orders in a human-oriented form: PRINT this, READ that, GOTO there, IF such-and-such. Words of this sort mean something to you; to the computer, however, they are just so many patterns of pulses with no more significance than SKLRGX or $#@!+?%.

The control section of a central processor acts on binary codes that are not only invisible but utterly meaningless to a person. Each binary code triggers some infinitessimally small action that serves as but one tiny step forward in an extensive sequence of events culminating in the addition of two numbers or the input of a character from a keyboard. It is possible and even fairly common to program at the machine level. The means of doing so is called *assembly language*, and is a tedious, time-consuming, error-prone process.

It's easier to program in a high-level language, such as BASIC, where a simple instruction, such as PRINT, generates the whole complex chain of machine codes leading to an output. To get from your PRINT to machine language, however, something has to happen.

That "something" is language translation. As the name suggests, it translates a human-oriented programming language into a CPU-oriented machine language. A language translator is itself a program whose purpose is to convert other programs from written form into executable form.

The written language that serves as its input is the *source*; the output is machine language. Every language translator has certain more or less inflexible rules for the way statements are formulated. These rules are the language's *syntax*, and minor differences in syntax account for the dialects of BASIC. Every translator produces a machine language for a particular make and model of CPU (its *target CPU*). You cannot use a language translator from an Apple II to produce machine language for the IBM PC because their CPUs are dissimilar. Likewise you cannot enter BASIC statements into a COBOL translator because their syntaxes differ. Some generalized translators, such as Microsoft BASIC, have been adapted for different target CPUs, so that the same source statements will work for Apple, Atari, Z8Ø, 8Ø8Ø, and other popular computer types, but you still have to make sure the translator is appropriate for the machine it is running on.

It would seem that language translation should be a universally straightforward process that everyone agrees on, but such is not the case. There are two fundamentally different approaches to the translation of programs, called *compilers* and *interpreters*. In a broad sense both accomplish the same thing; they take source language statements and convert them into a form that a computer can act on.

A compiler translates all the statements at one time, creating an executable machine-language file derived from, but independent of, the source program. Under CP/M, for example, if you compile a source program named PRINT.BAS, the compiler creates a machine-language file called PRINT.COM. To execute the program, you simply enter PRINT and it executes as though it were a system command. If you make a change in the program, you have to recompile to get the change into the executable copy. Once the program is finished, it never has to be translated again.

The alternative is an interpreter, which translates and executes source statements while the program is running. It does not produce a machine-language output file. Instead it interprets a statement and triggers the machine actions to carry out the intent of the statement, then interprets the next line in the program, and so on. The interpreter thus runs every time you execute your program. In fact, it loads your program into memory and processes it as input data, faithfully carrying out whatever "real" data-processing activities the instructions specify. Any changes you make to a program are immediately effective.

Most BASICs are interpreter-based. If you have a program named PRINT.BAS and the command to execute it is RUN PRINT, your language translator is an interpreter.

On some machines—notably low-cost home computers, such as Commodore and Atari—the BASIC interpreter is built into the hardware in a device called a ROM (read-only memory), which is a chip on one of the boards. It is a program, but it does not take up any memory in your machine and you don't have to load it from disk or a cassette. ROM-based interpreters usually start automatically when the system is turned on, giving you a message such as BASIC READY. A command turns off the interpreter if you want to do something not involving BASIC.

Digital Research sells a product called CBASIC that is somewhere between a compiled and an interpreted language. In this dialect the source code is semicompiled into a file of compact gibberish (an "intermediate language level") that must then be interpreted by a run-time program. The UCSD p-code languages work this way too. Although this approach is fairly common, it combines the negative aspects of both interpreters and compilers (slower running and the nuisance of recompiling for every little change).

Microsoft BASIC can be either interpreted or compiled. Most systems are implemented as interpreters, with the compiler available at extra cost. Few other BASIC products offer this flexibility (the Radio Shack parallel is really just Microsoft BASIC with Tandy's name on it). It is a real advantage, because program development and debugging is infinitely quicker and easier with an interpreter, and once the program works right you can compile it. Compiled programs always run faster than interpreted ones since the statements have already been translated, and they usually use less memory. On the other hand, if you are a casual user or a hobbyist you have to decide if saving a little running time is worth the added cost of the compiler.

CHAPTER 2

BASIC'S BASICS

A feel for the language: variables, assignment, input/output, control statements, loops, REMarks. The programming process. Preparing, entering, and running a program: setting up a working disk, entering a program, program names, debugging, prettyprint.

People write programs to tell a computer what they want it to do in a programming language such as BASIC, which expresses instructions in a mutually understandable fashion. Programming consists of developing a set of logical, sequential steps leading from a starting point to the achievement of the objective, and then translating those steps into the statements of a programming language and proving that they work.

This chapter covers the fundamentals of BASIC and of programming in general, laying down a foundation for the rest of the book. First we'll get a feel for BASIC and its ground rules by examining a simple program; then we'll discuss the programming process.

A feel for the language

One of the chief purposes of a computer is to do computations, hence its name. Obviously a computer does a great deal more than simple arithmetic, but it's both possible and useful to program it to act as an adding machine. The program in Figure 2.1(a) does just that. It also demonstrates most of the operations and principles of BASIC programming.

Before plunging into how this program works, let's examine it and discuss its general characteristics.

Perhaps the most noticeable feature is that every line has a number. BASIC requires line numbers in sequence (that is, you can't put line 125 in front of 120 or after 130). The line numbers indicate the order in which the statements are to be executed. Also, line numbers serve as a way to

```
10 REM  **  PROGRAM ADDMACH                    K. PORTER 12/6/82
20 REM  **  PERFORMS ADDING MACHINE FUNCTION IN BASIC.
30 REM  **  REPEATS UNTIL A ZERO ADDEND IS ENTERED.
40 REM  ----------------------------------------------------------
50 REM
60      PRINT "ADDING MACHINE"
70      PRINT
80      PRINT "FIRST NUMBER"
90        INPUT N1
100     IF N1 = 0 THEN GOTO 160
110     PRINT "SECOND"
120       INPUT N2
130     LET S = N1 + N2
140     PRINT "SUM ="; S
150     GOTO 70
160     END
```

(a)

```
ADDING MACHINE

FIRST NUMBER
? 5
SECOND
? 11
SUM = 16

FIRST NUMBER
? 854.62
SECOND
? 99.761
SUM = 954.381

FIRST NUMBER
? 0
```

(b)

Figure 2.1 (a) Program ADDMACH (b) Sample run.

refer to another instruction in the program, for example where line 150 points back to line 70.

Note that the line numbers increase by multiples of 10 and not in strict numeric progression. The program would work just as well if the lines were numbered 1, 2, 3..., etc., or 1000, 1050, 1384, and so on. The size of the increments doesn't matter, but numeric order does. *Every statement except the first and last must be preceded by a lower line number and followed by a higher line number*. Line numbers should increase by units larger than one because that makes it easy to insert additional lines if you need them. For example, you can add a new line 15 between lines 10 and 20. This is important in debugging (finding mistakes) and modifying programs.

The second thing to notice is that the program has a heading showing its name (ADDMACH), who wrote it and when, and what it does. Although the program will work without it, *always start a program with a header identifying it and stating its purpose.* This is for your benefit, not the computer's. As you write a program, its purpose is very clear; when you look at it months or even a few days later, it's seldom apparent on the basis of the instructions alone what the program does. A heading and explanatory remarks within the program (the latter discussed later) is central to the concept of *embedded documentation* stressed throughout this book. Don't punish yourself by omitting explanations and having to waste hours untangling gobbledygook.

This leads to the third general observation: the program is legible. Even if this is the first computer program you've ever seen, you should be able to read it and understand what it does and how. Maybe you don't comprehend the fine points and you wonder what line 70 is supposed to print, but at least the general flow should be apparent to you.

```
10 PRINT"ADDING MACHINE"
20 PRINT:PRINT"FIRST NUMBER":INPUTN1
30 IFN1=0THENGOTO50
40 PRINT"SECOND":INPUTN2:LETS=N1+N2:PRINT"SUM =";S:GOTO20
50 END
```

Figure 2.2 This program does the same as Figure 2.1, but notice how hard it is to read.

Program readability is as important as embedded documentation, and for the same reason: you owe it to yourself and to anyone else who might work with your programs. As shown in Figure 2.2, it is possible to write the same adding machine program in only five lines, but see how hard it is to read. *Good programmers write neat, readable programs.*

The structure of the adding machine program is as follows:

- Lines 10–50 are explanations for the benefit of people and ignored by the computer ("REM" instructs BASIC to disregard the rest of the line).
- Lines 60–120 prompt the user to enter two values called N1 and N2. Line 100 checks to see whether a 0 was entered and, if so, it stops the program by jumping to line 160.
- Line 130 calculates the sum of N1 and N2.
- Line 140 outputs the answer.

- Line 15Ø "loops back" to line 7Ø to repeat the program with new values for N1 and N2.
- Line 16Ø signifies the end of the program.

The program repeats any number of times, until a Ø is entered as the first number to be added. It will add any two numbers and display their sum. From it we can draw several observations about BASIC:

Variables——A variable in a program is any value that can change from one execution of the program to another, or as the program runs. In this program the variables are called N1, N2, and S, for "Number-1," "Number-2," and "Sum." The names themselves have no significance to BASIC; they could have been X, Y, and Z, or A1, A2, and A9, or anything else within the constraints of BASIC's rules for naming variables.

To BASIC itself, a variable name represents the memory address where the value is kept. You as the programmer do not need to know the address because BASIC looks after that for you. Therefore, it is convenient to think of a variable name in the algebraic sense of *x*, a symbol representing some value. S is the symbol for the sum of N1 and N2, and if BASIC wants to think of it as a memory address... well, that's what a programming language does; it bridges between your thought processes and the machine's. As we shall see more and more, the algebraic convention of referring to values symbolically is a fundamental of all programming.

In all dialects of BASIC, *a variable name can be any letter of the alphabet and it can be optionally followed by one digit*. Thus R, R1, R2, and J3 are four distinct and valid symbolic variable names representing four different values. On the other hand, 3J is not a valid name because it violates the naming rules. A program containing an invalid name will halt when it reaches that name. Microsoft and some other BASICs allow long variable names such as SUM and PAY.RATE, but many will not accept such names. All will, however, accept names conforming to the rule stated here, so if you want your programs to be portable to a different BASIC dialect, you would be well advised to stick by this rule even if yours allows long names. For that reason we'll use variable names conforming to the rule throughout this book.

Short names restrict your flexibility in selecting meaningful symbols; P1 is not nearly as self-explanatory as PAY.RATE, but it's about as good as you can get given the limitations of some BASICs. The following are suggestions for naming variables:

1. Select variable names that suggest (by initials) the values they represent. In a payroll program, H, T, and W are better for Hourly rate, Tax rate, and Withholding than would be J6, K, and Z.
2. As you plan and write a program, make a list of the variable names and their meanings. Include the list in the program heading so that

months later when you look at the program you can tell that B1 means "starting balance" and B2 stands for "ending balance." I did not do this in Figure 2.1(a) in order to avoid an overly complicated looking program.

Assignment——In BASIC *the assignment of a value to a variable is preceded by the instruction LET and always goes from right to left across the equals sign*. The statement

```
130    LET S = N1 + N2
```

means "let the symbol S represent the sum of N1 and N2." Arithmetic is implied in this statement, since N1 and N2 have to be added to satisfy it. Only one symbol is permitted to the left of the equals sign. It is *not* valid to say LET N1 + N2 = S, since this reverses the right-to-left direction of assignment and puts two symbols to the left of the equals sign.

For those who are punctilious about mathematical notation, it should be noted that an assignment (LET) statement is not an equation. In mathematics you cannot say that X = X + 1, but in BASIC it is perfectly legal to say LET X = X + 1. The effect of this instruction is to increase the present value of X by one, and it is frequently used in programs that count items or events.

In BASIC the symbol to the left of the equals sign is always the unknown. The expression to the right is evaluated to solve for the single value to the left. Thus an equation such as 7 = N − 2 *cannot* be written as LET 7 = N − 2 in BASIC; instead it must be rearranged to place the unknown to the left of the equals sign (LET N = 7 + 2).

Similarly, you have to rearrange complex equations to put the unknown to the left of the equals sign. To solve for x in the expression

$$3x^2 = (y^3 - 2y^2 + 5)^2$$

it is necessary to isolate x to the left of the equals sign. This is usually done by writing several interim steps that lead to the final value of x (the point being that you have to know how to work the problem before you can program it). Mathematics in BASIC will be discussed in detail in later chapters.

Most BASICs allow you to omit the actual word LET. It would be valid in Figure 2.1(a) to write

```
130    S = N1 + N2
```

This is called an implied LET; it does not change any of the rules regarding assignment.

Input/output——Figure 2.1(a) contains input and output operations (the INPUT and PRINT instructions). When BASIC encounters an IN-

PUT instruction it displays a question mark on the screen and stops until you key a response from the terminal. To signal that you have completed the response, press the ENTER (or RETURN) key. BASIC then resumes running and assigns the value you entered to the variable name specified in the INPUT statement. In line 90, for example, your keyboard entry is assigned to N1. That value is later used to compute the sum.

A simple question mark serves to alert you that the program expects an input, but it doesn't explain what the program wants. For that reason you should always precede an INPUT statement with a PRINT that tells you what to enter, as line 90 is preceded by the prompt in line 80.

BASIC is a highly interactive language, meaning that it's particularly well-suited for carrying on dialogs with the terminal user: asking questions, evaluating the responses, and immediately furnishing answers. As a result, PRINT is the most versatile instruction in the language.

In lines 60, 80, and 110, PRINT sends out the text that follows it in double quotes. (The PRINT statement normally displays output on the video screen, unless an instruction has been issued to divert the output to a printer.) In line 70, PRINT produces an empty line; or, in other words, it simply skips one line to create a visual break. In line 140, it prints both text and a variable. We could have combined lines 130 and 140 to create

```
130    PRINT "SUM ="; N1 + N2
```

and the sum would have been computed and printed, but not stored in memory (the computer would have "forgotten" it as soon as it was printed). We will discuss input/output in Chapter 5.

Control statements——A control statement is an instruction that influences the way the program runs. Figure 2.1(a) contains two control statements, at lines 100 and 150. The instruction at line 150 is an *unconditional branch*, more often referred to as a GOTO. Its form is

```
GOTO line number
```

Whenever it is encountered, execution jumps to the specified line number. If you name a nonexistent line number (GOTO 155 when there is no line number 155), BASIC "crashes" the program with the error message "Undefined line number."

The IF instruction at line 100 is a *conditional branch* or *decision*. Its general form is "IF (some condition is true) THEN (do something)." The "do-something" portion can be any other valid BASIC instruction. In this particular instance the IF statement is a conditional branch because, if the value of N1 is 0 when the statement is executed, control jumps to line 160. Otherwise (if N1 is not equal to 0) the specified condition is *not* true and execution "falls through" to line 110 without the GOTO being acted on. The branch is therefore conditional on the value of N1.

A noncontrol action (one that does not jump elsewhere in the program) can also occur in an IF statement, such as

```
350     IF N1 = N2 THEN PRINT "THE NUMBERS ARE
                        EQUAL"
```

In this case the quoted message is displayed if (and only if) N1 and N2 are equal, and then execution resumes at the next instruction. You could also write

```
425     IF N1 = 0 THEN LET N1 = S
```

which means that when N1 is 0, the value of S is assigned to it.

Control statements, of which there are several others in BASIC, will be covered in detail in Chapter 4.

Loops——Figure 2.1(a) contains one of the most important concepts in programming, the loop. A loop is a sequence of instructions that repeats until some condition is satisfied.

In Figure 2.1(a) the loop occurs between lines 70 and 150. When control reaches line 150, it jumps back to 70 and repeats the same instructions over again. Because this can potentially continue forever, it's necessary to establish a condition for terminating the loop. This condition, the *loop exit*, occurs with the IF statement at line 100. When you enter 0 as the first number to be added, the loop ends with a jump to line 160. In the adding machine program, line 160 happens to be the end, but it could just as well contain further instructions. The point is that *a loop must always have an exit.*

The main objective of a loop is to economize on program length. Loops have the added benefit of making a program "smart" by knowing how many times to perform an operation. Without a loop this program would execute one time. To add ten pairs of numbers it would need ten identical sets of instructions, and every time we ran the program we would have to enter ten pairs of numbers even if we had only one pair to add. With a loop the program is shorter and simpler, and we can stop it whenever it has added all the numbers we have at the moment.

Loops will be covered in Chapter 4.

REMarks——The final observation on Figure 2.1(a) concerns comments and open text embedded in the program. As discussed earlier, it is essential that you include explanations of the program's purpose and activities. You can place plain English—for your own benefit—into a program wherever it's appropriate by prefixing it with the REM instruction.

REM stands for remark. *Whenever BASIC encounters a REM, it ignores the rest of the line.* Therefore you can write anything you want to the right of a REM and it will have no effect on the way your program runs. The purpose of REM is to enable you to include explanatory comments so that later you don't have to decipher the instructions to figure out what the program does at one point or another. Use REMs freely.

In Figure 2.1(a) we confined all the REMs to complete lines at the beginning. You can also insert complete REM lines of text anywhere else in the program, among instructions. Even though BASIC disregards the contents of the line, a REM line needs a line number just like any other statement, and the number must be in proper sequence.

You can jump to a REM line with a GOTO or GOSUB (discussed later), and BASIC will automatically proceed to the first executable instruction after it. Figure 2.3 shows such an instance. When the computer arrives at line 1980 it jumps to line 1000, which is the first of several REM lines. Control then drops to line 1040, where it finds the first executable instruction.

```
1000 REM     ++++++++++++++++++++++++++++++++++++++++++++++++++++++++++
1010 REM     +        THIS IS THE START OF THE MAIN MENU              +
1020 REM     ++++++++++++++++++++++++++++++++++++++++++++++++++++++++++
1030 REM
1040    PRINT "MAIN MENU"
1050    PRINT "---------"
          .
          .
          .
1980    GOTO 1000
1990    ....
```

Figure 2.3 An instance where the program uses a GOTO to jump back to a REM line, after which control drops to the first executable line.

You can also place a REM on the same line with the instruction provided that the executable part of the line is to the left of the REM, and the REM is preceded by a colon. In the statement

```
185    LET A = Y - B :REM AGE = THIS YEAR - BIRTH
                              YEAR
```

BASIC executes the LET statement, but it doesn't try to do the operation to the right of :REM. This lets you explain individual lines, which is invaluable when you look at the program later.

Let me stress once more that a REM has *no* effect on the way a program runs. When I say that REMs explain the program, I don't mean that the text following the REMs starts popping up on the screen telling you what the program is doing at that instant. Rather, REMs simply make the program's printout more readable.

Although embedded documentation of programs using REMs is very important, it should be noted that it is also possible to carry it too far. Some programmers tend to get overzealous and document every single instruction and condition, to the point where the program becomes so cluttered with obvious statements that it would have been better to have included no comments at all. This is a matter of helping the reader to death, but it also raises the question of how much is enough. To that there's no easy answer. "Enough" is what aids in understanding without giving more information than necessary. Nobody reads voluminous remarks, anyway. In general, programs should be subdivided into logical sections, each preceded by a brief description of its purpose. Highlight important calculations with a remark. Explain unusual conditions and complicated logic sufficiently to establish the context when you read the program statements. As a broad guideline, no embedded remarks with the exception of the program heading should occupy more than two or three lines. The program examples in this book will provide a guide to how much embedded documentation is "enough."

Some BASICs, but not all, let you substitute an apostrophe for the letters REM. This definitely advances the cause of program readability, since the eye skips an apostrophe but becomes distracted by the pseudoword REM. On the other hand, use of the apostrophe limits the portability of programs to other BASICs. If portability is important, stick with REM even if your BASIC accepts apostrophes.

The Programming process

To program a computer is to direct an idiot. A computer, while appearing to be intelligent in the human sense, is really only following instructions thought out in advance by a person and provided for it in the form of a program. The appearance of intelligence is mere slavish obedience to a detailed set of orders. No computer has even the faintest glimmer of intelligence. A computer does not think, makes no judgements, and utterly lacks initiative. It will do anything it is told, subject only to the hardware capabilities at its disposal and its ability to understand instructions. If it encounters a situation it has not been programmed to deal with, it gives up. If told to do something incorrectly, it does it incorrectly. A computer is profoundly stupid.

Therefore it's entirely up to you as the programmer to think for the machine and verify that it's doing as you told it. Systems software—the BASIC translator and the operating system of the computer—buffer you from the details of system control, but no computer will ever say "You told me to multiply when you really meant to add." Nor will a computer correct faulty logic or fill in a missing step in even the most ridiculously obvious sequence of events. A computer knows nothing and it learns nothing from experience. It will tell you only if it doesn't understand

("Syntax error") or if you've told it to do something impossible, and even then it's not always reliable. Most microcomputers, for example, simply stop dead if you try to send output to a printer that's turned off or non-existent.

There's nothing you can do in a BASIC program about a turned-off printer (except to issue a message reminding the user to turn it on), but you *are* in total control of the logic and correctness of your programs. Because a computer is a methodical machine, the job of programming it demands a methodical approach and a methodical set of instructions.

In essence, the programming process breaks an overall, broadly stated task down into an orderly sequence of steps leading to the desired result. The complexity of the job and of the program itself are directly proportional to the complexity of the task to be performed. Because it is a subjective process that replicates the thoughts of an individual, programming is an art form in which there are very few absolutes and no "right way." Consequently, no one can tell you precisely how to program and give you the magic formula that will infallibly produce perfect machine solutions for every conceivable problem. The best one can do is to lay out a generalized, logical approach and leave it to you to adapt it to the specifics of a project.

In that spirit, then, let's construct a framework for the job of programming. These principles are as important as a knowledge of BASIC, so heed them well.

1. Write a brief general statement describing the purpose of the program and the results you expect from it.
2. Manually work a sample of the problem showing each step in its solution. Keep this sample handy.
3. From the sample, develop and write down a series of "one-liners" describing each step. If some steps are bypassed or performed only under certain circumstances, note them accordingly.
4. Using the outline from step 3, code the computer program in sections corresponding to the steps. If you're writing the program for someone else (or even for yourself and the program is complicated) insert an extra step here describing how to operate the program. Use it as a guide for programming the input/output.
5. Enter the program into the computer.
6. Run the program with the exact same data used in the manual sample and verify the results.
7. Correct errors in the program and repeat step 6 until you're satisfied that it works properly.
8. If the program bypasses or executes certain steps only under special circumstances, test it with data that exercise those conditions and verify the results (through further manual solutions, if necessary).
9. Save the program for "live" use.

If a program is complex, this general plan, especially in step 3, will have to be expanded. The "one-liners" describe the purpose of each *module* (section). When planning a long, difficult program, use the one-liners as statements of purpose for each of the modules, repeating steps 1, 2, and 3 to break the module down into subcomponents. This will yield a detailed outline of the program, from which you can then develop the BASIC statements to carry it out.

It's always harder to develop a program for someone else than for yourself. Communications between people often lead to misunderstandings, false starts, and revisions in programs. This makes it essential that you work closely with your "client" during the planning phase, and then stick by the agreements. Sometimes there's no alternative but to work closely with your client; if you're doing an economic analysis program and you don't know a thing about economics, you have to rely on your client for the necessary calculations and methods. When you *do* know about the subject of the program, guard against the tendency to let your own point of view and preconceptions dictate what the user gets. It may not be what he or she wants, and you'll waste your time and your client's good will.

Even when programming for yourself, you shouldn't short-cut this plan. Many people, notably those who know just enough to be dangerous, tend to sit down and start banging away on the terminal with only the fuzziest of plans in their heads. That might be an acceptable approach if you enjoy endless debugging and frustration, but it's an awful waste of energy. You owe yourself a quality product, so take a little time to develop a plan. The program development examples later in this book demonstrate the planning process in action.

Preparing, entering, and running a program

Before you start programming in BASIC you need to prepare a working disk and learn how to operate the BASIC interpreter. The iron rule of any software product is *never use the diskette you received from the vendor as a working disk*. You should first copy it, then store it in a safe, dust-free place, only using it thereafter to make replacement copies as each working copy wears out. Copyright statutes regarding software permit you to make copies for your own use, subject to the limitations and stipulations stated in documents accompanying the product. In most cases, however, it's illegal to make copies for your friends and business associates unless the vendor specifically says—in writing—that it's okay. Common sense applies here; if you bought the product, you have a right to do with it as you please, but that right doesn't extend to beating the software manufacturer out of his livelihood.

The first step on the road to BASIC proficiency is to set up the working disk, for which you use a blank diskette. Use your system's FORMAT program to prepare this diskette, name it "BASIC," and then load it with a copy of the operating system (CP/M in this case). The working disk doesn't need all the CP/M programs you got with the computer. For a bare-bones BASIC system disk, the only three programs you need are PIP, ED, and STAT. The computer manuals will tell you how to copy them, or you might convince your dealer to do it for you. (If you're using TRSDOS, select the "minimum system" option described in the manual, copy BASCOM, and skip the next two paragraphs; for IBM DOS or UCSD, study the manuals and figure out which programs are likely to be useful and copy them to the working disk.)

After you've prepared this much, put the working disk into the primary drive (drive A) and reset the system by holding down the CTRL key and typing C. (Some keyboards have a BREAK key that does the same thing. On the IBM PC, consult the manual for how to do a "warm boot.") Disk activity will occur, and the system prompt (A>, in CP/M) will appear on the screen. The diskette is now ready to be loaded with BASIC.

Now insert the vendor-provided BASIC disk into the B drive and enter the command (if using CP/M)

```
PIP BASIC.COM=B:MBASIC.COM
```

Press the ENTER (or RETURN) key after typing this command. *All* lines on all computers are ended this way. The command copies the BASIC interpreter from drive B to drive A. This procedure varies somewhat on non-CP/M systems. At any rate, when the system prompt (A>) appears again, take the vendor-provided BASIC disk out of the B drive and put it away. Your working disk is now fully prepared for operation.

To enter BASIC, type the command

```
BASIC
```

and press ENTER. The disk operates for a few seconds, and then several lines appear on the screen, identifying the version number, copyright, so many bytes free, etc. BASIC is now active.

Any time you power up your system and insert this diskette you have to type BASIC to make the interpreter active. Some versions of CP/M, TRSDOS, IBM DOS, etc., have an automatic feature that activates a program such as BASIC whenever the system is started. If you want to do this, consult the manuals.

BASIC signifies that it's open for business by displaying the prompt "OK" (the Apple computer issues] instead, and Radio Shack says "READY"). Any time you see this prompt on the line above the cursor you know BASIC expects you to enter something from the keyboard. That "something" can be either a direct command or a program line. As you complete an entry, press the ENTER (or RETURN) key to tell BASIC you've come to the end of that line.

With BASIC active, type the command FILES. BASIC will display a list of all the files on the working disk. FILES is an example of a direct command.

BASIC accepts both direct commands, which it executes immediately, and program statements, which it stores and executes as a group later in response to the RUN command. Any statement not preceded by a number is executed as a direct command; if a number precedes the statement, BASIC stores it in memory to be executed later. Direct commands and program statements can be mixed, so that you can enter some program lines, then a command or two, and then more of the program. No command (except for NEW) alters the program statements stored in memory. The command is acted on as soon as you've pressed ENTER, and the program lines are not. Type

```
PRINT 4+2
```

and as soon as you've pressed ENTER the number 6 appears. BASIC has acted on a direct command.

Now enter the program statement

```
100    PRINT 4+2
```

When you push ENTER nothing happens, because this is a program statement. In fact it's a complete one-line program, so if you type RUN, the answer 6 appears.

You can view the stored program lines by typing LIST. At this point only one program line is in memory, line 100 as shown above, so that's all that will appear in response to LIST. If there were several lines, they would all be displayed in the numeric order of the line numbers. The command LLIST has the same effect as LIST, except that it produces a program listing on the printer instead of on the display screen.

In a BASIC program the line numbers indicate the order of the program statements. They also serve as references, so that one statement can refer to another by its line number. These numbers, then, are extremely important. BASIC knows this, and if you enter lines that are not in numeric order it will rearrange them into the correct sequence for you.

As an example, we now have line 100 saved in memory. Type the program statement

```
90     PRINT "SUM OF 4+2"
```

which is being entered chronologically after line 100, and then type LIST. BASIC displays the program

```
90     PRINT "SUM OF 4+2"
100    PRINT 4+2
```

Here you can see that BASIC has put the lines into numeric sequence regardless of the fact that they were entered in the order opposite from that shown. It also executes the statements in numeric sequence, as you can see by typing RUN.

You can remove an existing line from a program by typing its line number and pressing ENTER. If you type a new line with the same number as an existing line, BASIC replaces the old with the new. This is the most frequently used method for correcting errors and making changes in programs. Type in

```
100    PRINT 4-2
```

and LIST. The program now reads

```
90     PRINT "SUM OF 4+2"
100    PRINT 4-2
```

because BASIC replaced line 100. Now when you enter the RUN command you get

```
SUM OF 4+2
2
```

Unfortunately, of course, this is wrong—the sum of 4+2 is 6, not 2. The error is not in what the program did, but in what it was instructed to do. There's a discrepancy between the quoted literal in line 90 and the computation in line 100. Computers do only as they're told, so it's your responsibility to make sure any program change is fully implemented by correcting *all* the relevant statements. In this case you can correct it by entering the replacement line

```
90     PRINT "DIFFERENCE OF 4-2"
```

Now when you LIST you'll see that line 90 has been replaced, and RUN will produce the proper description of the answer.

You can extend the LIST and LLIST commands by including a line number. The command LIST 100 produces only line 100, not line 90. Similarly, if you had a long program with many statements, you could list a portion of it by entering the LIST command with the range of line numbers you want to view. The command LIST 300–400 displays all the program lines between 300 and 400.

Usually after you've entered a program you want to save it so that you can call it back later and run it without having to rekey the whole works. This is done with the SAVE command. For the sake of this exercise let's call this little program by the name LEARNING. To save it, enter

```
SAVE "LEARNING",A
```

After you press ENTER there is brief disk activity and then BASIC displays the OK prompt. The SAVE command has placed the program into a disk file named LEARNING, but the original program itself is still in memory and capable of being run.

Let's talk about the ",A" following the program name. It tells BASIC to save the program statements exactly as you entered them and as they appear after a LIST. You don't have to include it in the SAVE command, but if you don't BASIC compresses the program into a bunch of gibberish. The program can still run, but it won't look like what you entered and you might not even be able to read it after you bring it back in from disk at some later time.

As we said, after a SAVE the program remains intact in the computer's main memory and you can still run it, list it, and change it. If you want to wipe the slate clean and enter a new program, type the command NEW. This completely erases the program statements BASIC has been keeping in memory. Enter NEW on your computer and then type LIST. BASIC displays no program lines because it's cleared away the two lines we saved. You can now enter a different program without fear that some lines left over from the old program will get mixed in with the new ones.

You can get the program back from disk by typing

```
LOAD "LEARNING"
```

After a brief pause while the disk drive works, BASIC replies OK. Do a LIST and you'll see that the program you entered earlier is back. You can run it or change it or whatever just as before. Unless you want to keep changes permanently, it's not necessary ever to save this program again. It remains intact on disk after a LOAD no matter what you do to it. If you do save a changed version under the same name, the new one replaces the old.

Another way of getting the program back from disk is

```
RUN "LEARNING"
```

BASIC then loads it from disk and immediately begins executing the program. This has exactly the same effect as the two commands

```
LOAD "LEARNING"
RUN
```

Most likely you don't want to clutter your disk with a program this trivial. It will remain there for all time, however, unless you tell BASIC to get rid of it. The KILL command does just that. To remove the program from the disk, enter

```
KILL "LEARNING"
```

The disk drive whirs for a moment and then BASIC says OK. The program has disappeared without a trace from the disk.

MBASIC provides a line editor (the EDIT command) that has a number of nifty features. It's also not the easiest thing to use. The most effective way of changing a program line is simply to retype it, since BASIC automatically replaces a line with a new line that has the same number. Once you've gotten a little more comfortable with BASIC and the computer, consult the manual and learn how to exercise the EDIT features.

For now you know enough to enter, fix, list, save, and run a real computer program. Practice by entering ADDMACH (Figure 2.1(a)), and save it under that name. We'll be referring to ADDMACH often over the next few chapters, so it's advisable to keep it available.

This book includes many program examples. Some you'll find immediately useful and some you won't. Regardless, you will learn much more about BASIC if you actually key in these programs and run and save them than if you simply glance over the listings and read the text. To paraphrase something some famous person once said, you can learn a little about fishing from a book, but you really learn about fishing by fishing.

Program names—Usually after you've written a program you want to save it for future use. This means you have to give it a name. To the computer, a program is just another file. It gets written onto the disk as a collection of information identified by a file name. You bring it back into the computer's memory for execution or editing with RUN or LOAD, followed by the file name. For example, the adding machine program is called ADDMACH. In most systems it's saved as a file named ADDMACH.BAS, and to run it you enter RUN "ADDMACH".

CP/M and most other microcomputer operating systems permit you to give files a two-part name. If you're working under a system other than CP/M, file naming details may differ and you'll have to check your manual to find out what they are. In CP/M the first part of the name can be up to eight characters in length. The first character has to be a letter of the alphabet, and the other seven can be either letters or numbers. The second part (the *suffix* or *filetype*) is optional. It has to be preceded by a period and can have up to three characters, again with the first character a letter and the other two either letters or numbers. The following are all valid CP/M file names:

ADDMACH.BAS	C12H34.X2
ADDMACH1.BAS	CALENDAR

The following are *not* valid file names for the reasons shown:

7ADDMACH.BAS	(Letter must be first)
ADDINGMACH.BAS	(Too many characters)
C12H34.2X	(Letter must be first in suffix)
CAL.END.AR	(Only one period allowed)

File name suffixes for programs are predetermined. Machine-language program files have the suffix .COM (for command), BASIC programs have the suffix .BAS, assembly language .ASM, and so on. The purposes of assigning preestablished suffixes to program files follow.

(1) Provide an easy means of identifying program files and the language in which they are written.
(2) Reduce the keying necessary to run or translate the program.

To illustrate point 2, if the adding machine program is saved as ADDMACH.BAS, you run it by entering RUN "ADDMACH". The RUN command assumes that .BAS is the suffix for a file named ADDMACH. Data files can have any suffix (or none), but the use of standard program file suffixes should be avoided for data files.

You save a program that has been keyed into the computer with the SAVE command (e.g., SAVE "ADDMACH"). When saving a program, be careful that you don't give it the name of a different program that has already been stored on the diskette. On any given diskette you can have only one file under a specific name; it is not possible to have two programs called ADDMACH.BAS on the same diskette. You can have programs named ADDMACH.BAS and ADDMACH1.BAS or two programs named ADDMACH.BAS and ADDMACH.ASM. The point is that there must be something unique about every file name on a disk. If you save a new ADDMACH.BAS on a disk that already contains an ADDMACH.BAS, the new one replaces the old one and you'll never be able to get the old one back.

A program's name should give a clue as to what it does. Who knows what RUN "XKJ2V" does? On the other hand, ADDMACH suggests an adding machine. The problem is, of course, that eight characters give precious little space in which to describe anything, so abbreviations are unavoidable, for example, ADDMACH.

If you were writing a payroll system of several programs, you might be inclined to call them PAYROLL1, PAYROLL2, etc., yet although that approach appears to make sense, in fact the sequence numbers give no hint about the functions of individual programs. The following might be preferable:

Name	*Purpose*
PAYUPDT.BAS	Update payroll records
TIMECARD.BAS	Enter weekly time cards
PAYCHKS.BAS	Produce paychecks
PAYREPTS.BAS	Print payroll reports

Sometimes a program almost names itself. The BASIC program I wrote to print manuscripts, program listings, correspondence, etc., is called

PRINTER. When I want to run off page copy I enter RUN "PRINTER", a command whose purpose is perfectly clear. Usually, however, some ingenuity is needed. Again drawing from my own program library, the word processing program I developed in assembly language for my use as a writer is named FSE. It probably signifies nothing to you now, but when you know it stands for Full Screen Editor the program name acquires a meaning. All program names should mean something.

Debugging—It's probably optimistic to hope that 10 percent of all programs run satisfactorily the first time. Because people are error prone, we almost always make mistakes in programming. Sometimes the computer calls our attention to mistakes and refuses to proceed until we fix them. Other times—don't lose sight of a computer's fundamental stupidity—the program runs merrily away, producing bizarre results, screwing up files, and otherwise going on the rampage. Or crashing in a disgraceful, bewildering mess, or locking itself forever into endless repetitions of the same loop. *Debugging* is the art of fixing program problems.

Program "bugs" fall into three general categories:

1. Syntax errors.
2. Semantic errors.
3. Logic errors.

Syntax errors are mistakes in forming instructions, in other words language errors. Some are obvious, such as misspelling keywords (RPINT instead of PRINT). Others are more subtle: forgetting to put quote marks around a message to be printed, or omitting REM before a comment, or leaving out parentheses in complex mathematical expressions.

The BASIC interpreter doesn't know what a statement containing a syntax error means, so when it finds one it stops the program and issues an error message. Unfortunately, because the interpreter doesn't understand the statement, the error message is seldom very helpful. In many cases, BASIC displays the offending statement and the catchall message SYNTAX ERROR. It's up to you to figure out what's wrong with the syntax and fix it. Usually that's easy, but occasionally it's not.

Let's cause a syntax error in ADDMACH.

1. Enter: 1ØØ   RPINT "SECOND"
2. Enter the command RUN.
3. The computer prints the heading ADDING MACHINE and asks for FIRST NUMBER.
4. After you enter it, the message "SYNTAX ERROR" appears.
5. To repair the bug, enter: 1ØØ   PRINT "SECOND"
6. Rerun the program. It should now function correctly.

Semantic errors occur as a result of inappropriate usage: you thought you entered one thing but you really entered another. Since a semantic error is a properly formed BASIC instruction, the interpreter doesn't detect it and yet the program behaves oddly. As an example, let's pretend that in ADDMACH you erroneously typed PRINT instead of INPUT in line 9Ø. To simulate the error, enter:

```
9Ø     PRINT N1
```

Then enter the RUN command. As you see, the computer immediately displayed the ADDING MACHINE title and the prompt FIRST NUMBER, but then it printed Ø and the startling message OK, meaning it has legitimately come to the end of the program.

Here's what happened: As far as BASIC is concerned the program is entirely correct, since there are no improperly formed statements. It's merely doing as you told it. What you told it was to PRINT (not INPUT) the value of N1. No assignment has been made to N1, so a zero value is assumed. This satisfies the comparison in line 1ØØ, which says that if N1 is equal to Ø then go to the end of the program. And that's just what it did.

Semantic errors fall in the category of forehead slappers: "Oy, how could I make such a dumb mistake?" They're not limited to incorrect instructions, nor are they the exclusive property of beginners. When I was testing the ADDMACH program (by conservative estimate the 1004th program I've written), it returned incorrect answers. I was ashamed; it is, after all, a very simple program and I am The Author. After some annoyed examination of the instructions, I discovered that in line 13Ø I'd typed N1 + N1, not N1 + N2. That, Gentle Reader, was a semantic error.

Logic errors are the most challenging. They occur when the method for solving the problem is just plain wrong. The most common program problem, logic errors span a broad spectrum of sin. In one case the program might run successfully but produce incorrect answers (if ADDMACH multiplied instead of added). In another case a logic error might cause the program to do something crazy (the conditional branch in line 1ØØ might jump to the start of the program instead of to the end). In other cases the defect might be much more serious, requiring a substantial rewrite of the program because of an elementary flaw in reasoning.

There's a fine line between semantic and logic errors. A semantic error is an honest mistake, whereas a logic error arises from wrong thinking. The symptoms of the two kinds of errors are often the same, and so is the technique for diagnosing the problems, which takes advantage of the interactive nature of BASIC.

Some pages back we mentioned that it's a good idea to step line numbers by tens. Figure 2.4(a) shows one reason why: we can insert PRINT statements to show the values of certain key variables at points through-

```
10 REM  **  PROGRAM ADDMACH                    K. PORTER 12/6/82
20 REM  **  PERFORMS ADDING MACHINE FUNCTION IN BASIC.
30 REM  **  REPEATS UNTIL A ZERO ADDEND IS ENTERED.
40 REM  -------------------------------------------------------
50 REM
60      PRINT "ADDING MACHINE"
70      PRINT
80      PRINT "FIRST NUMBER"
90        INPUT N1
100     IF N1 = 0 THEN GOTO 160
110     PRINT "SECOND"
120       INPUT N2
130     LET S = N1 + N1
135 PRINT "AT 140 ", N1, N2
140     PRINT "SUM ="; S
150     GOTO 70
160     END
```

(a)

```
ADDING MACHINE

FIRST NUMBER
? 19
SECOND
? 1
AT 140          19          1 <- Debugging
                                 statement
SUM = 38 <-
              Answer should be 20
FIRST NUMBER
? 0
```

(b)

Figure 2.4 (a) Program ADDMACH, with extra PRINT statement. (b) Sample run: Demonstrates the use of an extra PRINT for debugging.

out the program. In this case a semantic error (the one I actually made), calling for the sum of N1+N1, has occurred at line 130. We'll pretend we don't know that for the moment. At line 135 we've inserted a PRINT statement to show N1 and N2 at the point where they're added. The output of the program is shown, and obviously the answer is incorrect. Therefore, it seems likely that the calculation that produced the answer contains an error. Sure enough, on checking it we find that it does. To correct the error:

1. Enter: 130 LET S = N1 + N2
   (This new line replaces the old line 130 and corrects the error it contained.)

2. Enter: 135
   (By entering only the line number you delete the contents of that line and remove the unnecessary PRINT statement that helped in debugging.)

This is, of course, a simple example, but it illustrates one of the most useful techniques for trapping bugs. You should note a couple of things about line 135 and use them in real debugging. First, it is not indented like the other lines, thus making it stick out when you examine the program listing. Second, a message in the printed output of the statement identifies the line number where the observation is to occur. This is because we might want to distinguish between several such PRINTs inserted here and there in the program. Actually, a diagnostic message ought to indicate not only the line number but also the names of the variables and their values at that point. You'll learn more about how to form complex PRINT statements in a later chapter.

It's infinitely easier to debug a program when you have a hard-copy (printed on paper) listing of the program to refer to. A video screen simply doesn't let you see enough lines at one time, especially if the program jumps around. Also, you can mark up hard copy and run down the errors by tracing the flow through the instructions and manually working the problem in the margins. Any program of more than 50 lines is virtually impossible to debug without a printed copy to work on.

Prettyprint—This term is borrowed from Nagin and Ledgard's *BASIC WITH STYLE: Programming Proverbs* (Rochelle Park, N.J., Hayden Books, 1978), a work to be strongly recommended to everyone who writes computer programs. The thrust of prettyprinting is to make programs neat and readable. Nagin and Ledgard have given us a style manual that doesn't teach BASIC, but that certainly provides a rich set of ideals and rules for legibility.

BASIC is a remarkably flexible language. It doesn't care how many spaces you put between words, symbols, variables, etc., or how many comments you embed in your programs. Since it doesn't care, you might as well utilize that flexibility to your advantage. That's why it's there.

Figure 2.2 shows a sample of BASIC at its worst. Note especially line 3Ø (IFN1=ØTHENGOTO 5Ø). Such run-together statements are perfectly acceptable to BASIC, but not to the eye. Much better is

```
30      IF N1  =  0 THEN GOTO 50
```

or even

```
30      IF (N1  =  0) THEN GO TO 50
```

There's no reason to squeeze statements together. Some programmers think that compact code is somehow more efficient. They're right to the extent that a program so written will occupy a little less memory and run a few thousandths of a second faster. Who cares? If they're that concerned about machine efficiency, they shouldn't be writing in BASIC, a relatively slow programming language.

Little things add up to better programs. In the program examples in later chapters you'll see that modules are set apart by blank lines to provide visual breaks, that comments all begin at the same column instead of randomly, that equals signs are lined up, that identions show loops more clearly, and that other little fussy points improve the readability of the programs and thus their quality as a whole. Neatness is an important part of writing good programs.

CHAPTER 3

BASIC MATHEMATICS

Arithmetic. Literals, variables, and constants. Initialization. Signs. Exponents. Remainders. Precedence of operators. Factoring of expressions. Functions: square root, rounding and truncation. Functions in action. Data types. E notation. Investment comparison.

Inasmuch as computers deal chiefly with mathematics, BASIC, a general-purpose programming language, possesses powerful mathematical capabilities. Math in BASIC is not very different from the arithmetic we do on paper. For that reason, and because mathematical operations are fundamental to all programming, we will now begin in earnest with arithmetic up through the level of elementary algebra, that is, with the kind of math used in everyday life. A later chapter will discuss higher math using transcendental functions (values such as logarithms and sines that can't be calculated by using arithmetic).

Arithmetic

As in ordinary math, BASIC performs addition, subtraction, multiplication, and division. In Figure 2.1(a) we saw a sample of addition in the statement

```
130    LET S = N1 + N2
```

It should come as no surprise that the plus sign (+) is the operator for addition. Assignment passes to the left across the equals sign, so in this case the result of adding the values N1 and N2 is assigned to the variable S.

All other arithmetic operations are structured the same way. The form of every mathematical instruction in BASIC is:

```
LET [variable] = [expression]
```

where [variable] *must* be a symbolic variable name (e.g., S) and [expression] is another variable, a number, or a calculation. The following are examples of arithmetic expressions:

```
LET J = K        (J takes on the value of K)
LET J = 17.35    (J assumes the value 17.35)
LET J = K + L    (J becomes the sum of K and L)
LET J = K + 7    (J becomes the sum of K added to 7)
```

You *cannot* under any circumstances place an expression or an actual number to the left of the equals sign in a LET statement; for example, LET K + 7 = J, or LET 22 = J − 3. This is because BASIC assigns a memory location to the symbol at the left of the equals sign and that's where it puts the result of the expression to the right. You may think of the symbol as representing a value, but BASIC thinks of it as a place.

The arithmetic operators in BASIC are

+	Addition
−	Subtraction
*	Multiplication
/	Division

Probably the only one that comes as a surprise is the asterisk (*) for multiplication to avoid confusion with the use of X as a variable name.

The values worked on by operators are called *operands*, and the symbol to the left of the equals sign is the *result*. In LET S = N1 + N2, N1 and N2 are operands and S is the result. The order of operands in subtraction and division is as you might expect. In LET S = N1 − N2, the value assigned to N2 is taken away from that assigned to N1. Thus when N1 = 7 and N2 = 5, S = 7 − 5 = 2. Likewise, in division the first value is divided by the second. In LET Q = D1 / V, if D1 = 21 and V = 3, Q is 7. Figure 3.1(a) shows all the arithmetic operations.

Literals, variables, and constants

Possibly you noticed that in the examples of expressions above, the last one mixed a number with symbols (LET J = K + 7). As in algebra, it's perfectly all right to use actual numbers along with symbols. Such numbers are called *literals*, since they are specified literally.

BASIC deviates in one important respect from customary algebraic notation. In algebra, a number and a symbol can be written together to represent a value, as:

$$b = 2a$$

This notation implies multiplication, since the value of a must be multiplied by 2 to satisfy the equation. Implied relationships don't exist in

```
 10 REM  **  PROGRAM 'MATH'                     K. PORTER  12/12/82
 20 REM  **  TAKES TWO NUMBERS AND PERFORMS THE FOUR MAJOR ARITHMETIC
 30 REM  **      OPERATIONS ON THEM.
 40 REM  **  REPEATS UNTIL USER ENTERS '0' AS FIRST NUMBER.
 50 REM  ------------------------------------------------------------
 60 REM
 70 REM  **  SCREEN HEADING
 80 REM  **  --------------
 90      PRINT "MATHEMATICS"
100      PRINT "-----------"
110 REM
120 REM  **  GET THE OPERANDS
130 REM  **  ----------------
140      PRINT
150      PRINT "FIRST NUMBER (OR 0 TO STOP)... ";
160      INPUT N1
170      IF N1 = 0 THEN GOTO 480          REM     QUIT ON '0' INPUT
180      PRINT
190      PRINT "SECOND NUMBER... ";
200      INPUT N2
210      PRINT
220 REM
230 REM  **  ADDITION
240 REM  **  --------
250      LET R = N1 + N2
260      PRINT "SUM", R
270 REM
280 REM  **  SUBTRACTION
290 REM  **  -----------
300      LET R = N1 - N2
310      PRINT "DIFFERENCE", R
320 REM
330 REM  **  MULTIPLICATION
340 REM  **  --------------
350      LET R = N1 * N2
360      PRINT "PRODUCT", R
370 REM
380 REM  **  DIVISION
390 REM  **  --------
400      LET R = N1 / N2
410      PRINT "QUOTIENT", R
420 REM
430 REM  **  END OF LOOP
440 REM  **  -----------
450      PRINT
460      GOTO 120
470 REM
480 REM  **  END OF PROGRAM
490 REM  **  --------------
500      END
```

(a)

```
MATHEMATICS
-----------

FIRST NUMBER (OR 0 TO STOP)... ? 12

SECOND NUMBER... ? 6

SUM          18
DIFFERENCE   6
PRODUCT      72
QUOTIENT     2


FIRST NUMBER (OR 0 TO STOP)... ? 3.14159

SECOND NUMBER... ? 2.5

SUM          5.64159
DIFFERENCE   .64159
PRODUCT      7.85398
QUOTIENT     1.25664
```

(b)

Figure 3.1 (a) Program MATH. (b) Sample run.

BASIC. You must *always* specify the operation. Thus in BASIC this equation is written

```
LET B = 2 * A
```

Lengthy or complex constants can be a pain if they recur throughout the program. An example is π; BASIC doesn't include this classic value as part of its repertoire. To type 3.1415927 at numerous places is to invite errors or at least tedium. When a constant value recurs throughout the program, it's best to assign a variable name to it and then use that symbol in place of the number in calculations. For example:

```
50    LET P   = 3.1415927     REM   VALUE OF PI
 .             .
 .             .
 .             .
260   LET A1  = D * P         REM   AREA OF CIRCLE 1
 .             .
 .             .
 .             .
590   LET D2  = R / P         REM   DIAMETER OF CIRCLE 2
```

The statement at line 50 is called a *declaration*, since it declares that P represents 3.1415927. P is thus a *global constant* that retains its value throughout the program. We'll have more to say about global constants in later chapters.

If you use this technique, you must be careful not to alter the value of P (or whatever you choose to call the constant). If you do, your program will present you with some unpleasant surprises.

A literal number is any number—either specified in a program or entered from the keyboard in response to an INPUT statement—that is in plain digital form. In line 50 above, 3.1415927 is a literal number. When you ran the ADDMACH program, you entered literal numbers to be added.

There's nothing strange or mysterious about literal numbers in BASIC, but you should be aware of one rule: *Do not use commas in literal numbers*. To BASIC the number 32,531 is *two* numbers (32 and 531) because BASIC uses the comma as a separator character. Large numbers must therefore always be typed without commas (for example 32531).

Initialization

In computerese, *initialization* means the assignment of a starting value to a variable. When a program starts, BASIC automatically initializes all numeric variables as zeros and all string variables (alphabetics) as empty. A variable remains valueless until a LET, INPUT, or READ instruction assigns a value to it. As an example, in the statement

```
220    LET T = B + 6
```

if B has never been assigned a value it will be 0 at this point, so T will be equal to 6 after this instruction is executed. If this statement is part of a loop and there is a later instruction

```
370    LET B = T / 2
```

then B will take the value 3 (since T was earlier set to 6). When line 220 is again executed, T will become 9 because B now contains a value (3, if no other change has been made to T or B).

Signs

Numbers in BASIC can be either positive or negative. BASIC always assumes that a number is positive unless specified otherwise; that is, you don't have to (but you may if you wish) place a plus sign in front of a number to ensure that it's read as positive. To make a number negative, put a minus sign in front of it:

```
245     LET N3 = -12.75
```

BASIC keeps track of the sign of each value during the running of the program so that results are mathematically correct. Consider the following program fragment:

```
430     LET N3 = -17
440     LET M  =  12
450     LET A  =  M+N3
460     LET B  =  3 -A
```

The value developed for B is 8. This is because line 450 computes A as M + N3 = 12 + (−17) = −5. In line 460, B = 3 −(−5), which reverses the sign of −5 and maintains consistency with the rules of signs in arithmetic.

Exponents

An exponent is the power to which another number is raised. For example in the expression 9^4, the 4 is the exponent. In BASIC the exponentiation operator is an up-arrow (^), so the expression 9^4 is written as 9^4, as in

```
LET P4 = 9^4
```

You can also exponentiate using symbols:

```
LET P4 = T^4
LET P4 = T^L
```

Most BASICs also have a second exponentiation operator, a double asterisk (**), permitting the examples above to be written

```
LET P4 = 9**4
LET P4 = T**4
LET P4 = T**L
```

The operators ** and ^ are interchangeable

Remainders

Some dialects of BASIC, including Microsoft, have a special operator called MOD that calculates the remainder in the division of whole numbers. The technical term for remainder is *modulus*, hence the contraction MOD.

This operator is useful for eliminating errors caused by approximation. An example is 7 divided by 6, to which the answer is 1 with a remainder of 1. In BASIC, however, the division produces the rounded quotient 1.166667. Usually the remainder can be calculated by multiplying the fractional part of the quotient by the divisor (.166667 × 6), but in this case, since the fractional part is rounded, the calculation produces 1.000002 as a remainder, which is slightly inaccurate. Mathematicians call this phenomenon a *round-off error*. Because computers deal with numbers as absolute finite magnitudes, in cases such as this the remainder can never be calculated with complete accuracy.

MOD returns the remainder as a whole number. The statement

```
LET R = 7 MOD 6
```

assigns the value 1 to R. Usually, of course, symbolic variables are used in MOD statements, as in

```
LET R = N1 MOD N2
```

which gives R the value of the remainder no matter what values are assigned to N1 and N2.

Precedence of operators

Just as in ordinary math, in BASIC you can have a single expression that includes several different arithmetic operations; for example

$$y = ax^2 + bx - c$$

In this case, the expression involves multiplication, exponentiation, addition, and subtraction. The term *precedence of operators* refers to the order in which different kinds of operations are performed in a complex expression.

The precedence of operators in BASIC follows the rules of mathematics. BASIC repeatedly scans the expression from left to right, in each pass performing the operations that pertain to the present level of precedence, then dropping to the next level. When all operations have been performed and the expression has been resolved to a single value, the calculation is complete.

The precedence of operators is as follows:

Pass	*Operation*
1	Exponentiation
2	Multiplication and division in order occurring

3 MOD (if available)
4 Addition and subtraction in order occurring

To illustrate the precedence of operators, let's trace the solution to the equation cited above. In BASIC it's written

```
LET Y = A * X^2 + B * X - C
```

For this example, assume X = 2, A = 3, B = 4, and C = 5. Making the substitutions, the expression represents

```
LET Y = 3 * 2^2 + 4 * 2 - 5
```

BASIC solves it in three steps as follows:

```
1. LET Y =  3 * 4  +  4 * 2  - 5
2. LET Y =   12    +    8    - 5
3. LET Y =          15
```

The fact that BASIC handles single-line computations in steps is not apparent; the computer is so fast that the solution seems to appear instantly. It is not so important that you remember how the precedence of operators works as it is to remember that it exists.

Factoring of expressions

When performing calculations both by hand and in programming, we tend to think less in terms of the precedence of operators and more in terms of computation groups. In the example above ax^2 is one group and bx is another. The mathematical name for a grouping within an expression is *factor*.

In BASIC, just as in algebra, factors can be delineated by the use of parentheses. This makes the expression more legible. Thus we could (and should) have written the example as:

```
LET Y = (A * X^2) + (B * X) - C
```

By comparing the two statements you can see that although they are equivalent, the second one is easier to read because its component parts have been set apart from each other.

When BASIC encounters a factor within parentheses, it resolves that factor first. In this case, then, it computes the value of (A * X^2) before doing anything else. Next it calculates the factor (B * X). Finding no multiplication or division outside the factors, it then drops the precedence level to addition and subtraction, thus solving the equation in two steps rather than three as shown previously. Factoring therefore has the double benefit of making expressions more readable and the program slightly more efficient.

Factoring also permits you to override the precedence of operators. Consider the expression

$$d = a(b - c)$$

If we wrote this as

```
LET D = A * B - C
```

the precedence of operators would multiply A times B *before* subtracting C, producing an incorrect answer. Let's trace it, assuming that A = 5, B = 4, and C = 2:

```
LET D = 5 * 4 - 2
LET D =  20   - 2
LET D =     18        *** WRONG! ***
```

The answer should be 10, because according to the original equation we have to subtract *c* from *b* and *then* multiply by *a*.

Consequently, the precedence of operators has to be overridden by factoring (as it is in algebra) as follows:

```
LET D = A * (B - C)
```

BASIC then resolves the factor (B − C) *before* multiplying by A, leading to the correct answer. Note that the BASIC expression closely parallels mathematical notation.

Factors can also be *nested*, meaning that one factor can include other factors. In mathematical notation, nesting is indicated by varying the style of the brackets, as in

$$R = (a[b - c])^2 - 4$$

where square brackets delineate a factor nested within the larger factor indicated by parentheses. BASIC uses only parentheses, so this equation is programmed as

```
LET R = (A * (B - C))^2 - 4
```

To solve the equation, BASIC first resolves the lowest level factor (B − C), then the next higher level (A times the result of B − C), then exponentiates that result, and finally subtracts 4.

A rule that applies here is that *the number of right parentheses must always equal the number of left parentheses*. To write the expression above as

```
LET R = (A * (B - C)^2 - 4
```

results in a syntax error because BASIC cannot find the right boundary of one of the factors.

There is no theoretical limit to the levels of nesting, which allows you to write very complex factored expressions. For example, the equation

$$t = \frac{(ax^2 - bx + c)^2}{(x - 1)^3} . y$$

can be programmed as

```
LET T = ((((A * X^2) - (B * X) + C)^2) / (X - 1)^3) * Y
```

Nesting can be carried to ridiculous extremes, as this example demonstrates. For the sake of clarity it's better to break a complex equation of this sort down into several interim steps leading to the ultimate result. The following program fragment illustrates one approach:

```
220  LET  X1 = ((A *X^2) - (B * X) + C)^2
230  LET  X2 = (X - 1)^3
240  LET    T = (X1 / X2) *Y
```

This fragment, while less efficient, enhances the readability of the calculations and reveals the steps that solve the equation.

Functions

In both mathematics and BASIC, a *function* is a value that derives from another value (*argument*) in some predetermined way, so that for any value of the one there is a corresponding value for the other. For instance, a sine in trigonometry is a function of an angle because the measurement of the angle determines the value of the sine.

We'll discuss functions at length in Chapter 8. For now the scope will be limited to the arithmetic functions that yield square roots and rounded numbers.

Square root—The function SQR calculates the square root of a value or an expression. For example, the statement

```
LET F = SQR(16)
```

assigns the number 4 to F. Usually a variable or an expression is the argument of the SQR function:

```
LET G   = SQR(N), or;
LET P   = SQR(N + 3), or;
LET Y2  = SQR(D * (J + 2)^5)
```

In the second and third examples, BASIC resolves the expression before computing the square root.

The SQR function can be used as a factor, such as

LET A = (J * SQR(T / 4)) + 9

In this case T is divided by 4, its square root is multiplied by J, and the result is added to 9.

The SQR function only works for positive numbers, since the square roots of negative values are irrational numbers that exist in theory alone. A computer can only represent rational (actual) values.

```
10 REM  **  PROGRAM PYTHAG.BAS                    K .PORTER  12/15/82
20 REM  **  COMPUTES HYPOTENEUSE OF RIGHT TRIANGLE BASED ON LENGTHS OF
30 REM  **      TWO SIDES USING PYTHAGOREAN THEOREM.
40 REM  **  VARIABLES:       A, B  =  SIDES
50 REM  **                   C1, C2 =  HYPOTENEUSE (EXACT, ROUNDED)
60 REM  **                   X      =  INTERIM RESULT
70 REM  ---------------------------------------------------------------
80 REM
90      PRINT "PYTHAGOREAN THEOREM"
100     PRINT "-------------------"
110 REM
120 REM  **  GET SIDES, QUIT ON SIDE A = 0
130     PRINT
140     PRINT "SIDE A (0 TO STOP)... ";
150     INPUT A
160     IF A = 0 THEN GOTO 350
170     PRINT
180     PRINT "SIDE B... ";
190     INPUT B
200 REM
210 REM  **  COMPUTE HYPOTENEUSE
220     LET X  = A^2 + B^2              :REM     SUM OF SQUARED SIDES
230     LET C1 = SQR (X)                :REM     HYPOTENEUSE
240 REM
250 REM  **  ROUND TO NEAREST HUNDREDTH
260     LET C2 = INT (( C1 * 100 ) + .5 ) / 100
270 REM
280 REM  **  OUTPUT RESULTS
290     PRINT: PRINT
300     PRINT "HYPOTENEUSE = "; C1
310     PRINT
320     PRINT "APPROXIMATE = "; C2
330     GOTO 120                        :REM     LOOP UNTIL A = 0
340 REM
350 REM  **  END OF PROGRAM
360     END
```

Figure 3.2 Program PYTHAG.BAS.

Figure 3.2 shows one application of the SQR function.

Rounding and truncation—In computerese, *truncation* means to chop off the fractional part of a number and reduce it to the next lower integer (whole) number. To *round* is to adjust the fractional part to the nearest higher or lower value. If we truncate 5.7, the result is 5; if we round 5.7, the result is 6, but if we round 5.2, the result is 5.

The function that performs both truncation and rounding is INT, short for "integer." The argument—either a number, a variable, or an expression—is enclosed in parentheses after INT in the form INT(argument). If V3 = 727.685, the instruction

```
LET W = INT (V3)
```

assigns 727 to W. When the argument is an expression, BASIC first resolves it and then truncates the result. If J = 2.6 and P2 = 1, the statement

```
LET A = INT (J + P2)
```

assigns the number 3 to A, since 2.6 + 1 = 3.6 and its truncated value is 3.

INT merely deletes any digits to the right of the decimal point. It does *not* alter the high-order portion of the number. Thus INT(7) is 7, *not* 6.

You cannot use INT (or any other function) on the left side of the equals sign in a LET statement. The instruction

```
LET INT(X) = (J * 9) + 6
```

is a syntax error. To achieve the desired result this statement must be written

```
LET X = INT ((J * 9) + 6)
```

The INT function can be used as a factor, for example

```
LET A = (I * INT(B / 7)) + R
```

In this case the first step is to find the integer value of (B/7). This is then multiplied by I and the result is added to R in order to compute the value assigned to A.

Rounding exploits the truncation function's ability to handle expressions. To round a value, add 0.5 to the argument, as

```
LET E2 = INT (L + .5)
```

If L = 2.3 then L + .5 = 2.8. Truncation returns a value of 2, which is nearest to 2.3. If L = 2.8, however, L = .5 = 3.3 which, when truncated, returns the number 3, and that is nearest to 2.8. Rounding is that simple.

But now let's suppose you have monetary amounts and you need to round to the nearest penny. If you simply add 0.5 and truncate you'll round instead to the nearest dollar. Since bookkeepers are persnickety about pennies, this just won't do.

To round to the nearest penny, multiply the amount by 100, round, and then divide the result by 100. In the following program fragment, line 620 computes interest (P * I1 is principal times interest rate in this case) and line 630 rounds the interest amount using this method.

```
620    LET M = P * I1
630    LET A = INT ((M * 100) + .5) / 100
```

Suppose the principal comes to $633.46 at 14.25 percent interest. This makes the interest amount M = 90.28605. Line 630 rounds this amount as follows:

```
M * 100              =   9028.605
9028.605 + .5        =   9029.105
INT (9029.105)       =   9029
9029 / 100           =   90.29
```

The value A thus becomes $90.29, which is the nearest penny amount to 90.28605.

You can round to different decimal points by varying the constant. To round to the nearest tenth, multiply and divide by 10; to the nearest thousandth, by 1000, etc.

Functions in action

Probably few of us recall much about the Greek mathematician Pythagoras, except that he invented a thing called the hypoteneuse and left behind a theorem about it with which to torture school kids. How well we all remember sweating over the Pythagorean theorem, looking up square roots in long boring tables! That was in the days before computers.

The Pythagorean theorem is, in fact, an elegantly simple concept embodied in the formula

$$c^2 = a^2 + b^2$$

which means that the square of the hypoteneuse is equal to the sum of the squares of the other two sides of a triangle. Another way of saying it is that to find the hypoteneuse, you square the sides, add them together, and take the square root of the result.

Figure 3.2 finds the hypoteneuse of a right triangle using the Pythagorean theorem. It produces both an exact result and an approximate length rounded to the nearest hundredth of a unit. The program repeats until a 0 is entered for side A.

The program plan is as follows:

Name—PYTHAG.BAS

Purpose—Compute the hypoteneuse of a right triangle based on the lengths of the two sides, using the Pythagorean theorem.

Steps
1. Get side A. If Ø stop, else continue.
2. Get side B.
3. Compute the hypoteneuse:
   a. Add the squares of the sides (A and B)
   b. Take the square root to find the hypoteneuse.
4. Print the result:
   a. Exact result as calculated.
   b. Rounded to nearest 1/1ØØ.
5. Repeat.

Figure 3.2 shows the program as developed and includes sample output from it.

Data types

BASIC is a *weakly typed* language, a feature that makes it easier to learn and use than other programming languages. In Pascal, COBOL, PL/I, and other popular languages, every program has to begin by declaring the names and data types of all the variables it uses. In BASIC, on the other hand, a variable name doesn't exist until the first time it's actually used, and its name implies its type (alphabetic or numeric). In effect, you don't have to give BASIC advance notice of the names and types of your programs' variables.

The term *type* refers to the representation of a variable within the computer. Externally (during input/output) all variables are either decimal numbers or alphabetic characters. The I/O processing, however, translates between these familiar formats and an internal binary representation more compatible with electronic circuitry. The details of how this is implemented are neither relevant to BASIC programming nor within your control; hence, they are beyond the scope of this book. Nevertheless, types have some external effects on your programs and if you wish you may specify data types for variables. Indeed, sometimes it's necessary to do so.

All BASICs have two fundamental types called string and numeric. A *string* variable contains alphabetic data. It is usually designated by a dollar sign suffix attached to the variable name (e.g., L$ or A4$). This tag notifies BASIC that it is a string and therefore subject to special processing rules. The handling of strings is so different from that of numbers that an entire chapter (Chapter 7) is devoted to it.

The numeric type is the focus in the present chapter. Microsoft BASIC supports three numeric types called integer, single-precision floating point, and double-precision floating point.

The *integer* type is easiest to deal with, both for us and for the computer. An integer is any whole number (i.e., no decimal point) such as 7, Ø, −258, or 29322. Note than an integer can be either positive or negative. If no sign is specified, BASIC assumes it's positive. It is permissible but pointless to prefix a number with a plus sign. The range of integers in BASIC is −32768 to +32768 (−32K to +32K).

Floating-point numbers are values, such as 3.14159, 99.44, and −212.4, that have a decimal point somewhere among their digits. Because its position is variable (contrasted with integers, where it always follows the last digit of the number), the decimal point "floats," hence the term.

Single and double precision have to do with the number of digits that can be represented in a variable. Double precision is actually more than twice as "precise" as single; it contains up to 17 digits in addition to the decimal point and sign, while single precision holds up to 7 plus the decimal and sign. A floating-point number can represent an integer simply by placing the decimal point after the lowest order digit.

Actually, single- and double-precision numbers can both represent the same range of values. What differs about them is the number of *significant digits* possible in their written forms (*significant digits* are the "leading" numbers of a value). The absolute range of values for floating-point BASIC numbers (in scientific notation) is $1.\emptyset \times 1\emptyset^{-38}$ to $1.\emptyset \times 1\emptyset^{38}$. Since a single-precision variable has up to seven significant digits but can represent a number of up to 39 digits, rounding limits its accuracy to the following range:

Smallest:	.ØØØØØØ1
Largest:	9,999,999

Double precision, with 17 significant digits, accurately represents the following smallest and largest values:

Smallest:	.ØØØØØØØØØØØØØØØØ1
Largest:	99,999,999,999,999,999

Numbers smaller or greater than these limits are approximate, but unless you're doing something awfully exotic, that shouldn't concern you very much.

BASIC automatically rounds to the nearest decimal point when computing a value that exceeds the number of digits possible within the type format. If the result of dividing 1Ø by 6 is single precision, for example, BASIC rounds the quotient to 1.666667, since seven digits can be accommodated. It does this by calculating an eighth (low-order) place and then adjusting the seventh digit as necessary.

In Microsoft BASIC all numeric variables automatically become single precision unless you specify otherwise. There are two ways of defining the type of a variable: by declaration or by a type-identifying suffix.

1. *Type declarations:* A declaration is a statement placed near the start of the program to define the type(s) of the variable(s) named. The general form is

   DEF*typ* [list]

   where *typ* is an abbreviation for the type and [list] is one or more variable names used in the program. When two or more names are included in [list], they're separated by commas; for example,

   DEFINT A3, L, R2

   declares the variables A3, L, and R2 as integers. The declaration statements and their types are:

DEFSTR	String
DEFINT	Integer
DEFSNG	Single precision
DEFDBL	Double precision

   Once defined, a variable remains of that type for the duration of the program. You can subsequently redefine the type of a numeric variable with the functions CINT, CSNG, and CDBL, but this is not a good idea.

2. You can avoid declarations and still define types by affixing an indentifying tag to the name of the variable. For example, A3$ is a string variable by dint of having the $ tagged to its name. The suffixes and their types are as follows:

$	String
%	Integer
!	Single precision
#	Double precision

The suffix makes the named variable not only of a defined type but unique as well. Thus B$, B%, B!, and B# are four entirely distinct values to BASIC.

As a result, if you use a suffix the first time you name a variable, you *must* be consistent and remember to include it every time the variable is used thereafter. If you have defined a double-precision variable V# and at some point you forget the # and call it simply V, BASIC will think you mean a different variable from V# and it will assign this "new" variable the value Ø. This can lead to monumental problems in debugging.

Declarations and type suffixes are mutually exclusive; if you use one, don't use the other for the same variables. Declarations offer the advantage of establishing once and for all the type of the variable(s), and thereafter you are spared the nuisance of remembering which type symbols go with which names.

The entire type business is a nuisance. Declaring single precision for numerics is pointless since it's automatic anyway. Integer values are processed more quickly by BASIC, but integers are useful only for counters and other control values in programs. The time savings might net out to a few hundredths of a second in a long-running program. It's not worth the trouble.

Types *are*, however, necessary under three circumstances:

1. To identify strings as distinct from numerics.
2. When working with amounts of money represented by more than six digits.
3. When working with extremely large or extremely small values in scientific/mathematical applications (then use double precision).

You can mix numeric types in arithmetic, for example, multiplying a single-precision number by an integer to obtain a double-precision answer. You can also change the type of a value (but not of a variable name) by assigning the content of one variable type to another. For example,

```
LET A# = B!
```

moves a single-precision value into a double-precision variable. If you move a complex value to a less complex type, however, some accuracy is usually lost, as when changing a floating-point number into an integer involves the truncation of any fractional part.

You can *never* mix strings and numerics in computations. The statement

```
LET N = A$ + B
```

is a syntax error because the plus sign with numerics means addition, whereas with strings it means concatenation (hooking together two strings to make one).

Therefore, except for strings, big money, and cases where extraordinary precision is required, avoid the use of types in BASIC. The negligible increase in program running time is far outweighed by your savings in sheer aggravation.

Throughout this book, I will follow the convention of naming string variables with the $ suffix and letting ordinary numerics be single-precision numbers, except for large monetary amounts.

E notation

When BASIC has calculated a very large or small quantity, it outputs the number in modified scientific notation. This is called "E notation" because the portion "× 10" is abbreviated "+E." Thus the number 1.307+E9 stands for 1.307×10^9, and 2.5512−E7 represents 2.5512×10^{-7}. You can also enter numbers in this form from the keyboard.

E notation appears in conjunction with single-precision numbers. With double precision the letter is replaced by a D, but it means the same thing.

If you find scientific notation distracting or hard to read, you can force BASIC to reformat results into conventional form with the PRINT USING instruction described in Chapter 5.

Investment comparison

Now let's tie together some of the things we've discussed about computations in BASIC.

John Smith has just inherited $30,000. After paying inheritance taxes, settling some bills, and taking a nice vacation, John decides to invest the remaining $20,000. He shops around and finds that there are two opportunities that appeal to him: nontaxable municipal bonds and interest-bearing accounts of deposit.

Like most of us, John's never paid a lot of attention to things of this sort, since he's never had a substantial amount of money to invest before. Looking into the two alternatives, he discovers a significant difference between them.

Municipal bonds pay a lower rate than deposit accounts and money in bonds doesn't compound. The municipalities will send him an annual check for interest rather than accumulating it and then having to pay him interest on a larger amount each year. On the surface it seems to John that a deposit account is a better deal, but—as his stockbroker has pointed out—he won't have to pay income tax on interest from the bonds.

The deposit account pays higher interest that will compound as long as John leaves his money in the account. Thus the amount will grow each year and so will the interest John earns. The problem is that he'll have to pay income tax on the interest.

John makes a pretty decent living, from which the IRS has helped itself to 35 percent on the average over the past few years. Assuming that his income, and with it his tax rate, will continue to rise, he decides to plan on a 40 percent bracket in the future. With that bracket in mind, is John better off with the bonds or the accounts of deposit?

If these two alternatives were the only ones to consider, the job would be fairly simple. John has discovered, however, that many governmental jurisdictions offer tax-free bonds at varying interest rates, and financial institutions compete with each other chiefly through the rates they pay on deposits. The two types of investments need to be compared with each other to find which is the more advantageous in view of tax issues. With a multitude of choices he could spend so much time figuring out trade-offs that he'd lose some of the interest he could be earning.

John decides to write a program on his personal computer to help speed the process of selection. He calls the program COMPINV (short for "comparison of investments"), and Figure 3.3 shows the notes he writes to himself in developing it. John's program as developed from these notes appears in Figure 3.4(a). To test the program, he uses two cases he's already worked up by hand. The following are the cases as he computed them, and the results of the program's calculations are shown after the program listing.

Having verified his program, John can now use the COMPINV program to evaluate various plans over differing periods of time at any tax rates and amounts he wishes. So can you.

Program name: COMPINV.BAS

Purpose: Compute net values of two alternative investments over *n* years:

1. Non-compounding tax-free municipal bond offering.
2. Compounding taxable deposit of account.

Assumptions:

1. Broker fees not considered.
2. Interest paid out from bonds will be reinvested, but the payoff from that won't be considered here (to offset broker fees).

Input variables:	Names:
1. Amount of investment	A
2. Interest rate on bond (for example .Ø75 per year)	I1
3. Interest rate on deposit account	I2
4. My tax rate (.4Ø)	T
5. Period in years	N

Procedure:

1. Enter variables.
2. Calculate value of bond investment after n years:
   a. Revenue (R1) = (Interest rate * amount) * years
   b. Value of investment (V1) = Revenue + amount
3. Calculate future worth of account after n years:
   [Note: future worth factor for a compounded amount = (1 + interest rate) to the power of years, e.g. 12% over five years is $(1.12)^5$]
   a. Worth at end of n years (W1) = Amount * factor
   b. Tax bite on interest (T1) = (Worth − amount) * my tax rate.
   c. Net value (V2) = Worth − tax bite.
4. Round values to nearest penny.
5. Output results.
6. Repeat until amount of investment = Ø.

Manual Solution

	Case 1	Case 2
Amount of investment	$20,ØØØ	$20,ØØØ
Interest on bonds	.Ø75	.Ø9
Interest on account	.12	.11
Tax rate	.4Ø	.4Ø
Period in years	5	5
Bonds after 5 years	$27,5ØØ	$29,ØØØ
Account after 5 years	$29,148	$28,221

Figure 3.3 Program plan.

```
100 REM  ** COMPINV.BAS                          JOHN SMITH   12/19/82
110 REM  ** COMPARES NET VALUES OF TWO INVESTMENTS OVER 'N' YEARS.
120 REM  ** FIRST INVESTMENT IS TAX-FREE NON-COMPOUNDING MUNICIPAL BOND.
130 REM  ** SECOND INVESTMENT IS A COMPOUNDING ACCOUNT WITH TAXABLE
140 REM  **        DIVIDENDS.
150 REM  -----------------------------------------------------------
160 REM
170      PRINT "NON-TAXABLE BOND VERSUS TAXABLE COMPOUNDING ACCOUNT"
180      PRINT "---------------------------------------------------"
190      PRINT
200      PRINT "AMOUNT OF INVESTMENT...........";
210        INPUT A
220      IF A = 0 THEN GOTO 510
230      PRINT "INTEREST ON NON-TAXABLE BOND...";
240        INPUT I1
250      PRINT "INTEREST ON TAXABLE ACCOUNT....";
260        INPUT I2
270      PRINT "YOUR TAX RATE AS A PERCENTAGE..";
280        INPUT T
```

```
290     PRINT "PERIOD IN YEARS...              ";
300       INPUT N
310 REM --------
320 REM  **  COMPUTE VALUE OF BOND INVESTMENT
330     LET R1 = (I1 * A) * N                  :REM     TOTAL REVENUES
340     LET V1 = R1 + A                        :REM     VALUE AFTER N YEARS
350 REM --------
360 REM  **  COMPUTE VALUE OF TAXABLE COMPOUNDING ACCOUNT
370     LET W1 = A * (1 + I2)^N                :REM     COMPOUNDED VALUE
380     LET T1 = (W1 - A) * T                  :REM     TAX BITE
390     LET V2 = W1 - T1                       :REM     NET AFTER-TAX VALUE
400 REM --------
410 REM  **  ROUND NET VALUES TO NEAREST PENNY
420     LET V1 = (INT ((V1 * 100) + 0.5)) / 100
430     LET V2 = (INT ((V2 * 100) + 0.5)) / 100
440 REM --------
450 REM  **  OUTPUT RESULTS
460     PRINT: PRINT
470     PRINT "VALUE OF NON-TAXABLE INVESTMENT  $";V1
480     PRINT "VALUE OF COMPOUNDING INVESTMENT  $";V2
490     PRINT: PRINT
500     GOTO 190
510 REM --------
520     END
```

(a)

```
NON-TAXABLE BOND VERSUS TAXABLE COMPOUNDING ACCOUNT
---------------------------------------------------

AMOUNT OF INVESTMENT........... 20000
INTEREST ON NON-TAXABLE BOND... .075
INTEREST ON TAXABLE ACCOUNT.... .12
YOUR TAX RATE AS A PERCENTAGE.. .4
PERIOD IN YEARS...              5


VALUE OF NON-TAXABLE INVESTMENT  $ 27500
VALUE OF COMPOUNDING INVESTMENT  $ 29148.1



AMOUNT OF INVESTMENT........... 20000
INTEREST ON NON-TAXABLE BOND... .09
INTEREST ON TAXABLE ACCOUNT.... .11
YOUR TAX RATE AS A PERCENTAGE.. .4
PERIOD IN YEARS...              5
```

```
VALUE OF NON-TAXABLE INVESTMENT  $ 29000
VALUE OF COMPOUNDING INVESTMENT  $ 28220.7


AMOUNT OF INVESTMENT........... 0
```

(b)

Figure 3.4 (a) Program COMPINV.BAS. (b) Sample run.

CHAPTER 4

CONTROL STATEMENTS

GOTO. IF . . . THEN . . . decisions. ELSE. Relational operators. Multiple comparisons. Loops: FOR/NEXT, nested loops, other loop structures. Menus and multiple conditions: the ON . . . GOTO . . . instruction. Other control statements.

As we've already seen, the instructions in a BASIC program are sequentially numbered to establish their order. The normal flow of a program takes the statements in numeric order from low to high, and when there are no more statements the program stops.

Many times, however, we need to alter this straight-through sequence. In most of the program examples up to this point we've used a simple loop structure to make the program repeat until a 0 is entered at the keyboard. This demonstrates one situation in which sequential execution is altered to suit circumstances. There are many other cases as well.

This chapter deals with control statements. *A control statement is an instruction that influences the way the program runs*, or, in other words, that alters the normal order of execution. Because control statements enable a program to evaluate circumstances and modify its own behavior accordingly, they form the basis for decision making and "intelligence" in machines.

GOTO

The simplest of the control statements is GOTO, which causes execution to jump to the specified line number. We've already seen GOTOs in the figures in Chapters 2 and 3.

The GOTO instruction is called an *unconditional branch* because no condition determines whether or not it's performed. When BASIC encounters it, control immediately and unquestioningly transfers out of the normal sequence and resumes at the named line number. The form of the GOTO instruction is

GOTO *n*

where *n* is a line number within the range of the program. If you specify a nonexistent line number, execution halts with the message "Undefined line number."

Note that you must explicitly state a line number in a GOTO; you cannot use a variable. The sequence

```
720    R = 220
730    GOTO R
```

won't work, and BASIC will reject it as a syntax error.

If you use the Microsoft BASIC interpreter's RENUM command to resequence a program's line numbers, it will also change the line numbers in GOTO statements to keep them pointed to the proper places. Most other interpreters furnish a similar service.

The GOTO statement is so simple it's easy to abuse it, and this has given rise to a great controversy in the programming profession. The chief complaint against GOTOs is that they obscure the flow and structure of programs. This is indisputably true, as Figure 4.1 demonstrates. The program (a revision of Figure 3.2) works, but following its flow is difficult. The problem increases manyfold when the program listing runs several pages and you have to flip back and forth tracing GOTOs.

The result of the uproar over GOTOs has been a sort of allergic reaction that strives to eliminate the irritant. This effort is called structured (or sometimes "GOTO-less") programming. Languages such as Pascal, the darling of structured programming, discourage the use of GOTOs to the extent that the instruction doesn't exist at all in some implementations, and it's inconvenient to utilize it in others. This is carrying things a bit far, but it proves that it's possible to write a program without GOTOs.

In contrast, the instruction set and the characteristics of BASIC make it difficult to write a program *without* GOTOs. Nevertheless, GOTOs should be used sparingly. If you find that your programs jump around a lot because of the liberal use of GOTOs, you need to question your programming techniques.

IF . . . THEN . . . decisions

We've also met up with the IF...THEN... statement in earlier program examples. This instruction makes a decision and acts on it, as in

```
160    IF X = 3 THEN GOTO 210
```

The general form of IF...THEN... is

IF (a condition is true) THEN (take action)

```
10 REM  **  PROGRAM PYTHAG.BAS                    K. PORTER  12/15/82
20 REM  **  COMPUTES HYPOTENEUSE OF RIGHT TRIANGLE BASED ON LENGTHS OF
30 REM  **      TWO SIDES USING PYTHAGOREAN THEOREM.
40 REM  **  VARIABLES:      A,  B  =  SIDES
50 REM  **                  C1, C2 =  HYPOTENEUSE (EXACT, ROUNDED)
60 REM  **                  X      =  INTERIM RESULT
70 REM  ------------------------------------------------------------
80 REM
90      GOTO 160
100 REM
110 REM  **  COMPUTE HYPOTENEUSE
120     LET X  = A^2 + B^2
130     LET C1 = SQR(X)
140     GOTO 380
150 REM
160 REM  ** GET SIDES, QUIT ON SIDE A = 0
170     PRINT
180     PRINT "SIDE A (0 TO STOP)... ";
190     INPUT A
200     IF A = 0 THEN GOTO 420
210     PRINT
220     PRINT "SIDE B... ";
230     INPUT B
240     GOTO 110
250 REM
260 REM  ** PRINT RESULTS
270     PRINT: PRINT
280     PRINT "HYPOTENEUSE = "; C1
290     PRINT
300     PRINT "APPROXIMATE = "; C2
310     GOTO 160
320 REM
330 REM  ** PRINT SCREEN HEADING
340     PRINT "PYTHAGOREAN THEOREM"
350     PRINT "-------------------"
360     GOTO 160
370 REM
380 REM  ** ROUND TO NEAREST HUNDREDTH
390     LET C2 = INT (( C1 * 100 ) + .5) / 100
400     GOTO 260
410 REM
420 REM  ** END OF PROGRAM
430     END
```

Figure 4.1 How not to structure a computer program. Try following the trails of GOTOs, and then multiply the problem by several pages.

In the preceding example, if the present value of the variable X is 3, then execution jumps to line 210. If X has any other value (even 3.000001), the branch is *not* taken and execution "falls through" to the next instruction, presumably line 170 in this example.

Any expression can be stated as the condition of an IF, and any resulting action can be specified for THEN, so long as the action is a valid BASIC instruction. IF... THEN... is thus a compound statement. For example,

```
IF X = ( SQR(( N * 3 ) + 1 )) THEN PRINT "X ="; X
```

In this example N is multiplied by 3, the result is added to 1, and the square root is calculated. This value is then compared with the current value of X. If the two are the same, the PRINT statement is executed. On the other hand, if X is not equal to the computed value, the PRINT statement is ignored.

Its flexibility makes IF... THEN... one of the most useful instructions in BASIC. It adds the dimension of decision-making to programs, permitting them to alter events based on circumstances, as in the earlier program examples where the programs stopped if some value was zero and ran otherwise.

You can use an IF... THEN... not only to control events, but to prevent errors that might crash a program. Suppose, for instance, that A can be any number including zero, and you have the instruction

```
110     LET P = T1 / ( A * 2 )
```

If A = 0 when this instruction is executed, division by zero is attempted and the program crashes. To prevent this you can code

```
100     IF A = 0 THEN LET A = .000001
110     LET P = T1 / ( A * 2 )
```

This sequence wards off disaster by assigning a very small value to A only when A = 0.

Multiple statements can be executed in the THEN clause, but you should use care. In the preceding example you might want to issue an advisory message when A = 0, as well as preventing the error. You can then write

```
100     A = 0 THEN LET A = .000001: PRINT "DZ ERROR
                     AT 110"
110     LET P = T1 / ( A * 2 )
```

Here if A is not zero, line 110 is executed immediately, but if A is zero, the correction is made *and* the message is issued by the PRINT instruction. In a multiple statement of this kind, when the IF clause is not true, control moves to the next *line*.

Caution is essential because it's easy to fall into the trap of unnecessary complication. If a whole bunch of things have to happen when the condition is true, thus making for a long convoluted IF statement, it's usually better to restructure using a conditional GOTO. In the following rewrite of the example the symbol <> means "not equal to."

```
100     IF A <> 0 THEN GOTO 130
110        LET A = .000001
120        PRINT "DZ ERROR AT 130"
130     LET P = T1 / ( A * 2 )
```

When A is *not* zero in this instance, BASIC skips down to line 130; when it *is* zero, lines 110 and 120 are executed.

The uses of IF... THEN... are almost endless. In the following section and throughout the rest of this book you will see the instruction used in numerous ways, and as you develop your own programs you'll find it indispensible.

ELSE

The IF... THEN... statement can be extended by an ELSE clause that serves as a catchall condition. It really means "otherwise," and the statement following ELSE is executed whenever the condition in the IF clause is not true. For example,

```
200     IF A = B THEN GOTO 300 ELSE GOTO 400
```

directs execution to line 300 if and only if A = B. If the comparison fails (if A <> B), execution jumps to line 400.

Relational operators

Because IF... THEN... statements involve comparison, a wider range of expressions is permitted in the IF clause than in a LET instruction. So far, except for the example above, we have only used the "equals" relationship, as in

```
IF A = B THEN GOTO 200
```

Above we introduced the "not-equals" relationship in the statement

```
IF A <> 0 THEN GOTO 130
```

This concept is extended in IF... THEN... statements to encompass "less than" and "greater than." The symbols signifying these comparisons are called relational operators, and they are:

Symbol	*Meaning*
<	Less than
=	Equal to
>	Greater than
<>	Not equal to
<=	Less than or equal to
>=	Greater than or equal to

IF always causes a comparison between the quantities on either side of the relational operator. The result is either true or false if the THEN clause is executed; if false, the THEN clause is ignored and execution moves to the ELSE or to the next line of the program; for example,

```
IF A < B THEN LET X = X + 1
```

If A = 7 and B = 9, then it is true that A < B, so the value of X is increased by 1 as instructed in the THEN clause. However, when A = 11 and B = 9, it is false to say that A < B; A is in fact greater than B, so the comparison fails and X remains unchanged.

The second case (A = 11 and B = 9) would be *true* in

```
IF A > B THEN LET X = X + 1
```

because it tests for A being *greater than* B.

You can use calculated expressions on either side of a relational operator, such as

```
IF (( A * B ) + 6) <> (A * C ) THEN GOTO 1140
```

BASIC computes the values of each expression and then compares them to determine whether they satisfy (true) or do not satisfy (false) the relational operator.

In the case of less than (<) and greater than (>), the result is false when the compared values are equal. That's why the operators <= and >= exist. The statement

```
IF X <= Y THEN GOTO 100
```

is read "if X is less than or equal to Y then go to 100."

You *cannot* use two relational operators in the same IF clause. In mathematical notation it is valid to write

$$0 \leqslant a \leqslant 7$$

meaning that *a* represents a number in the range of 0 to 7. In BASIC, however, the statement

```
140    IF 0 <= A <= 7 THEN GOTO 200
```

is a syntax error because only one relational operator can be used at a time. This range check could be written as

```
140    IF A <= 0 THEN GOTO 150
145    IF A <= 7 THEN GOTO 200
150    ...
```

Multiple comparisons

Although you cannot use two relational operators in connection with a single comparison, you can make multiple comparisons in a single IF clause, using the conjunctions AND and OR. The case above ($0 \leq a \leq 7$) could be written

```
IF A >= 0 AND A <= 7 THEN GOTO 300
```

and BASIC would consider the statement true only if A were in the range of 0 through 7, and would only go to line 300 if both comparisons proved true. Similarly, we could reject the statement as false and branch if A were outside the range, by writing

```
IF A < 0 OR A > 7 THEN GOTO 400
```

When A is within the range, the next instruction is executed.

Such multiple conditions need not involve the same variable. It's perfectly okay to write

```
IF A > 0 AND B = 7 AND C < 12 THEN STOP
```

The program then halts when all three conditions are satisfied; otherwise, it keeps running.

Loops

The loop is one of the most useful features in computer programming. You'll recall from the figures in Chapters 2 and 3 that a loop is a sequence of statements that repeatedly executes until a condition is true. The loop exit in the figures occurred when a zero was keyed.

In those programs, all of them variations on ADDMACH (Figure 2.1), a simple test using an IF... THEN GOTO... was adequate for loop control. The person operating the program controls the loop by entering or not entering 0 as the first value in each *iteration* (repetition).

Often, however, it's more desirable to have automatic loop control, in which the loop itself knows how many times it needs to repeat. For that, BASIC provides a pair of "book end" statements (one at the start of the loop, the other at the end) called FOR and NEXT. You can also control loops in other ways, as we show in the following sections.

FOR/NEXT loops—FOR and NEXT are two separate but related statements that serve as the boundaries of a loop. They are the most frequently used method in BASIC for loop control.

The FOR instruction identifies the start of the loop by assigning a variable to serve as a loop-control value and specifying the range of that control variable. For example,

FOR L = 1 TO 10

assigns L as the control variable and specifies that the loop will repeat ten times. The first time L = 1, the second time L = 2, the third L = 3, etc.

Any number of lines of instructions can follow the FOR statement, and there is no restriction on what they can do, with one exception: *within a loop the value of the loop-control variable must never be altered.* Therefore, in this case, the value associated with L can be used in calculations and for other purposes, as long as it never appears to the left of the equals sign in a LET statement.

A loop follows the normal sequence of instructions, which can include GOTOs and IF... THEN GOTOs..., until it comes to a NEXT statement. NEXT identifies the end of a loop begun by a FOR, and it contains the name of the control variable. In this case, it is written

NEXT L

```
100 REM  ** PROGRAM 'SQUARES'                K. PORTER   12/27/82
110 REM  ** COMPUTES AND PRINTS SQUARES OF A SERIES OF NUMBERS
120 REM ---------------------------------------------------------
125 REM
130       PRINT "SQUARES OF A SERIES OF NUMBERS:"
140       PRINT
150       FOR L = 1 TO 10
160         LET S = L^2
170         PRINT L, S
180       NEXT L
190       END
```

(a)

```
SQUARES OF A SERIES OF NUMBERS:

 1             1
 2             4
 3             9
 4             16
 5             25
 6             36
 7             49
 8             64
 9             81
 10            100
```

(b)

Figure 4.2 (a) Program SQUARES. (b) Sample run.

When BASIC encounters a NEXT, it increases the value of the loop variable and compares it with the upper limit specified in the matching FOR (in this instance, 10). When the new value *exceeds* the upper limit (L = 11), the loop is completed and execution moves to the statement after NEXT. Until then, BASIC jumps back to the instruction following the FOR and repeats the sequence.

Figure 4.2(a) illustrates the FOR/NEXT loop structure. This program loops ten times, each time printing the loop variable's value and its square. Enter it into your computer, because we're going to use it to demonstrate other loop features.

The range of values for the loop variable can be anything you specify, and not simply 1 to some higher number. If you replace line 130 with

```
130    FOR L = 12 TO 28
```

and run, it produces a list of all numbers from 12 to 28 and their squares. You can also go from negative to positive values for the loop variable, as

```
130    FOR L = -5 TO 5
```

or from a negative number to another negative number (as long as you increase value by addition). In a loop beginning with

```
130    FOR L = -25 TO -10
```

the values of L are −25, −24, −23... −10 during successive iterations. Try these statements on the computer.

The loop variable does not have to be an integer. Enter the statement

```
130    FOR L = 5.5 TO 19.5
```

and run, and you'll see that L goes from 5.5 to 6.5 to 7.5, etc. The value of the loop counter automatically increases in each iteration by 1.

The successive addition of 1 to a loop-control variable is an example of a default, because it just happens until you override it. In computerese, *a default is an action that automatically occurs unless otherwise specified.* To specify increments of other than 1 in a loop, you add a STEP clause to the FOR, as

```
130    FOR L = 1 TO 21 STEP 2
```

Try it and you'll see that L increases by 2 (the increment specified in the STEP clause).

You can also reverse the sequence of steps so that the loop counts downward rather than upward.

```
130    FOR L = 10 TO 1 STEP -1
```

decreases the value of L in each iteration. Note that in this case the upper and lower boundaries must also be reversed (from a higher to a lower number). To decrease a value successively is called *decrementing.*

The loop variable can be incremented and decremented not only by integral steps, but by fractional amounts as well. The instructions

```
130     FOR L = .1 TO 1 STEP .1
```

produces .1, .2, .3, etc., and

```
130     FOR L = .3 TO -.3 STEP -.1
```

sets successive values of L at .3, .2, .1, etc., down through −.3.

The range and step of a loop can be specified using variables and expressions in the FOR statement, and this is where a program starts to become "smart." As a simple example, enter

```
125     LET X = 10
130     FOR L = 1 TO X
```

run the program and you'll see that it functions as it did originally (L ranges from 1 to 10). Replace line 125 with

```
125     LET X = 15
```

and run again. Because X is the upper limit of the loop variable, the program now loops 15 times.

Now suppose that we always want the loop variable to have a range of 10 so that the loop ends when the variable becomes 10 more than it was originally, but we want to specify its starting and stepping values. To do this, enter

```
123     PRINT "STARTING VALUE...";
125       INPUT V
127     PRINT "STEPPING VALUE...";
128       INPUT N
130     FOR L = V TO (V+10) STEP N
```

Run the program, entering 5 as the starting value and .5 as the step value. The loop executes 20 times, with L starting at 5, then going to 5.5, then to 6, etc., until it reaches 15.

Run the program several times, entering various values. The loop itself decides how many times it needs to repeat. If you enter a very small step value, say .001, the loop will execute many times. Conversely, if you step by a large value it will make few iterations. When the stepping value is more than 10, it makes only one pass, since the step bumps the loop variable past its upper limit after the first iteration.

Nested loops—It's often necessary to place one loop inside another so that the inner loop repeats several times for each pass of the outer loop. This is called *nesting*. Nesting, which is especially useful for the manipulation of arrays (discussed in Chapter 6), occurs often throughout programming.

```
100 REM  ** PROGRAM 'NESTING'                        K. PORTER  12/26/82
110 REM  ** DEMONSTRATES NESTING OF FOR/NEXT LOOPS
120 REM -------------------------------------------------------------------
130 REM
140     PRINT "NESTED LOOPS"
150     PRINT "------------"
160     PRINT
170     PRINT "PASS","L1","L2"
180     PRINT "----","--","--"
190     LET V1 =  3                    :REM     UPPER LIMIT OF L1
200     LET V2 = 10                    :REM     UPPER LIMIT OF L2
210     FOR L1 = 1 TO V1
220       PRINT
230       FOR L2 = 1 TO V2
240         LET P = (( L1 - 1 ) * V2 ) + L2
250         PRINT P, L1, L2
260       NEXT L2
270     NEXT L1
280     END
```

Figure 4.3 Program NESTING.

Figure 4.3 demonstrates nested loops. The FOR and NEXT at lines 210 and 270 define the outer loop (L1), and the FOR/NEXT pair at lines 230 and 260 control the inner loop (L2). Note the use of indentions to clarify the loop structure; BASIC doesn't care about indentions, but they enhance readability.

In this example the outer loop repeats three times. During each pass of the outer loop, the inner loop goes through ten iterations. Thus the instructions at lines 240–250 are executed 30 times, as you will see when you enter and run the program. A break in the printout occurs at the start of each iteration of the outer loop because of the PRINT statement at line 220. Line 240 calculates how many times it itself has been executed, and line 250 prints this count and the values of the two loop variables.

You can modify the behavior of this program by changing either of the values for V1 or V2 at lines 190 or 200, and then running the program again. The output will show you what the program is doing and the effects of altering loop-control variables.

One ironclad rule about nested loops is that *you must always use different control variables for each loop*; that is, you can't have L as the control variable for two loops at the same time.

When you nest loops you must take care not to overlap them. The following shows overlapping loops:

```
┌─ 100    FOR A = 1 TO 10
│┌─ 110    FOR Z = 1 TO 20
││        .
││        .
││        .
│└─ 400    NEXT A
└── 410    NEXT Z
```

This sequence won't work because it's logically inconsistent; it attempts to terminate the outer A loop while the inner B loop is still being performed. The outcome varies from one BASIC program to another. Some issue an error message, such as "UNMATCHED FOR" or "NEXT WITHOUT FOR", and stop, while others lock into an endless loop. Regardless, overlapping loops never work. *A NEXT statement must always refer back to the most recent unterminated FOR.*

In this connection, there is no limit to the depth of nesting. One loop may be inside another, which is within another, which is nested in yet another, etc. Obviously, the greater the depth of nesting the longer the program runs.

You can combine NEXT statements when two or more loops end at the same point, so long as the loop variables are named in the proper order (opposite the order given in FOR instructions). In Figure 4.3 we could eliminate line 260 and code line 270 as

```
270    NEXT L2, L1
```

This tends to obscure the loop structure implied by the indentions, however, since to the eye it would appear that the inner loop isn't properly terminated.

The outer loop's variable can be used to control the inner loop. Figure 4.4(a) illustrates this by printing a histogram (Figure 4.4(b)) in which the number of asterisks in each bar is determined by and thus graphically shows the current value of the outer loop variable. (The semicolon at the end of line 230 means "print this character but don't end the line.") The inner loop therefore prints one asterisk for each unit value from 1 to the current setting of the outer loop variable A. Give it a try, and then change the value of J in line 190 and see what happens.

Other loop structures—As we saw in Chapters 2 and 3, it's possible to construct loops without the FOR/NEXT instructions. ADDMACH and the other programs built to the same model repeated until a zero was entered at the keyboard.

That type of loop and the FOR/NEXT loop differ chiefly in where the loop exit test occurs. In ADDMACH it takes place near the start of the loop (as soon as there's a condition to test), whereas in a FOR/NEXT loop the test occurs at the end so that the loop either repeats or control

```
100 REM  **  PROGRAM HISTO1                              K. PORTER 12/22/82
110 REM  **  PRODUCES A HISTOGRAM. LENGTH OF EACH BAR IS DETERMINED
120 REM  **     BY THE VALUE OF THE OUTER LOOP VARIABLE.
130 REM  ------------------------------------------------------------
140 REM
150     PRINT "HISTOGRAM #1"
160     PRINT "------------"
170     PRINT
180 REM
190     LET J = 12                          :REM     UPPER LIMIT OF LOOPS
200     FOR A = 1 TO J                      :REM     OUTER LOOP
210       PRINT A,
220       FOR B = 1 TO A                    :REM     INNER LOOP
230         PRINT "*";                      :REM     HISTOGRAM BAR
240       NEXT B
250       PRINT                             :REM     END OF LINE
260     NEXT A
270     END
```

(a)

```
HISTOGRAM #1
------------

 1          *
 2          **
 3          ***
 4          ****
 5          *****
 6          ******
 7          *******
 8          ********
 9          *********
 10         **********
 11         ***********
 12         ************
```

(b)

Figure 4.4 (a) Program HISTO1. (b) Sample run.

falls through ("out the bottom") to the first instruction outside the loop. Another major difference is that in the ADDMACH model the value N1 is only incidentally used for loop control, while in a FOR/NEXT loop a variable is specifically assigned as a control value and its other uses are only incidental to that purpose.

It's possible to construct a FOR/NEXT-type loop without using the actual FOR/NEXT instruction pair. If you do, you have to include state-

```
100 REM  ** PROGRAM 'SQUARES'                       K. PORTER   12/27/82
110 REM  ** COMPUTES AND PRINTS SQUARES OF A SERIES OF NUMBERS
115 REM  **     USING A DO-UNTIL LOOP
120 REM -------------------------------------------------------------
125 REM
130      PRINT "SQUARES OF A SERIES OF NUMBERS:"
140      PRINT
150      LET L = 1                              :REM     INITIALIZE
160 REM
170 REM  ** LOOP
180        LET S = L^2                          :REM     PROCESS
190        PRINT L, S
200        LET L = L + 1                        :REM     INCREMENT
210      IF L <= 10 THEN GOTO 170               :REM     TEST (UNTIL L = 10)
220      END
```

Figure 4.5 Program SQUARES, DO UNTIL loop.

ments to perform the control functions that are automatically done by FOR/NEXT. The stages of such a loop are:

1. Initialize the loop-control variable.
2. Perform the process that is the loop's purpose.
3. Increment the loop-control variable.
4. Test for loop termination.

Figure 4.5 is SQUARES (Figure 4.2), rewritten to loop without a FOR/NEXT. The stages of the loop are labeled by REMs. Enter it into your computer and run it. Because it's more convenient to use the FOR/NEXT instructions in counted loops, you'll probably seldom write a program of this sort.

This construction *is* useful, however, when we want to control the loop based on a value it calculates. For example, let's say we wanted to print a list of all the squares and their roots in order up to the first one past 1000. To demonstrate this in Figure 4.5, change the loop test by entering

```
210      IF S <= 1000 THEN GOTO 170
```

and run the program. The loop is now controlled by the value of S, so it repeats until the square exceeds 1000. This kind of loop is called a DO UNTIL, since it repeats until its control variable (the square, in this instance) exceeds 1000. FOR/NEXT loops are also DO UNTILs.

An alternative form of loop is the DO WHILE. As an example of a DO WHILE loop, suppose we want the SQUARES program to produce a list

```
100 REM  ** PROGRAM 'SQUARES'                         K. PORTER   12/27/82
110 REM  ** COMPUTES AND PRINTS SQUARES OF A SERIES OF NUMBERS
115 REM  **     USING A DO-WHILE LOOP
120 REM ---------------------------------------------------------------
125 REM
130     PRINT "SQUARES OF A SERIES OF NUMBERS:"
140     PRINT
150     LET L = 1                                  :REM     INITIALIZE
160 REM
170 REM  ** LOOP
180       LET S = L^2                              :REM     PROCESS
190       IF S > 1000 THEN GOTO 230                :REM     'DO-WHILE' TEST
200       PRINT L, S
210       LET L = L + 1                            :REM     INCREMENT
220     GOTO 170                                   :REM     LOOP END
230     END
```

Figure 4.6 Program SQUARES, DO WHILE loop (but this is not the best way to program it).

of all squares less than 1000: in other words, to repeat while the square is less than that value. One way to do this is to change the basic structure of the loop by moving the exit test, as shown in Figure 4.6. Although this program works, it embodies some poor programming practices. For instance, it's generally not a good idea to exit from the middle of a loop; also, this example needs two GOTOs to make it work. The DO WHILE loop is simplified and improved by using a compound IF... THEN... for the exit test, as shown in Figure 4.7.

```
100 REM  ** PROGRAM 'SQUARES'                         K. PORTER   12/27/82
110 REM  ** COMPUTES AND PRINTS SQUARES OF A SERIES OF NUMBERS
115 REM  **     USING A DO-WHILE LOOP
120 REM ---------------------------------------------------------------
125 REM
130     PRINT "SQUARES OF A SERIES OF NUMBERS:"
140     PRINT
150     LET L = 0                                  :REM     INITIALIZE
160 REM
170 REM  ** DO WHILE S <= 1000
180       LET L = L + 1                            :REM     INCREMENT
190       LET S = L^2                              :REM     PROCESS
200     IF S <= 1000 THEN PRINT L, S: GOTO 170
210     END
```

Figure 4.7 Program SQUARES, DO WHILE loop (better example than Figure 4.6).

There are three things to note about Figure 4.7. First, the base value L is set to zero in line 15Ø instead of to one. This is because, second, we moved the increment step to line 18Ø, before the process, so that the first thing the loop does is to increase the base value for the process. The third change is in line 2ØØ. Here a multiple action occurs; if the square is less than or equal to 1000, a line of print is produced *and* the loop repeats. When S rises above 1000, *neither* action occurs. Thus the loop "does while" S ≤ 1ØØØ.

Menus and multiple conditions

Interactive programs in BASIC frequently offer the user a multiple-choice *menu* from which to select an action. The user picks one of the actions by entering the number associated with it, and the program then carries out that choice.

To illustrate a menu, suppose we decide to expand our old friend ADDMACH (Figure 2.1) into a full-blown calculator program. Given two numbers, the program will let us choose what we want to do with them. The menu for the program will read:

```
1  Addition
2  Subtraction
3  Multiplication
4  Division

   Enter selection (Ø to stop)...
```

To subtract we enter 2, to multiply 3, etc. The program then performs the appropriate calculation and displays the answer. We can stop the program by entering Ø.

The program has to be able to evaluate the menu choice (we'll call it C) and take the action it specifies. In this case, there are six possible alternatives:

One of the four selections shown.
A Ø to stop the program.
A selection that is not one of the above.

This is called a *multiple condition*, the "condition" resulting from the selection keyed by the user.

Based on what we already know, we could code this multiple condition with a series of IF statements:

```
IF C = 1 THEN LET S = N1 + N2
IF C = 2 THEN LET S = N1 - N2
IF C = 3 THEN LET...etc.
```

This approach is feasible in the case of a simple program, but it leads to difficulties in more complex applications. What if some choices require a number of instructions? Then we would have to make some IFs conditional GOTOs, leading to an inconsistent structure and a hard-to-follow flow. What if there were 30 menu choices? Would we want 30 IFs in a row? In addition to blurring the program's structure, so many IFs would dramatically slow execution when we pick a number at the tail end of the list.

Obviously this is leading up to something, and we arrive there with the introduction of the ON...GOTO... instruction. This instruction is specifically designed to handle multiple conditions, such as menu selections, by *vectoring* (pointing) execution to different places based on a variable's current value.

In the case of the CALC menu above, we can follow the menu selection with the instruction

    ON C GOTO 1000, 2000, 3000, 4000

When C = 1, this statement transfers control to line 1000; when C = 2, to line 2000; when C = 3, to line 3000, etc.

The line numbers that receive control based on the value of C are not numerically significant, but their order is. This instruction could just as well read

    ON C GOTO 325, 190, 762, 10

and, if C = 1, the program jumps to line 325, if C = 2, to 190, etc.

```
100 REM  ** PROGRAM 'CALC'                       K. PORTER  12/29/82
110 REM  ** PERFORMS CALCULATOR FUNCTION ON ANY TWO NUMBERS.
120 REM  ** PROGRAM REPEATS UNTIL A ZERO IS ENTERED AS N1.
130 REM  ** VARIABLES:
140 REM  **             N1      FIRST INPUT
150 REM  **             N2      SECOND INPUT
160 REM  **             R       RESULT
170 REM  **             C       MENU CHOICE
180 REM -------------------------------------------------------
190 REM
200      PRINT "CALCULATOR:"
210      PRINT "-----------"
220 REM
230 REM  ** GET INPUTS, QUIT ON N1 = 0
240      PRINT
250      PRINT "FIRST NUMBER (0 TO QUIT)...";
260        INPUT N1
270      IF N1 = 0 THEN GOTO 1000
280      PRINT "SECOND NUMBER...";
290        INPUT N2
300 REM
```

```
310 REM  ** MENU
320      PRINT
330      PRINT "MENU:"
340      PRINT "-----"
350      PRINT
360      PRINT "1 ADDITION"
370      PRINT "2 SUBTRACTION"
380      PRINT "3 MULTIPLICATION"
390      PRINT "4 DIVISION"
400      PRINT
410 REM
420 REM  **  GET MENU SELECTION
430      PRINT "SELECT BY NUMBER...";
440        INPUT C
450 REM
460 REM  **  VALIDATE AND MAKE SELECTION
470      IF C < 1 THEN GOTO 1000               :REM     QUIT
480      IF C > 4 THEN GOTO 420                :REM     RANGE ERROR - REPEAT
490      ON C GOTO 500, 600, 700, 800
495 REM
500 REM  **  ADDITION (MENU #1)
510      LET R = N1 + N2
520      GOTO 900
530 REM
600 REM  **  SUBTRACTION (MENU #2)
610      LET R = N1 - N2
620      GOTO 900
630 REM
700 REM  **  MULTIPLICATION (MENU #3)
710      LET R = N1 * N2
720      GOTO 900
730 REM
800 REM  **  DIVISION (MENU #4)
810      LET R = N1 / N2
820 REM
900 REM  ** PRINT RESULTS AND REPEAT
910      PRINT
920      PRINT "ANSWER = "; R
930      PRINT
940      GOTO 230
950 REM
1000 REM **  END OF PROGRAM
1010     END
```

Figure 4.8 Program CALC.

The control variable of the ON...GOTO... (in this example, C) must be an integer with a value greater than Ø, and there is a correlation between its range of values and the positions of the target line numbers in the GOTO list. Thus, *for every potential value of the control variable, there must be a corresponding line number that is positionally significant.* This means that even if we had selection numbers 1, 2, 3, and 5 (and we knew that a 4 would never reach this statement), we would still have to include a "dummy" line number for the 4, because when C = 5 the ON...GOTO... instruction will transfer control to the fifth line number in the list.

The ON...GOTO... is thus vulnerable to unexpected control values. In the example instructions above, there are four line numbers corresponding positionally to the range of four menu selections. If C has somehow become less than 1 or greater than 4 when this instruction is executed, the program will crash.

We interrupt this discussion of ON...GOTO... to state a relevant general rule on programming: *You must* always *protect your programs from crashing due to unexpected data.* The case in point here is someone who selects menu item 9 when there are clearly only four choices. Although this program is relatively simple, in more complex programs a sudden crash because of an error can be catastrophic. Therefore when the program requires a fixed range of values in order to function properly, it's good programming practice to make sure the variable chosen is within that range. Because ON...GOTO... is less forgiving than any other instruction in BASIC with respect to a fixed range of control values, you have to check the control value before the statement is executed.

In Figure 4.8, a menu-driven calculator program, validation of the control value occurs in lines 470 and 480. Line 470 directs the program to halt when C = 0 (or a negative number). If C is greater than 4, line 480 forces the user to rekey a choice by jumping back to the menu selection routine at line 420. The effect of these two statements is to filter out unexpected values of C before execution arrives at the ON...GOTO... in line 490.

Note what happens now. If the user has chosen subtraction (selection number 2), the ON...GOTO... transfers control to the second line number in its list, which is line 600. Execution therefore bypasses the intervening lines (495 through 530), and the subtraction is done in line 610. With that finished, line 620 branches to line 900, where the answer is displayed. The program then loops back to 230 for the next computation.

It's necessary to end the section of each selected action with a GOTO (lines 600–620) that jumps to a common point (lines 900+), because otherwise BASIC will continue to execute consecutive lines even though they're part of another selection. For instance, if the GOTO at line 620 were left out, the subtraction would be done but then multiplication would ensue, and if line 720 were also missing, division would follow that. The program would thus only return the quotient of N1/N2 no matter which menu selection you made.

Other control statements

This concludes the detailed discussion of control statements for the moment. Four other control instructions have been deliberately omitted from this chapter. We'll come back to them at the points where they become pertinent. They are:

1. ON ERROR GOTO, in Chapter 9.
2. GOSUB
3. RETURN
4. ON...GOSUB...

(Items 2–4), in Chapter 8.

CHAPTER 5

TERMINAL INPUT/OUTPUT

An overview of terminal I/O. Keyboard input: INPUT, prompts, LINE INPUT. Displayed output: PRINT, inserting blank lines into output, literals, string variables, numeric output, output control with semicolons and commas, tabulation, formatted output with PRINT USING, application. Page copy. Odds and ends: WIDTH, POS, WRITE, SPC, SPACE$, LSET, RSET.

BASIC owes its popularity among nonprofessional programmers not only to its ease of use but also to its interactive nature. It's especially well-suited for conducting dialogs with a terminal user, in which information is exchanged in the form of a conversation.

BASIC communicates with people through three types of external machinery, or *terminals*, all of which can be and usually are accessible to it. These terminals are a keyboard, a display screen, and a page printer. The keyboard is an input device and the display and printer are outputs. Collectively they're referred to as I/O devices (for input/output) and the reading and writing operations that talk with them are called *terminal I/O*.

The INPUT and PRINT instructions accomplish all terminal I/O in BASIC. The purpose of this chapter is to discuss these two remarkably versatile instructions and their variations.

An overview of terminal I/O

Although a detailed knowledge of how I/O works is not a requisite to writing INPUT and PRINT statements in BASIC, a general overview of the processes is helpful in understanding what happens when you put them into a program.

In Chapter 1 we briefly mentioned the operating system, a special program that lives for the most part invisibly somewhere in the memory of your computer. Its job is to control the system by bridging between BASIC software and the computer's hardware. There are many operating systems; on micros CP/M is still the most prevalent (though the mass production of many inexpensive computers is bound to change this), but this discussion is equally applicable—with a few differences in details—to all other systems as well.

The BASIC interpreter reduces your program statements to machine language codes that can be executed by the CPU (Central Processing Unit), but it does not directly control the computer hardware. Certain control tasks—terminal I/O chief among them—are the duties of the operating system.

The operating system has an entry point, a memory address to which control is transferred by BASIC in the same manner as a GOTO and which serves as its "doorway." In CP/M this entry point is at memory address 5; it's a different location in other operating systems. When BASIC requests a service from CP/M, it places information related to the desired function into the CPU registers and then it calls address 5. The operating system acts on the information in the CPU by performing the requested service. When it's finished it returns to the instruction following the one that called it; thus BASIC regains control. This is not really much different from GOTOs that transfer control within your BASIC programs; the BASIC interpreter and the operating system form a partnership that functions as though they were a single program.

But of course they're not one entity. The statement

```
920    PRINT "ANSWER ="; R
```

actually involves four distinct components: the statement itself, the BASIC interpreter, the operating system, and the output device.

The common denominator among these elements is an area set aside in memory as a *buffer*. There's nothing special about a buffer; it's simply a block of memory locations that functions as a drop box for passing information from one element to another.

To execute line 920, BASIC first moves the quoted text (ANSWER =) into the buffer from the line as you typed it. Next it converts the value of R from internal binary format into digits and writes them into the buffer after the equals sign. Since there's nothing more to print, it places an end-of-line marker after the last digit.

Now it's ready to print. To do this under CP/M, it loads a 9 into register C, signifying a display operation, places the buffer's starting address into the DE register pair, and calls CP/M by transferring control to address 5. This transfer automatically saves the location of the next instruction in the BASIC interpreter as a return address.

CP/M takes over by evaluating the code in register C and executing an operation similar to ON... GOTO... that accesses the instructions for writing to the display. It uses the address in registers DE to find the buffer where BASIC built your line of output. Reading the characters from the buffer one at a time, it sends them to the display. At the end of the line, CP/M sends the carriage return and line-feed characters to the display, moving the cursor to the start of the next output line. It then retrieves the return address and uses it to restore control to BASIC at the point where the interpreter left off. (Printed output sent to a page printer is handled in exactly the same way, except that the destination is different.)

A keyboard entry is indicated by the BASIC instruction INPUT, as in Figure 4.8

```
260     INPUT N1
```

BASIC and the other elements also use a buffer for inputs, sometimes the same one as for outputs, at other times (depending on the implementation) a different one. Whichever, when the BASIC interpreter comes to line 260, it places the buffer address into registers D and E and a code 10 into register C, indicating a read-keyboard operation, and calls CP/M at location 5.

CP/M jumps to a different set of instructions to obtain input. First it sends a question mark to the display to prompt the user, and then it starts asking the keyboard if it has any data to send. Each time a key is pressed, the character is sent to the CPU and a signal turns on. CP/M then moves that character into the next address in the buffer. At the same time, it sends the character to the display so that the user sees what he or she keyed. When the ENTER key (or RETURN) is operated, CP/M considers the input completed. At the start of the buffer it records the number of characters entered, then restores control to BASIC by jumping to the return address.

BASIC processes the input buffer in one of two ways. If it contains alphabetic data (the variable name in the INPUT statement ending with a $ or declared a string), it simply moves the indicated number of characters elsewhere. If the data are numeric, BASIC converts them into internal binary format. In either case, it places the input into a memory area whose address is represented by the variable name.

Although these I/O operations seem (and in fact are) quite complicated, the speed of the computer is so great that they're accomplished in a few hundredths of a second.

Keyboard input

The BASIC instruction that accepts a keyboard entry is

```
INPUT [list]
```

where [list] is one or more variable name(s) that will receive the data item(s) keyed. When two or more names are specified, they have to be separated by commas:

```
INPUT A, B1, G
```

The INPUT instruction in this form prompts by issuing a question mark and the BASIC program halts until a response has been keyed, terminated by operation of the ENTER (or RETURN) button. After a response to the instruction above, the display might show

```
?221,37.14,9
```

221 is assigned to the variable A, 37.14 to B1, and 9 to G. And now we see why commas can't be included in large numbers.

As a matter of general programming practice (and despite the capabilities of the INPUT instruction) *you should request input of one item at a time*. For one thing it confuses the user to have to key two items, then five, then one, and so forth, in successive entries. For another, BASIC behaves strangely when an entry has too many or too few items, and sometimes it fails to explain that the number of items is incorrect. Also, it's difficult to read multiple responses, as the sample entry above demonstrates.

Another practice you should follow concerns prompting for input. An INPUT statement such as

```
INPUT N1
```

sends a question mark to the display screen and waits for a keyboard entry; it does not explain *what* it expects. In the absence of any explanation, the user can be confronted by a question mark and wonder what on earth he or she is supposed to enter. Therefore, *any INPUT request should explain what the program expects*. Previous sample programs, such as ADDMACH (Figure 2.1) and CALC (Figure 4.8) illustrate this practice with a PRINT statement preceding every INPUT.

As a convenience in setting up prompts, BASIC offers a variant of the INPUT statement that combines PRINT and INPUT in one instruction. The statement

```
210     INPUT "FIRST NUMBER (Ø TO STOP)... "; N1
```

is exactly equivalent to

```
210     PRINT "FIRST NUMBER (Ø to STOP)... ";
220     INPUT N1
```

The advantage of the first example over the two-line PRINT/INPUT sequence in reducing program size is obvious.

There is one constraint on this combined INPUT instruction: you cannot use a variable in the text of the prompt. The following shows the proper way to prompt using a variable in the prompt message:

```
610    FOR P = 1 TO 5
620       PRINT "ENTER VALUE NUMBER"; P
630       INPUT E
  .
  .
  .
690    NEXT P
```

In the first two iterations of this loop, the prompt reads:

```
ENTER VALUE NUMBER 1?
ENTER VALUE NUMBER 2?
```

If you tried to use the variable P in the input prompt with

```
620    INPUT "ENTER VALUE NUMBER"; P; E
```

BASIC would become confused, thinking you expected *two* values to be entered. Not only that, but any number you entered would alter the loop-control variable P. An instruction such as this won't generate an error message, but it will cause the program to malfunction. Therefore, *the prompt in an INPUT statement must always be exactly as you want it to appear.*

A semicolon after a prompt is significant. In sample line 210 above, the trailing semicolon means "don't go to a new line after printing this message." Your input thus appears directly after the prompt. An example of the display where you've entered 27.5 in response to this statement is

```
FIRST NUMBER (0 TO STOP)...? 27.5
```

If you *do* want the entry to appear on the next line after the prompt, leave the semicolon off. The display then reads

```
FIRST NUMBER (0 TO STOP)...
? 27.5
```

When you include the prompt in an INPUT statement, the entry *always* appears on the same line as the prompt, as in the first of the two examples immediately above.

Line Input—Sometimes an item of data has to have a comma in it regardless of what BASIC thinks. An example is the name John Jones, Jr. Another is word processing applications in which a line might have any number of commas. The intolerance of the INPUT instruction for commas could greatly complicate programming for these cases.

Fortunately, BASIC has a LINE INPUT instruction that disables the comma-checking feature of the INPUT statement. LINE INPUT treats an entry as a single alphabetic (string) variable that is one item of data from the first character to the end of the line, including commas. The form of this instruction is

```
LINE INPUT S$
```

where S$ is any string variable name.

The LINE INPUT statement can only specify one variable name, since it considers the entire entered line as one data item, and the variable must be a string (it can't be numeric).

As does the INPUT instruction, LINE INPUT has a prompting option. For instance, you can code

```
110    LINE INPUT "LAST NAME? "; N2$
```

and the resulting prompt and entry might read

```
LAST NAME? JONES, JR.
```

Note that a question mark is *not* automatically generated by LINE INPUT. This is unlike the regular INPUT instruction. With LINE INPUT if you want a question mark in your prompt, you have to include it in the text yourself.

You can thus use LINE INPUT in lieu of the regular INPUT when you specifically *don't* want a question mark in the prompt. If it happens that the input is numeric—LINE INPUT receives only strings, don't forget—you can convert the entry to numbers using the VAL function discussed in Chapter 7.

Displayed output

As you've no doubt already figured out, the PRINT instruction normally produces output on the display screen and not on the printer. In fact, it can also send output to page copy; we'll discuss how later in this chapter.

PRINT is the most versatile instruction in the BASIC language. It prints text, variables, numerics, and any mixture of them. It also performs calculations, rounds results, and formats the output. As we've said, it routes information to the display or the page printer; it can also write to files (although we won't discuss that until Chapter 10). This one instruction has so many features and options that most of the rest of this chapter is devoted to them.

Inserting blank lines into output—The readability of output is usually enhanced by leaving blank lines under headings, before and after significant items, and elsewhere. The simplest form of the PRINT instruction does this. You merely code

```
PRINT
```

with nothing after it, and BASIC sends an empty line to the output device (actually it sends a carriage return/line-feed sequence to move the cursor or print head to the start of the next line).

For the sake of program brevity, when you want to insert several blank output lines you can combine the appropriate number of PRINTs in one program line. The statement

PRINT: PRINT: PRINT

skips three lines on the output. The colons separating the PRINTs make this statement equivalent to individual PRINTs on three consecutive program lines. If you want to insert several blank lines into your output, you can also write

FOR X = 1 TO 15: PRINT: NEXT X

This constitutes a loop that writes 15 blank output lines and saves a lot of coding.

Literals—A literal is any text printed exactly as specified. Literals must be enclosed in double quotes, as in

PRINT "THIS IS A LITERAL"

The effect of this instruction is to produce output reading

THIS IS A LITERAL

Note that the quote marks don't appear in the output.

```
10 REM  **  PROGRAM ADDMACH                    K. PORTER 12/6/82
20 REM  **  PERFORMS ADDING MACHINE FUNCTION IN BASIC.
30 REM  **  REPEATS UNTIL A ZERO ADDEND IS ENTERED.
40 REM  -------------------------------------------------------
50 REM
60      PRINT "ADDING MACHINE"
70      PRINT "*************************************************"
80      PRINT "FIRST NUMBER"
90        INPUT N1
100     IF N1 = 0 THEN GOTO 180
110     PRINT "SECOND"
120       INPUT N2
130     PRINT "*************************************************"
140     LET S = N1 + N2
150     PRINT "SUM ="; S
160     PRINT "*************************************************"
170     GOTO 70
180     END
```

(a)

```
10 REM  ** PROGRAM ADDMACH                  K. PORTER 12/6/82
20 REM  ** PERFORMS ADDING MACHINE FUNCTION IN BASIC.
30 REM  ** REPEATS UNTIL A ZERO ADDEND IS ENTERED.
40 REM  ----------------------------------------------------
50 REM
60      LET B$ = "*********************************************"
70      PRINT "ADDING MACHINE"
80      PRINT B$
90      PRINT "FIRST NUMBER"
100       INPUT N1
110     IF N1 = 0 THEN GOTO 190
120     PRINT "SECOND"
130       INPUT N2
140     PRINT B$
150     LET S = N1 + N2
160     PRINT "SUM ="; S
170     PRINT B$
180     GOTO 80
190     END
```

(b)

```
ADDING MACHINE
*********************************************
FIRST NUMBER
? 28
SECOND
? 13.5
*********************************************
SUM = 41.5
*********************************************
*********************************************
FIRST NUMBER
? 365.25
SECOND
? 88.51
*********************************************
SUM = 453.76
*********************************************
*********************************************
FIRST NUMBER
? 0
```

(c)

Figure 5.1 (a) Uses several lines of asterisks to separate parts of the program's output [not as good as part (b)].
(b) Sets up a line of asterisks used repeatedly in the program as a constant [better than part (a)].
(c) Sample run of parts (a) and (b).

Literals are useful for report identification, column headings, and other fixed information. All the figures in this book print literals because it's good practice always to *identify what the output is.*

You can most easily underline literals with a following line of hyphens, for instance

```
230    PRINT "THIS TEXT IS UNDERLINED"
240    PRINT "-----------------------------------------"
```

Some displays and printers do true underscoring, but not all, and usually it takes some sleight of hand to turn the underline feature on and off. The use of hyphens works universally, but of course it takes two lines of print to do it.

String variables—A string variable is alphabetic text that is subject to change at various times during execution. It can also be a constant assigned to a variable name; for example,

```
100    LET A$ = "A$ IS A CONSTANT"
 .
 .
 .
180    PRINT A$
```

When line 180 is executed, it prints the output

```
A$ IS A CONSTANT
```

These two statements have the same effect as printing a quoted literal in line 180.

At first glance it would seem that there's little reason to take this approach when a quoted literal will do the same thing with fewer lines. In a short program that's usually true. In a long program, however, it's better to assign literals to variable names at the start. That way if you want to change the literal, you don't have to hunt for it.

Also, when the same literal is printed at two or more points in the program, it makes sense to assign it to a variable name. For instance, it's attractive to separate sections of output with lines of asterisks that provide visual breaks. Many programmers laboriously recode a line of asterisks at each such point, as in Figure 5.1(a), wasting effort and memory space. They would do better to declare the literal once and then print it as a string variable wherever needed, as in Figure 5.1(b). Both of these samples are revisions of ADDMACH (Figure 2.1) reworked to separate the input and results sections of output with one line of asterisks and iterations of the loop with two.

String variables are printed the same way as constants assigned to variable names. For example,

```
220     LINE INPUT "NAME... "; N$
.
.
.
580     PRINT N$
```

Line 580 prints the name you entered at 220. The string can also be acquired in other ways (from a file or a DATA statement) that will be discussed in subsequent chapters.

Numeric output—In the figures we've seen many cases of printing numerics. The simplest form of this instruction is

```
PRINT N
```

where N is a numeric variable. You can use the same form to print a literal number without the use of quotes. The statements

```
PRINT 7
PRINT "7"
```

are exactly equivalent; both produce 7 in the output.

When PRINT includes a mathematical expression, BASIC first resolves the expression and then prints the result, but *without* saving it as a variable. In the statements

```
210     LET J = 6
.
.
.
375     PRINT J + 3
```

BASIC prints the number 9 at line 375. Note that because the sum of J + 3 isn't assigned to a variable as in a LET statement, it's unavailable to subsequent instructions. In effect, the result of an expression in a PRINT is "assigned" to the output device.

The expression can be as complex as any in a LET statement.

```
210     LET J = 26
.
.
.
375     PRINT INT (SQR (J * 2) / 3)
```

This fragment evaluates the expression at line 375 and prints the answer: 2 in this case.

In single-precision numbers, BASIC prints the six most significant digits; in double precision, seventeen. When the value is a whole number, it omits the decimal point. A fractional value is carried out to six digits in total, but trailing zeros to the right of the decimal point are left off. Thus the number 3.71200 is printed as 3.712, but the number 3.71201 appears as it is. BASIC rounds numbers that can be approximately expressed in six digits, so that 3.712001564 is printed as 3.71202. Single-precision values over 99,999 or less than .00000005 appear in E notation.

This characteristic can be a problem in monetary output. The amount 97.1 is obviously $97.10, but it looks funny. In addition, a loop that prints a column of figures aligns the *first* digits and not the decimal points, producing

```
97.1
3.16
274.29
```

These problems, which pertain mostly to financial programming, are overcome by the PRINT USING statement discussed a few pages hence.

Output control with semicolons and commas—In some of the figures you might have noticed and wondered about the use of semicolons and commas in PRINT statements. More than simply punctuation, these symbols govern the behavior of the PRINT instruction and give you considerable flexibility in controlling output.

The comma is a zoning character when included in a list of items to be printed, as in SQUARES (Figure 4.2):

```
170        PRINT L, S
```

This instruction, you will recall, produced two columns of output on the screen. We also used it for three-column output in NESTING (Figure 4.3) with the statement

```
250    PRINT P, L1, L2
```

The concept of a zone in BASIC has to do with the vertical subdivision of the display screen or printed page into units of 16 columns (print positions) each. The 16-column zones thus divide an 80-column display into five vertical areas beginning at print positions 1, 17, 33, 49, and 65.

When two items in the list of a PRINT statement are separated by a comma, BASIC takes that to mean that they belong in consecutive zones. The instruction

```
PRINT L, S
```

places the value associated with L starting at column 1, and the value associated with S starting in column 17. The intervening print positions between the last character of one and the start of the other are filled with spaces.

Because the comma is actually a PRINT control character, it can be used in ways that appear a bit peculiar until you understand its true function. For instance

```
PRINT ,L,,8
```

places the value of L at column 17 and the digit 8 at column 49. Too many commas can cause problems. The statement

```
PRINT A, B, C, D, E, F
```

produces *two* lines of output because:

A is at column 1
B is at column 17
C is at column 33
D is at column 49
E is at column 65
F is at column 81

Column 81 doesn't exist (neither does 65 on some displays), so BASIC continues at the first column of the next line on the display (or printer) when it's used up all the print positions in the current line.

A semicolon has quite a different effect than a comma. It has two purposes, depending on where it occurs in the PRINT list. Between items it means "leave no space;" at the end of the list it means "print the list but don't go to the next line." In Figure 4.4 (HISTO1) the statement

```
230    PRINT "*";
```

tells BASIC to print an asterisk without ending the line. BASIC outputs one asterisk, advances the cursor or print head, and suspends further output until the next execution of a PRINT. In this program the instruction lies within a loop, so the same PRINT repeatedly executes, once for each iteration. The printed line is ended after the loop exit with the PRINT at line 250.

If you separate items in a PRINT list with semicolons, BASIC prints them with no intervening spaces. Type NEW and enter this sequence of instructions:

```
100    LET X1$ = "ALL"
110    LET X2$ = "RUN"
120    LET X3$ = "TOGETHER"
130    PRINT X1$; X2$; X3$
RUN
```

The resulting output reads

```
ALLRUNTOGETHER
```

This is because a semicolon tells BASIC to load the preceding value into the next available location in the buffer. Note that in this case the PRINT statement has no trailing colon, so the cursor moves to the start of the next line. If the line ended with a colon, the cursor would remain at the end of the output.

Now rework this program by entering

```
100     LET X1$ = "NOT"
130     PRINT X1$, X2$, X3$
RUN
```

The resulting output reads

```
NOT          RUN          TOGETHER
```

This shows the effects of commas and semicolons in PRINT lists.

When you print a positive numeric variable after a semicolon, BASIC puts one space in front of it. This space is reserved for the sign, so a minus (−) appears here when the number is negative, but in positive values BASIC suppresses the plus sign by replacing it with a space character. Thus the statement

```
PRINT "THE ANSWER IS"; F
```

produces the output

```
THE ANSWER IS 9
```

when F = +9, but when F = −9 it produces the line

```
THE ANSWER IS-9
```

If you definitely want a space before the number, make it part of the quoted literal. To avoid running together the text and the numeric variable in the preceding example, code

```
PRINT "THE ANSWER IS  "; F
```

(Note the space between IS and the quote marks.) In the case of positive and negatives values of F, you will get

```
THE ANSWER IS    9
```

or

```
THE ANSWER IS   -9
```

You can mix commas and semicolons, literals, strings, and numeric variables in the same PRINT statement, and also do calculations. Figure 5.2(a) computes the cubes of the series 1–10. Note line 160, which demonstrates these capabilities

Tabulation—Although the comma is a simple way to force output into a tabular format, often it's necessary to squeeze the columns closer together than the comma permits, or you want to skip to a print position other

```
100 REM  ** PROGRAM 'CUBES'                          K. PORTER 1/3/83
110 REM  ** COMPUTES AND PRINTS CUBES OF THE SERIES OF NUMBERS 1..10
120 REM ------------------------------------------------------------
130 REM
140      LET A$ = "CUBE IS"
150      FOR V = 1 TO 10
160        PRINT "IN LOOP"; V; " (BASE VALUE)", A$; V^3
170      NEXT V
180      END
```
(a)

```
IN LOOP 1  (BASE VALUE)      CUBE IS 1
IN LOOP 2  (BASE VALUE)      CUBE IS 8
IN LOOP 3  (BASE VALUE)      CUBE IS 27
IN LOOP 4  (BASE VALUE)      CUBE IS 64
IN LOOP 5  (BASE VALUE)      CUBE IS 125
IN LOOP 6  (BASE VALUE)      CUBE IS 216
IN LOOP 7  (BASE VALUE)      CUBE IS 343
IN LOOP 8  (BASE VALUE)      CUBE IS 512
IN LOOP 9  (BASE VALUE)      CUBE IS 729
IN LOOP 10  (BASE VALUE)     CUBE IS 1000
```
(b)

Figure 5.2 (a) Program CUBES. (b) Sample run.

than a multiple of 16. For this you can use the TAB function in a PRINT instruction.

As with the INT and SQR functions, TAB requires a value enclosed in parentheses, as in TAB(20), which skips to the twentieth print position in the line. The value can be a literal number, a variable, or an expression. The following are all valid:

```
TAB(20)
TAB(V)
TAB((V * 12) +7)
```

The argument of the TAB function is assumed to be an integer, and if it's not, TAB rounds it. If J = 12.28 and you code

```
PRINT TAB(J) A$
```

BASIC advances to column 12 and begins A$ there, but if J = 12.78, the output begins at column 13.

TAB *must* appear within the list of a PRINT statement; it cannot stand alone as an individual instruction. You can include several TABs in the same line intermixed with printable items. Semicolons may optionally be used to separate TABs and data items; they have no effect in connection with TABs. Thus you can code

```
PRINT "LEFT"; TAB(35); "CENTER"; TAB(70); "RIGHT"
```

or

```
PRINT "LEFT" TAB(35) "CENTER" TAB(70) "RIGHT"
```

and the instructions are exactly equivalent. This statement produces the output line

```
LEFT                              CENTER                              RIGHT
```

TAB only advances the print position to the right. You can't move to the left from the current column. In the statement

```
PRINT TAB(20) "LAST" TAB(1) "FIRST"
```

BASIC honors the first TAB, but since it can't tab to the left on the same line it jumps to the next line to produce

```
                   LAST
FIRST
```

instead of the desired output line

```
FIRST              LAST
```

Note also that TAB specifies a print column relative to the *first* character position in the line, and not relative to the *current* position. Therefore you don't have to adjust for inconsistent tabbing if you have variable-length data items. When you want the next item to appear at column 40, you simply write TAB(40), and the only possible glitch is if in some lines you've already passed column 40 at this point.

Figures 5.3(a) and 5.4(a) show two applications of the TAB function. Figure 5.3(a) is purely a demonstration in which the value of the loop-control variable determines the number of columns tabbed, and is then printed.

Figure 5.4(a) is much more sophisticated. It prints a table showing the products of all values from 1 to M (in the example M = 15) multiplied by all values from 1 to 9.

The TAB computations in lines 210 and 300 are deliberately made complex in this sample program to illustrate the flexibility available. Line 300, in particular, is more complicated than it really ought to be; it would have been better to have written it as the following three statements:

```
300    LET P = R * C                : REM  PRODUCT
303    LET T = ((C - 1) * 5) + 8    : REM  TAB LOCATION
307    PRINT TAB(T); P;
```

```
100 REM  **  PROGRAM 'TABDEMO'                          K. PORTER  1/3/83
110 REM  **  DEMONSTRATES THE TAB FUNCTION
120 REM ------------------------------------------------------------
130 REM
140     PRINT "TAB DEMONSTRATION"
150     PRINT "-----------------"
160     PRINT
170     LET M = 20                          :REM    UPPER LIMIT OF LOOP
180     FOR T = 1 TO M
190       PRINT TAB(T); T
200     NEXT T
210     END
```

(a)

```
TAB DEMONSTRATION
-----------------

  1
   2
    3
     4
      5
       6
        7
         8
          9
           10
            11
             12
              13
               14
                15
                 16
                  17
                   18
                    19
                     20
```

(b)

Figure 5.3 (a) Program TABDEMO. (b) Sample run.

After you've entered and run this program, let's examine the TAB calculation to see why it has to be as involved as it is. Note that in the output the left column is wider than the others to make it visually distinct as the base value for each row, separating it from the products. This first column is eight spaces wide, thus explaining the (+ 8) factor in the

```
100 REM  **  PROGRAM 'TIMESTAB'                          K. PORTER  1/3/83
110 REM  **  PRINTS TIMES TABLES IN A MATRIX 'M' ROWS BY 9 COLUMNS
120 REM -----------------------------------------------------------------
130 REM
140     LET M = 15                                :REM     NUMBER OF ROWS
150     PRINT "TIMES TABLES FOR";M;"BY 9 VALUES:"
160     PRINT
170 REM
180 REM  **  PRINT COLUMN HEADINGS
190     PRINT "BASE x";
200     FOR C = 1 TO 9
210       PRINT TAB(((C - 1) * 5) + 8) C;
220     NEXT C
230     PRINT                                     :REM     END HEADING LINE
240     PRINT                                     :REM     EXTRA LINE
250 REM
260 REM  **  GO FOR M ROWS X 9 COLUMNS
270     FOR R = 1 TO M                            :REM     OUTER (ROW) LOOP
280       PRINT R;                                :REM     ROW VALUE
290       FOR C = 1 TO 9                          :REM     INNER (COL) LOOP
300         PRINT TAB((( C - 1 ) * 5) + 8) (R * C);
310       NEXT C
320       PRINT
330     NEXT R
340     END
```

(a)

```
TIMES TABLES FOR 15 BY 9 VALUES:

BASE x  1    2    3    4    5    6    7    8    9

 1      1    2    3    4    5    6    7    8    9
 2      2    4    6    8    10   12   14   16   18
 3      3    6    9    12   15   18   21   24   27
 4      4    8    12   16   20   24   28   32   36
 5      5    10   15   20   25   30   35   40   45
 6      6    12   18   24   30   36   42   48   54
 7      7    14   21   28   35   42   49   56   63
 8      8    16   24   32   40   48   56   64   72
 9      9    18   27   36   45   54   63   72   81
 10     10   20   30   40   50   60   70   80   90
 11     11   22   33   44   55   66   77   88   99
 12     12   24   36   48   60   72   84   96   108
 13     13   26   39   52   65   78   91   104  117
 14     14   28   42   56   70   84   98   112  126
 15     15   30   45   60   75   90   105  120  135
```

(b)

Figure 5.4 (a) Program TIMESTAB. (b) Sample run.

expression; it's an offset for the columns of products.

The products forming the elements of the table are each in a column five spaces wide. The first product begins at position 8 and each column is another five to the right from there. Thus, computing TAB positions for three consecutive values of C:

C = 1:	((1 − 1) × 5) + 8 = 8
C = 2:	((2 − 1) × 5) + 8 = 13
C = 3:	((3 − 1) × 5) + 8 = 18

These results satisfy the spacing requirements.

Usually tabbed printing is not this complicated, and you merely set a few fixed TAB stops in a PRINT statement, such as

```
PRINT A$ TAB(25) N1 TAB(4Ø) G
```

which, every time it executes, places the string A$ at print position 1, the value of N1 at position 25, and the value of G at 4Ø.

We'll often encounter TAB in subsequent figures.

Formatted output with PRINT USING—The output controls we've covered so far provide a rich and flexible set of options for formatting results, but they fail to address some commonly accepted conventions. It's customary, for example, to use two decimal places for cents ($1.6Ø and not $1.6), immediately precede money amounts with a dollar sign, and line up the decimal points (not the first digits) in columns of figures. There are also others less commonly recognized, such as preceding amounts on checks with asterisks. For professional-looking output, BASIC offers the powerful formatting instruction PRINT USING.

The form of this instruction is

```
PRINT USING [image]; [list]
```

where [image] is a symbolic representation of the output buffer, and [list] is the items to be printed.

As we discussed earlier, BASIC builds the output line in a buffer according to the parameters of the PRINT statement. The image specifies exactly how the buffer is to be constructed with regard to the placement and treatment of output items. It does this through various special symbols and is therefore a symbolic image of the output line.

The first symbol we'll talk about is #, which represents one digit. The designation #### stands for a four-digit integer number; ### means a three-digit integer. The statement

```
PRINT USING "####"; H2
```

puts the last digit of the value of H2 in the rightmost place of the four-digit field. If this instruction is in a loop, it prints a column of numbers aligned on the last digits; for instance,

```
   2
2472
  16
 291
```

where these are successive values of H2. Note that any unused digit positions are filled with spaces.

You have to specify a numeric field with enough #'s to accommodate the largest potential value of the number it will contain. In the example above, four digits is the maximum size, and the largest number has four places. Suppose, however, that you coded the instruction

```
PRINT USING "###"; H2
```

and printed the same list. The buffer is too small for the largest value of H2, so you get the output

```
  2
%2472
 16
291
```

The largest value is still printed, but misaligned and with % preceding it to denote an error in sizing the buffer. This happens as a result of inadequate planning; the programmer didn't anticipate the largest number that would be output by the PRINT USING.

Now let's say we want to print two columns of numbers as we did in the SQUARES program (Figure 4.2, line 170). The first number will always be less than 100, so a two-digit field will suffice for it. The second number will be the square of the first, and since the largest two-digit value is 99, the largest second number will be 99^2, or 9801. Therefore we have to provide a four-digit field for it. Ten spaces will separate the last digit of the first column and the first digit of the second which are called L and S. To code this, write

```
170 PRINT USING "##          ####"; L, S
```

Each time BASIC executes this instruction it prints the value of L in the first field, the value of S in the second, and leaves ten spaces between them. Any unused digit positions at the start of the second field count as part of the field even though they're filled with spaces, so the proper alignment holds true. When L is in the range 1–15, this statement produces the list:

1	1
2	4
3	9
4	16
.	.
.	.
.	.
15	225

If you think of the buffer image in the PRINT USING statement as a template, the last line of this list overlays on it as follows:

```
##   ####   Buffer image
1 5   2 2 5  Data (L, S)
```

When a numeric field has a decimal point, specify it at the appropriate place in the image. To print a maximum six-digit number D with two decimal places, code

PRINT USING "####.##"; D

This forces BASIC to print trailing zero(s) in the decimal field. It also aligns a list on the decimal points when in a loop. For three successive values of D it will print

```
  22.7Ø
   1.ØØ
3621.Ø4
```

BASIC rounds the fractional part of the number to fit within the number of decimal places. Thus if D = 221.837, this PRINT USING produces 221.84 since there are two places in the decimal portion.

As we've already said, you can't enter or code large numbers with embedded commas, such as 32,216.29; you have to write it as 32216.29. You can, however, print out numbers with PRINT USING in groups of three digits separated by commas, as in

PRINT USING "##,###.##"; J

For consecutive values of J, this will produce a list such as

```
 3,1ØØ.12
   214.4Ø
32,216.29
```

Note that the comma is automatically omitted where it's inappropriate. You can also include it in an integer field, as in

PRINT USING "##,###"; I

In monetary amounts, you can place a floating dollar sign in front of the first digit of the amount by using the $$ symbol. The dollar sign changes position according to the number of digits to the left of the decimal point. The symbol signifies a floating dollar sign, and the second $ also furnishes an extra digit position. The instruction

```
PRINT USING "$$#,###.##"; A2
```

in a loop will produce a list such as

```
 $3,100.12
   $214.40
$32,216.29
```

To discourage fraud, checks are often printed with leading asterisks in the amount field. This is done with the **$ symbol, which also adds *two* digit positions to the buffer. The statement

```
PRINT USING "**$,###.##"; V
```

prints successive checks with amounts such as

```
*$3,100.12
***$214.40
$32,216.29
```

When the PRINT USING instruction outputs a negative quantity, it normally places the minus sign immediately ahead of the first digit. If you prefer to have it *after* the last digit instead, you can code an instruction such as

```
PRINT USING "###-"; Y
```

The minus sign only prints when the number is negative. In positive values it is replaced by a space character.

Literal text can be included in the image exactly as it should appear in the output, such as

```
PRINT USING "AMOUNT OF PAYMENT $$##.##"; P
```

If the payment P is $112.28, this statement produces

```
AMOUNT OF PAYMENT $112.28
```

Since they control the way BASIC fills the buffer, the following characters cannot be included in literal text specified in the image:

```
#  **  !  \  ,  $$  +  -
```

String variables are placed in the buffer with a pair of backslashes (\). The text begins with the first backslash and ends with the second, as in

```
PRINT USING "\              \"; T$
```

This statement will print the first eight characters of any string value for T$, since there are two backslashes and six spaces between them, for a total of eight print positions. When T$ has fewer than eight characters, the right-hand unused positions are filled with spaces. This has the effect of aligning alphabetic text on the first character in repeated executions, which is consistent with normal formatting practices.

You can also specify literal text in the list portion of the PRINT USING instruction, in place of inserting it inside the buffer image and in place of a string variable; for instance,

```
PRINT USING "\                \ #"; "NUMBER", N
```

When N = 9, this statement produces the output

```
NUMBER 9
```

You should allocate enough space to accommodate the longest expected string. Unlike numeric overflow flagged by a %, however, BASIC doesn't tell you whether the string was too long for the field. It simply truncates any right-hand characters that it can't fit in. For example, suppose we have a loop to print a list of last names with the instruction

```
PRINT USING "\            \"; N2$
```

We've allocated space for seven characters. The following shows the effect on several names:

N2$	*Printed*
JONES	JONES
STADLER	STADLER
ANDERSON	ANDERSO
SHAUNNESSY	SHAUNNE

If the truncation is unacceptable, the length of the field has to be increased to accommodate the longest expected name.

As an alternative to the fixed-length alphabetic field, you can specify a variable-length field with the symbol & (ampersand). When this symbol appears in the image it tells BASIC to "use as much space as you need to hold the whole string." This has the advantage that it doesn't arbitrarily truncate the string to fit within so many character positions, but it has the disadvantage that any fields to the right of the & will vary in position as the length of the string varies. For example, in three successive executions of the statement

```
PRINT USING "###  &  $$##.##"; A, B$, F
```

the results might read

```
231  JOHANNSEN    $251.88
 31  AMOS     $118.50
559  MARTIN     $88.43
```

Thus the & for a variable-length string field is only useful as the last field in an image, or if you don't care about maintaining a columnar format to its right.

The backslash symbols provide for a minimum string field length of two characters (USING "\\"). When you want to print a single character, use the symbol ! (exclamation point). This symbol prints one character, and if the value specified for it is a string, it prints only the first character, as in

```
PRINT USING "FIRST CHARACTER OF \        \ IS !"; N$, N$
```

When N$ = TYLER, this statement prints the line

```
FIRST CHARACTER OF TYLER IS T
```

These format specifications can be freely mixed. A daily accounts receivable program might contain the instruction

```
PRINT USING "PAYMENT NO. ## FROM \        \ $$#.##"; P, N$, A
```

This will produce a report reading

```
PAYMENT NO.  3 FROM JOHNSON      $36.50
PAYMENT NO. 15 FROM SMITH         $9.12
PAYMENT NO.  8 FROM BROWN        $24.96
```

Note that the variable names must be specified in the order of their appearance in the buffer image.

The preceding example shows a rather long buffer; it can be even longer, as when a formatted line of print spans the width of the screen or a sheet of paper. Also, sometimes the same image is used in two or more separate PRINT USINGs. For these reasons it's often convenient to assign the buffer image to a string variable name, for example

```
100    LET I$ = "PAYMENT NO. ## FROM \        \ $$#.##"
 .
 .
 .
230    PRINT USING I$; P, N$, A
```

These two statements are equivalent to the preceding example, in which the image was specified in the PRINT USING instruction itself. Now, however, you can have another statement

```
625    PRINT USING I$; A4, J$, Q
```

that uses the same buffer image but with different variables. This simplifies the program, saves space, and relieves you of the burden of rekeying the same image at each point where it's used.

Application—To put some of this newly discovered formatting power to practical use, let's rejoin our friend John Smith. Since we left him two chapters ago John has made a profitable investment, but he's also suffered a setback. His car died of old age and his wife thinks the living room furniture is soon to follow. Not wanting to disturb his investment, John decides to borrow the money he needs for the car and furniture.

He has called around to find out the interest rates being charged by several lenders, but he's not yet sure how much he'll need. To some extent he'll govern his tastes by the monthly payment, which in turn is determined by the amount he borrows and the repayment period of the loan. Rather than constantly calling banks to get quotes for specific amounts and time periods, John decides to write a program that will give him some ranges. Figure 5.5 shows his program plan.

This program computes a series of loan prices based on 1... N years' repayment periods, so John decides to call it LNPRICES. Figure 5.6 shows the code developed from these notes. John has incorporated some interesting features into it.

Lines 22Ø and 23Ø define buffer images for PRINT USINGs. The first is for the pricing report (line 69Ø). The other (D1$) will be used for printing a dollar amount with a floating dollar sign. We'll discuss this particular image further in a moment.

First, though, note line 39Ø. If a Ø loan amount is entered, the program quits. The overall structure, therefore, follows the same general pattern as ADDMACH and several other program examples we've seen.

Now look at what John's done in line 42Ø. He knows that the entry of interest rates can be tricky; is the user supposed to input .1425 or 14.25? He's included an instruction that lets the user enter either one. If an interest percentage greater than 1 is input, line 42Ø changes it to a decimal fraction, but if .1425 (or whatever) is entered, it's left as is.

Just to make the report prettier, John reads the input back out in lines 46Ø–59Ø. Note the use of TABs to present a tidy column of data. Especially note lines 5ØØ–51Ø. Here he prints a literal and tabs to position 2Ø, and then he utilizes a PRINT USING with D1$ mentioned earlier to give the dollar amount of the loan a more conventional appearance than it had at input.

The TABs in lines 5ØØ, 53Ø, and 55Ø go to different print positions because of the differing widths of the data. The object of this game is to line up the units position of each number on the output. Line 53Ø tabs one to the left of line 55Ø (even though the output of two-digit numbers starts in the same print position) because a number not produced by a

1. Purpose—Calculate monthly payments for each of a series of years, based on an amount borrowed (B) at a given interest rate (I).

   Produce a report showing the terms and, for each year in the series, the number of years for repayment, the monthly installment, and the total of all payments.
2. Inputs:

	Name:
Amount borrowed	B
Interest rate	I
Maximum years in series	N

3. Calculations:
   a. Monthly interest = I / 12
   b. Total number of payments = Years × 12
   c. Monthly payment (M1) =

   $$B\left[\frac{I}{1-(1+I)^{-y}}\right]$$ where I = mo. int, Y = years × 12

   [d. Total of all payments (T1) = M1 × 12 × years]
4. Procedure:
   a. Get the inputs:
      If amount B = 0, quit.
      If interest rate is a %, divide by 100.
   b. For each year (Y = 1 to N)
      (1) Calculations as in 3 above.
      (2) Format and print a report line.
   c. Repeat from 4a until B = 0.
5. Manual solution for test case:
      Borrowed (B) = $10,000
      Interest (I) = 15%
      Test years = 5
   a. Mo. int. I = .15 / 12 = 0.0125
   b. Total payments Y = 5 × 12 = 60
   c. M1 = $10000 × (.0125 / (1 − (1.0125)^(−60))) = $237.90
   d. T1 = $237.90 × 12 × 5 = $14,274.00

Figure 5.5 John Smith's program plan.

PRINT USING is preceded by a space. These three lines of print represent different approaches; John should have used one consistent method, but he wanted to try out some alternatives.

The rest of the program contains no surprises. Lines 610–700 comprise a loop that calculates and prints the loan price for each repayment period from 1 to "N" years.

```
110 REM  **  PROGRAM 'LNPRICES'                    JOHN SMITH  1/5/83
120 REM  **  CALCULATES MONTHLY LOAN PAYMENTS FOR EACH OF A SERIES OF YEARS.
130 REM  **  INPUTS:    AMOUNT BORROWED           B
140 REM  **             INTEREST RATE             I
150 REM  **             MAXIMUM YEARS             N
160 REM  **  VARIABLES: MONTHLY PAYMENT           M1
170 REM  **             TOTAL OF ALL PAYMENTS     T1
180 REM  **             YEARS OF CURRENT TERM     Y
190 REM --------------------------------------------------------------
200 REM
210 REM  **  CONSTANTS
220     LET I1$="LOAN OF ## YEARS   MO. PMT $$###.##   TOTAL PMTS $$#,###.##"
230     LET D1$ = "$$#,###.##"
240     LET L1$ = "AMOUNT OF LOAN"
250     LET L2$ = "INTEREST RATE"
260     LET L3$ = "MAXIMUM YEARS"
270     LET B$= "********************************************************"
280 REM
290 REM  **  HEADING (MAIN LOOP STARTS HERE)
300     PRINT B$
310     PRINT
320     PRINT "LOAN PRICING"
330     PRINT "------------"
340     PRINT
350 REM
360 REM  **  INPUT
370     PRINT L1$  TAB(17);
380       INPUT B                             :REM     AMOUNT OF LOAN
390       IF B = 0 THEN GOTO 760              :REM     QUIT IF 0 ENTERED
400     PRINT L2$  TAB(17);
410       INPUT I                             :REM     INTEREST RATE
420       IF I > 1 THEN LET I = I / 100       :REM     ADJUST PERCENTAGE
430     PRINT L3$  TAB(17);
440       INPUT N                             :REM     MAX YEARS TO STUDY
450 REM
460 REM  **  TOP OF REPORT SHOWS INPUTS
470     PRINT
480     PRINT B$
490     PRINT
500     PRINT L1$  TAB(20);
510       PRINT USING D1$; B                  :REM     AMOUNT
520     PRINT
530     PRINT L2$  TAB(24); I * 100; "%"      :REM     INTEREST AS PERCENT
540     PRINT
550     PRINT L3$  TAB(25);
560       PRINT USING "##"; N                 :REM     MAX YEARS
570     PRINT
```

(continued)

```
580     PRINT B$
590     PRINT
600 REM
610 REM  **  COMPUTE LOAN PRICES FOR 1 TO N YEARS
620     LET I = I / 12
630     FOR Y = 1 TO N
640       LET M1 = B * (I / (1 - (1 + I)^(-Y * 12)))
650       LET M1 = INT((M1 * 100) + .5) / 100
660       LET T1 = (M1 * 12)* Y                    :REM     TOTAL OF PAYMENTS
670 REM
680 REM  **  PRINT REPORT
690       PRINT USING I1$; Y, M1, T1
700     NEXT Y
710 REM
720 REM  **  AT END OF N YEARS
730     PRINT
740     PRINT B$
750     GOTO 290                                 :REM     REPEAT UNTIL B = 0
760     END
```

(a)

```
*******************************************************
AMOUNT OF LOAN     $10,000.00

INTEREST RATE            14.75 %

MAXIMUM YEARS            10
*******************************************************
LOAN OF  1 YEARS  MO. PMT  $901.41  TOTAL PMTS $10,816.90
LOAN OF  2 YEARS  MO. PMT  $483.68  TOTAL PMTS $11,608.30
LOAN OF  3 YEARS  MO. PMT  $345.43  TOTAL PMTS $12,435.50
LOAN OF  4 YEARS  MO. PMT  $277.04  TOTAL PMTS $13,297.90
LOAN OF  5 YEARS  MO. PMT  $236.59  TOTAL PMTS $14,195.40
LOAN OF  6 YEARS  MO. PMT  $210.10  TOTAL PMTS $15,127.20
LOAN OF  7 YEARS  MO. PMT  $191.57  TOTAL PMTS $16,091.90
LOAN OF  8 YEARS  MO. PMT  $178.01  TOTAL PMTS $17,089.00
LOAN OF  9 YEARS  MO. PMT  $167.76  TOTAL PMTS $18,118.10
LOAN OF 10 YEARS  MO. PMT  $159.81  TOTAL PMTS $19,177.20
*******************************************************
```

(b)

Figure 5.6 Program LNPRICES. (b) Sample run.

From the output John can select a loan period with a monthly payment that fits in with his budget, and he can play around with borrowing different amounts at varying interest rates.

Page Copy

The route to the page printer varies from one BASIC to another. CBASIC and some others have companion instructions that function as positions of a toggle switch and, in fact, are called printer toggles; the LPRINTER statement turns on access to the printer so that all subsequent PRINT statements generate page copy until a CONSOLE statement is executed, thereby flipping the toggle back to the display screen.

Microsoft BASIC uses a different approach. It has the LPRINT instruction, which is absolutely identical to PRINT and all its variations with the sole exception that it routes output to the printer instead of to the screen. If you want to produce a line of print on paper, you simply substitute LPRINT for PRINT. As an example, enter and run the following on your computer:

```
100    PRINT "THIS LINE IS DISPLAYED"
200    LPRINT "THIS LINE IS PRINTED"
```

As you see (if you have Microsoft BASIC) the literal in line 100 appears on the screen and that in line 200 comes out on paper.

The LPRINT instruction has the USING capabilities for formatting output, and they work the same as PRINT USING. Commas and semicolons have the same effect with PRINT and LPRINT. Thus, LPRINT and PRINT are the same in every way, except for their destinations.

For most programming these separate instructions are just fine, but they become a real nuisance if you want to produce the same output report on both the screen and hardcopy. Then you have to code the same group of instructions twice, once using PRINT and the other time using LPRINT. This wastes a lot of energy and space, especially for complex reports.

For CP/M users, however, there's good news. You don't have to use LPRINT at all if you don't want to (although it's usually convenient to do so). CP/M maintains a piece of control information in memory address 3 called the IOBYTE, in which the assignment of I/O devices is indicated by bit settings. BASIC provides methods for manipulating individual memory locations, called PEEK and POKE; they'll be discussed in Chapter 12.

For now I'll let you in on a secret without explaining how it works. To redirect all subsequent PRINTs to the printer, you can issue the program instructions

```
LPRINT: POKE 3, (PEEK(3)+1)
```

The LPRINT initializes the printer (sets it up to receive). The POKE/PEEK sequence changes the IOBYTE at location 3 so that all output is now routed to the printer and not to the screen.

```
110 REM       Same as 5.5, except allows for optional printout on request.
120 REM  **  PROGRAM 'LNPRICES'                           JOHN SMITH  1/5/83
130 REM  **  CALCULATES MONTHLY LOAN PAYMENTS FOR EACH OF A SERIES OF YEARS.
140 REM  **  INPUTS:    AMOUNT BORROWED         B
150 REM  **             INTEREST RATE           I
160 REM  **             MAXIMUM YEARS           N
170 REM  **  VARIABLES: MONTHLY PAYMENT         M1
180 REM  **             TOTAL OF ALL PAYMENTS   T1
190 REM  **             YEARS OF CURRENT TERM   Y
200 REM ----------------------------------------------------------------
210 REM
220 REM  **  CONSTANTS
230     LET I1$="LOAN OF ## YEARS   MO. PMT $$###.##   TOTAL PMTS $$#,###.##"
240     LET D1$ = "$$#,###.##"
250     LET L1$ = "AMOUNT OF LOAN"
260     LET L2$ = "INTEREST RATE"
270     LET L3$ = "MAXIMUM YEARS"
280     LET B$  = "**********************************************************"
290 REM
300 REM  **  HEADING (MAIN LOOP STARTS HERE)
310     PRINT B$
320     PRINT
330     PRINT "LOAN PRICING"
340     PRINT "------------"
350     PRINT
360 REM
370 REM  **  INPUT
380     PRINT L1$  TAB(17);
390       INPUT B                                 :REM    AMOUNT OF LOAN
400       IF B = 0 THEN GOTO 900                  :REM    QUIT IF 0 ENTERED
410     PRINT L2$  TAB(17);
420       INPUT I                                 :REM    INTEREST RATE
430       IF I > 1 THEN LET I = I / 100           :REM    ADJUST PERCENTAGE
440     PRINT L3$  TAB(17);
450       INPUT N                                 :REM    MAX YEARS TO STUDY
460     LET D9 = 0                                :REM    PRINT TO DISPLAY
470 REM
480 REM  **  TOP OF REPORT SHOWS INPUTS
490     IF D9 <> 0 THEN POKE 3,(PEEK(3)+1)        :REM    TURN ON PRINTER
500     PRINT
510     PRINT B$
520     PRINT
530     PRINT L1$  TAB(20);
540       PRINT USING D1$; B                      :REM    AMOUNT
550     PRINT
560     PRINT L2$  TAB(24); I * 100; "%"          :REM    INTEREST AS PCT
570     PRINT
580     PRINT L3$  TAB(25);
590       PRINT USING "##"; N                     :REM    MAX YEARS
```

```
600     PRINT
610     PRINT B$
620     PRINT
630 REM
640 REM  **  COMPUTE LOAN PRICES FOR 1 TO N YEARS
650     LET I = I / 12
660     FOR Y = 1 TO N
670       LET M1 = B * (I / (1 - (1 + I)^(-Y * 12)))
680       LET M1 = INT((M1 * 100) + .5) / 100
690       LET T1 = (M1 * 12) * Y                :REM    TOTAL OF PAYMENTS
700 REM
710 REM  **  PRINT REPORT
720       PRINT USING I1$; Y, M1, T1
730     NEXT Y
740 REM
750 REM  **  AT END OF N YEARS
760     PRINT
770     PRINT B$
775     LET I = I * 12
780     IF D9 = 0 THEN GOTO 850
790 REM
800 REM  **  IF COMPLETING PAGE COPY
810     PRINT CHR$(12)                          :REM    EJECT PAGE
820     POKE 3, (PEEK(3)-1)                     :REM    RESTORE DISPLAY
830     GOTO 300                                :REM    REPEAT UNTIL B = 0
840 REM
850 REM  **  QUERY IF WANT PRINTOUT
860     PRINT
870     INPUT "WANT PRINTED COPY (Y/N)"; X$
880     IF X$ = "Y" THEN LET D9 = 9: GOTO 490   :REM    PRINT IF YES
890     GOTO 300                                :REM    REPEAT UNTIL B = 0
900     END
```

Figure 5.7 Same as Figure 5.6, only with this version you can get an optional printout on request.

To restore output to the screen and "turn off" the printer, issue the following instruction:

POKE 3, (PEEK(3) − 1)

These two statements have the same effect in Microsoft BASIC as CBASIC's LPRINTER/CONSOLE instruction pair. They function as flips of a toggle switch.

To repeat: these instructions are for CP/M only. *DO NOT USE THEM IF YOUR COMPUTER IS NOT WORKING UNDER CP/M!* If you don't know, find out.

There are any number of times when you might want to build printer toggling into a program. One such case is shown in Figure 5.7. This is the same loan pricing program developed in Figure 5.6, but it contains the added ability to print out the displayed results. The additions to implement this feature are in lines 460, 490, and 780–900.

The program needs to have a way of knowing whether the printer is toggled on, so the variable D9 is created for this purpose. D9 is set to zero when the output goes to the display and to a nonzero value (9, in this case, but any nonzero value will do) when the printer has been toggled on. Thus in the first pass through this program line 460 sets D9 to 0, so the POKE at line 490 is not executed and the output is displayed.

At line 780 on the display pass, control jumps to line 850 and begins a routine asking the user if he or she wants a printed copy of the display. If the user replies Y (for yes), D9 is changed to a nonzero value and the program repeats from line 490.

There, because D9 is not zero, the printer is toggled on by the POKE sequence and the entire output report goes to the page printer. Returning to line 780, the comparison fails, so lines 800–830 gain control. Line 810 sends a form feed to the printer to eject the page, and 820 toggles the printer off and reactivates the screen with another POKE. Control then reverts to line 300, where another input sequence begins on the screen.

The user can thus select any reports he or she wants printed and skip those that are not worth keeping. This is a useful trick for holding down program size in Microsoft BASIC under CP/M.

Odds and ends

In addition to the capabilities already discussed, Microsoft BASIC offers a few enhancements to control output.

You can limit the length of output lines with the WIDTH instruction. It takes the form

```
WIDTH 15
```

when you want to hold line lengths to 15 characters. As long as this statement is in effect no output line on the screen will be longer than 15 characters. Any time a sixteenth is output, BASIC forces it to the next line. This has the following effect:

```
100    WIDTH 10
110    PRINT "ABCDEFGHIJKLMNOPQRSTUVWXYZ"
       RUN
A B C D E F G H I J
K L M N O P Q R S T
U V W X Y Z
```

You can change the output line length anywhere in the program by issuing another WIDTH instruction.

An alternate form of this instruction is

```
WIDTH LPRINT 15
```

which fixes the length of lines sent to the printer by LPRINTs.

Another way of limiting line length is through the POS(X) function. This is useful if you're building an output line with a succession of PRINTs, each ending with a semicolon. POS(X) returns the next available column position in the line. The argument (X) has no effect on the current value of a variable named X. As the line builds you can check its length against some limit, and when it exceeds the limit you print the present line and go to the next as follows:

```
IF POS(X) > 55 THEN PRINT
```

In this case, when the line has grown to more than 55 characters, it's printed and a new line is begun. The equivalent of POS(X) for the page printer is LPOS(X).

Microsoft BASIC has an instruction WRITE that's somewhat like PRINT, but with slightly different characteristics. WRITE has no USING extension, but it otherwise operates pretty much the same as PRINT. However, when you include a list of variables after WRITE, each variable is separated from the others by commas. The following illustrates the difference between PRINT and WRITE with the same lists:

```
100    LET A = 1: LET B = 5: LET C$ = "STRING"
110    PRINT A, B, C$
120    WRITE A, B, C$
RUN
 1             5              STRING
1,5,"STRING"
```

Note also that the WRITE instruction produces the string with quote marks around it. This instruction is not particularly useful for screen output, but as we shall see later in the book it *is* useful in file processing.

The functions SPC and SPACE$ provide output spacing capabilities. SPC(12) inserts 12 spaces into the output line, starting at the current print position. TAB, on the other hand, changes the current column position to that specified, so that TAB(22) lines up the next output field on column 22, whereas SPC(22) sticks 22 spaces into the line. SPC is therefore not useful for tabulated columnar output, as the following demonstrates:

```
100    LET A$ = "JONES": LET A = 34
200    LET B$ = "ANDERSON": LET B = 27
300    PRINT A$ TAB(20) A
400    PRINT B$ TAB(20) B
500    PRINT A$ SPC(20) A
```

```
600     PRINT B$ SPC(20) B
RUN
JONES                                        34
ANDERSON                                     27
JONES                    34
ANDERSON                           27
```

SPACE$(6) actually creates a string containing six space characters. When used in an assignment statement, it loads the string variable.

```
LET S$ = SPACE$(20)
```

creates the string S$ consisting of "   ". In a PRINT statement it is equivalent to SPC(20), so that line 500 above can be written as

```
500     PRINT A$; SPACE$(20); A
```

The LSET and RSET instructions (which are really for file processing and will be discussed in Chapter 11, "Random Files") can be used in connection with SPACE$ for formatting strings. LSET moves one string into another at the extreme left end; RSET moves it to the extreme right end. In both cases, the length of the target string prevails, and the unused positions are filled with spaces. The following illustrates this by creating the kind of "sports scoreboard" display often seen on television newscasts.

```
100     LET T$ = SPACE$(20)
110     LET I = 21: LET I$ = "IOWA"
120     LET N = 14: LET N$ = "NORTHWESTERN"
130     RSET T$ = N$
140     PRINT USING "& ##"; T$, N
150     RSET T$ = I$
160     PRINT USING "& ##"; T$, I
```

This fragment produces the display:

```
NORTHWESTERN  14
        IOWA  21
```

As we said back at the start of this chapter, BASIC has remarkably flexible output capabilities. The fact that this is the longest chapter in this book serves as testimony to the power and—admittedly—to the complexities of the facilities at your disposal for creating imaginative, attractive output. The figures have also attempted to give you a glimpse of what you can do with these facilities.

CHAPTER 6

DATA, LISTS, AND ARRAYS

The DATA statement. Lists: subscripts, DIM, ERASE, sorting, minimum subscript. Arrays and matrices: two-dimensional, multidimensional, array characteristics.

BASIC provides very flexible facilities for specifying, organizing, and processing large amounts of data with relatively simple instructions. Lists and arrays in particular treat masses of data in almost exactly the same ways that individual items are handled. It's our purpose in this chapter to discuss the manipulation of grouped data.

The DATA statement

Up to this point we've entered data into programs with the LET statement or through keyboard entry in response to an INPUT. These two methods, while useful, possess some shortcomings:

- Once you've assigned a value through a LET statement, you have to write another LET to change it. This becomes a real problem if the value changes with every iteration of a loop or at various stages in the program.
- The trouble with keyboard entry of successive values is that you have to keep conversing with the machine all the time. It can't continue without you. Also, you can lose track of where you were when you have a number of items to enter and process. And finally, the values you enter are lost as soon as the program ends.

One solution to these difficulties is to use files, which are collections of information stored on a diskette so that they can later be read and processed by a program. Considerable attention is given to files in Chapters 10 and 11.

For the time being let us consider the DATA statement, which enables us to build data directly into a program. The DATA statement is a sort of surrogate input file.

Any number of DATA statements can be placed anywhere in a program. A DATA statement requires a line number and has the form

```
DATA [list]
```

where [list] is any number of data items separated by commas, for example,

```
1000    DATA 7, 256.3, 29, 9999
```

This list contains four numeric values that can be read into the program and then processed just as though you'd entered them from the keyboard or assigned them to variables with a LET.

To move values from a DATA statement to a variable, BASIC has the instruction

```
READ [vlist]
```

in which [vlist] is a list of variable names that will receive the items from the DATA statement. To read the numbers in line 1000, you can code

```
800    READ A, F1, B, X
```

and 7 will be assigned to A, 256.3 to F1, 29 to B, and 9999 to X. This has precisely the same effect as writing

```
LET A  = 7
LET F1 = 256.3
etc.
```

The question is, therefore, Why bother? And the answer is that we don't have to read all the values from DATA statements at once. They can be read one or two or however many at a time. Each time a READ is executed, BASIC fetches the item following the last one read. Consequently, we could process the numbers in the DATA statement with a loop, such as

```
530    FOR T = 1 TO 4
540      READ V
 .        .
 .        .
 .        .
610    NEXT T
```

In the first iteration the READ assigns 7 to V, in the second it assigns 256.3 to V, etc., by sequentially reading values from the DATA statement at line 1000.

This loop could also read two values at a time with

```
540    READ V1, V2
```

In the first iteration it assigns 7 to V1 *and* 256.3 to V2; in the second iteration 29 is assigned to V1 and 9999 to V2.

In the third iteration, however (assuming there are no other DATA statements after line 1000), it runs into a snag. The READ instruction can't read past the last item of data, so it halts the program with the message "Out of data in 540." This is an effective means of stopping the program, but it's not very orderly or professional simply to let it crash this way. In a moment we'll discuss a tidier way to handle the end-of-data condition.

First, though, let's talk about pointers. In computerese a *pointer* is a record maintained by software to indicate the location of something. A pointer is neither a physical object nor one that is visible, but instead a sort of "note" the software "jots down" for its own reference purposes, ordinarily showing the memory address where an item of information is stored. BASIC automatically keeps a data pointer when a program contains DATA statements. You aren't consciously aware of it, but it's there. When the program starts, the data pointer points at the first item in the first DATA statement. Each time a READ is executed anywhere in the program, BASIC fetches the item indicated by this data pointer and then advances the pointer to the next item. If a two-item READ is executed (READ V1, V2), BASIC reads the next two items and advances the pointer twice.

This has some peculiar implications in the structuring of programs. Consider the following program fragment:

```
220      READ A
230    DATA 29, 37, 15
 .
 .
 .
360      READ B
370    DATA 66, 22, 0
380      GOTO 220
```

At first glance it would seem that the READ at 220 reads from the DATA statement at 230 and the READ at 360 takes data from line 370. In fact this is not so.

This instruction sequence is a loop, since line 380 refers back to 220. In the first pass the data pointer points to the first item (29) in line 230. The READ at 220 advances the pointer to the next item (37). Then line 360 gets executed, reading 37 into the variable B (and *not* 66 from line 370 as you might expect). Thus in the second pass through this loop, line 220 reads 15 (the *third* item) from line 230, and line 360 reads the *first* item from line 370. This is because a READ *anywhere* in the program obtains the next unread data item.

Note that the data pointer skips from the end of line 230 to the start of 370. When all items have been read from a DATA statement, BASIC automatically scans down the program seeking another DATA statement. When it finds one it locks onto the first item in this new DATA line. If it doesn't find one, the next READ instruction cannot be performed and consequently the program crashes in the attempt.

The two points to be noted are that:

1. Items are read sequentially from DATA statements no matter where the READ is, or how many different READs a program has.
2. You can scatter DATA statements at will throughout the program (although this is poor practice; you should group all DATA statements in one place so they're easy to find and obvious as to contents).

Now, regarding the orderly handling of the end-of-data condition: Just as programs on the ADDMACH model tested for a 0 input, so READ instructions can test for a unique end-of-data value (such as 0 or 99999) that would not occur in "real" data. The following program fragment suggests one such approach.

```
 620   READ A1
 630   IF A1 = 0 THEN GOTO 9999
  .    .
  .    .
  .    .
 740   GOTO 620
1000   DATA   29, 67, 331.2, 48
1010   DATA  251, 17.3
9998   DATA  0                 :REM         END OF DATA
9999   END
```

In this model, all DATA statements are grouped starting at line 1000 and continuing for as long as necessary to contain the data. The last two lines of the program are always as shown in 9998 and 9999. Line 9998 is fixed as the end-of-data indicator, so that other data lines (1000–9997) can be added, deleted, or reworked as necessary without concern for the end-of-data flag. Line 9999 is the known and fixed end-of-program point.

Up in lines 620–740 a loop reads and processes items from the DATA statements. At line 630 it tests for the end of data (the 0 value presupposes that a 0 will never legitimately appear as data; it could be any other value that is *not* valid data). When the end-of-data condition is detected, control jumps to the known END.

In addition to numerics, DATA statements can contain strings. Each string should be enclosed in quotes, as in

```
1000    DATA "THESE ARE", "3 STRINGS", "IN A DATA
                STATEMENT"
```

Suppose this data statement is in a program containing the loop

```
100    FOR B = 1 TO 3
110      READ A$
120      PRINT A$
130    NEXT B
```

As this loop executes, it will read and print out:

```
THESE ARE
3 STRINGS
IN A DATA STATEMENT
```

There is no READ instruction to parallel LINE INPUT for string data items containing commas, but that's okay since a string is defined by the quotes. In the sequence

```
200     READ N$
 .       .
 .       .
 .       .
1020    DATA "BROWN, JAMES"
```

the string N$ is taken from quote to quote, including the comma, as one item of data.

You can mix numerics and strings in DATA statements, but be careful if you do. Say you have several records in a home budgeting program, with each record showing the name of a creditor, the monthly payment, and the date of the month due. The DATA statements might read:

```
1000     DATA "MORTGAGE",         525,    10
1010     DATA "JC PENNEY",         45.25, 25
1020     DATA "SEARS, ROEBUCK",    60,    15
```

The READ statements have to be carefully organized for mixed data of this kind, since the first READ assigns to a string variable and the next two to numeric variables, then the next to a string again, etc. If you get bollixed up and try to read a string into a numeric or vice versa, your program will have a nervous breakdown. The best approach in this case is to structure your data consistently and to READ all the items in a record at once, as in

```
READ C$, P, D
```

In cases of this sort, the end-of-data indicator has to be revised from a simple 0 to reflect the data organization. One suggestion:

```
220     READ C$, P, D
230     IF P = 0 THEN GOTO 9999
 .       .
 .       .
 .       .
9998    DATA "", 0, 0
9999    END
```

Sometimes it's necessary to read all the data more than once during a program run. When that's the case, you can reset the data pointer all the way back to the very first item with the instruction RESTORE.

In the case of the budgeting program, let's say you want to produce a list of all creditors first and then go back and do some further processing on the payments and dates due. The following fragment illustrates the use of RESTORE in doing this.

```
150  READ C$, P, D
160    IF P = 0 THEN GOTO 190
170    PRINT C$
180  GOTO 150
190  RESTORE               :REM BACK TO START OF DATA
200  READ C$, P, D
210    etc.
```

Note that in line 150 you have to read all the data items in each record even though you're only interested in one of them. Line 160 tests for the end of data; if it's not yet, line 170 prints the creditor name and loops back. At end of data, line 160 jumps to the RESTORE in line 190. Processing then continues from line 200 onward by rereading the same data.

Microsoft BASIC furnishes an extension to the RESTORE instruction that lets you specify the line number of the DATA statement you want to return to. This is useful when you have two or more classes of data: say, the creditors and payment data in lines 1000 through 1050 and your paydays and projected earnings for the next year in lines 1080 through 1150. After you've read through all the data, you can go back to the payday data with

```
RESTORE 1080
```

You could also use this statement to jump forward in the data, if you wanted to read the payday information first. After that has been processed, you can get back to the start of data in line 1000 with a simple RESTORE.

The DATA statement is most useful when there are large amounts of information to be sequentially processed by a program. If you save a program containing DATA statements, they become a permanent part of the program. Thus over time you can add to the data, delete from it, and edit it as it changes.

Lists

A computerized list is conceptually the same as a list you make with pencil and paper, an enumeration of related but different items of information. For example, a list of the months is:

January
February
March
April
  etc.

You can relate the number designation of any month to the name of that month by reading the list entry corresponding to the number: the third month is March because that's the name in the third entry of the list. A way of representing it symbolically is MONTH(3). February would be MONTH(2), September MONTH(9), etc.

Similarly, in BASIC we can call the list of months M$, and the third entry in M$ would be written as M$(3), the second entry as M$(2), and the ninth as M$(9). This provides you with a way of symbolically representing any item in a list, and the program can directly access the numbered entry without having to read sequentially through the preceding entries.

By way of nomenclature, the parenthesized numeric entry indicator (N) in M$(N) is called a *subscript* or sometimes an *index*. M$(N) is therefore a subscripted variable, and the collection of items it represents is called an indexed list.

Each entry in an indexed list is actually a complete, separate item of data, just as February and March are individual months and Jack and Jane are different people. A list merely gathers them for convenience as related elements of information.

Although you don't have to declare data types in BASIC, it is necessary to declare subscripted variables and list lengths by telling BASIC their names and the maximum number of entries in each list in the program. This is done using the DIM instruction, short for DIMension. In the case of the list of months, we'd declare it by writing

```
160     DIM M$(12)     :REM     LIST OF MONTHS
```

This statement tells BASIC to "reserve space for a list of twelve string entries called M$."

When it encounters this statement, BASIC allocates an area in memory and loads it with twelve empty strings (an "empty string" being alphabetic text with a length of zero characters). It remembers that this area is called M$. Henceforth for the rest of the program, *any reference to the list name must include a subscript indicating an entry within the specified length of the list.* You cannot, for example, access M$(15), since there are only 12 entries declared for this list. If you attempt to access an entry outside the list size, you get the error message "Subscript out of range".

A DIM statement for a given variable name can only be declared once in a program. In the case of M$, you can't later issue the instruction

```
480     DIM M$(25)
```

because M$ has already been dimensioned, and if you do you'll get the error message "Redimensioned array". Consequently, as a matter of programming practice *you should declare all DIMs at the start of the program.*

It is possible in Microsoft BASIC to undo a DIM with the ERASE instruction. To do away with M$(25), code

```
ERASE M$
```

```
100 REM  **  PROGRAM 'MONAME'                              K. PORTER 1/7/83
110 REM  **  PRINTS THE CORRESPONDING MONTH NAME FOR ANY NUMBER BETWEEN
120 REM  **    1 AND 'C1'
130 REM ----------------------------------------------------------------
140 REM
150    LET C1 = 12                              :REM     ENTRIES IN LIST
160    DIM M$(C1)                               :REM     LIST OF MONTHS
170 REM
180 REM  **  LOAD MONTH NAMES INTO LIST
190    FOR L = 1 TO C1
200      READ M$(L)
210    NEXT L
220 REM
230 REM  **  PROGRAM HEADER
240    PRINT "MONTH NUMBER/NAME CROSS-REFERENCE"
250    PRINT "---------------------------------"
260 REM
270 REM  **  INPUT/LOOKUP/OUTPUT LOOP
280    PRINT
290      INPUT "MONTH NUMBER (0 TO STOP)... "; I
300      IF I = 0 THEN GOTO 9999
310      IF I > C1 THEN GOTO 350
320      PRINT "MONTH NUMBER"; I; "IS "; M$(I)
330    GOTO 280
```

```
340 REM
350 REM  **  INVALID MONTH NUMBER (ERROR HANDLER)
360     PRINT "MONTH NUMBER"; I; "DOESN'T EXIST, YOU DUMMY"
370     GOTO 280
380 REM
390 REM  **  DATA IS THE NAMES OF THE MONTHS
1000    DATA    "JANUARY","FEBRUARY","MARCH","APRIL","MAY","JUNE","JULY"
1010    DATA    "AUGUST","SEPTEMBER","OCTOBER","NOVEMBER","DECEMBER"
9999    END
```

(a)

```
MONTH NUMBER/NAME CROSS-REFERENCE
---------------------------------


MONTH NUMBER (0 TO STOP)...  5
MONTH NUMBER 5 IS MAY

MONTH NUMBER (0 TO STOP)...  2
MONTH NUMBER 2 IS FEBRUARY

MONTH NUMBER (0 TO STOP)...  13
MONTH NUMBER 13 DOESN'T EXIST, YOU DUMMY

MONTH NUMBER (0 TO STOP)...  12
MONTH NUMBER 12 IS DECEMBER

MONTH NUMBER (0 TO STOP)...  0
```

(b)

Figure 6.1 (a) Program MONAME. (b) Sample run.

You can then redimension M$ to a different size, or use it as a nonsubscripted variable.

Another good habit to develop is to *use a symbolic constant to declare the list length and to limit the subscripts referring to that list.*

This is shown in Figure 6.1(a), which displays the month name for any number from 1 to 12. Line 150 assigns the constant 12 to C1, which is then used in line 160 to dimension the list M$, in line 190 for loading the list from DATA statements, and again in line 310 to protect the user from his or her own mistakes.

This constant C1 accomplishes two laudable purposes. First, it enforces consistency throughout the program with respect to the size of M$. Second, it enhances the maintainability of the program. Should Congress pass a law establishing the new month of Thirtember, the revised calendar can be implemented in this program with only two changes: LET C1 = 13 in line 150, and add a DATA statement at line 1030 showing the new month name. Try it, and then see what you get by entering a month number 13.

Note also that in lines 200 and 320 the subscript of M$ is a variable. BASIC assumes that a variable subscript is an integer and just to make sure, it rounds a floating-point variable before indexing the list with it. Thus month number 3.49 returns MARCH, but 3.5 returns APRIL. You can also use a computed expression as a subscript, but that's a poor practice unless you're absolutely convinced the result won't exceed the range of entries in the list, and even then it should be avoided for the sake of program simplicity and readability.

Lists can also be of any numeric type, so L(N), L#(N), and L%(N) are all valid subscripted variables. The point is that *all the elements in a given list must be of the same data type.* You can't mix numerics and strings in the same list. If you have corresponding alphabetic and numeric items (e.g., the names and ages of a group of people), you'll need two lists—one of strings, the other of numerics—to hold the items. The two lists will have corresponding entries in this case (if properly set up), so that age(5) will show the age of name(5).

In addition to cross-referencing, lists are useful in rearranging data. One of the classic applications of computers is *sorting*, switching data items around into alphabetic or numeric order. Figure 6.2, a list sort, accepts up to 20 numbers in any order and rearranges them into numeric sequence. This program has some interesting features that merit consideration. Line 130 establishes the constant N as the list size, which is enforced the same way as in Figure 6.1(a). If you want to make the list larger, change the value assigned to N and the program handles the rest.

The data entry loop at 240–280 accepts numbers and puts them into the list until either a 0 is entered or until N items have been keyed. In either case, the loop counter K is always one value higher than the number of items entered (since a FOR/NEXT loop ends when the counter is greater than the upper limit of its range), so in line 320 it is decreased by one to show the actual number of items in the list.

The sort in lines 340–440 works as follows:

1. A variable F is initialized at 0.
2. The first item in the list is compared with every succeeding item.
3. If any item is lower in value than the first, the two are switched by:
   a. moving the first item to the variable F;
   b. moving the lower value item to first place in the list;
   c. moving the item held in F into the position formerly occupied by the one just moved.
4. When all entries have been compared with the first and swapped as appropriate, the process is repeated, starting with the second item and its successors.
5. When the second-to-last item has been compared with the last

```
100 REM  ** PROGRAM 'SORTNUM'                              K. PORTER  1/5/83
110 REM  ** ENTERS, SORTS, AND PRINTS A LIST OF UP TO 'N' NUMBERS
120 REM ---------------------------------------------------------------------
125 REM
130     LET N = 20                                :REM     LIST MAX LENGTH
140     DIM A(N)                                  :REM     LIST SPACE
150 REM
160 REM  ** HEADER AND INSTRUCTIONS
170     PRINT "NUMBER SORT"
180     PRINT "-----------"
190     PRINT
200     PRINT "ENTER UP TO"; N; "NUMBERS TO BE SORTED"
210     PRINT "   STOP INPUT BY ENTERING 0"
220     PRINT
230 REM
240 REM  ** DATA ENTRY LOOP
250     FOR K = 1 TO N
260       INPUT A(K)
270       IF A(K) = 0 THEN GOTO 300               :REM     SORT ON 0 ENTRY
280     NEXT K
290 REM
300 REM  ** SORT PREPARATION
310     PRINT "SORTING"
320     LET K = K - 1
330 REM
340 REM  ** SORT THE LIST INTO ASCENDING ORDER
350     LET F = 0                                 :REM     RESET SWAP FLAG
360       FOR L1 = 1 TO (K - 1)
370         FOR L2 = (L1 + 1) TO K
380           IF A(L1) <= A(L2) THEN GOTO 420     :REM     IF IN PROPER ORDER
390           LET F     = A(L1)                   :REM     ELSE SWAP ITEMS
400           LET A(L1) = A(L2)
410           LET A(L2) = F
420         NEXT L2
430       NEXT L1
440     IF F <> 0 THEN GOTO 350                   :REM     REPEAT UNTIL NO SWAPS
450 REM
460 REM  ** PRINT SORTED LIST
470     PRINT "************************************************************"
480     PRINT
490     PRINT "SORTED RESULTS:"
500     PRINT
510     FOR L1 = 1 TO K
520       PRINT A(L1)
530     NEXT L1
540     END
```

Figure 6.2 Program SORTNUM.

entry, F is checked to see whether it is still zero. If not, the process is repeated all over from the beginning (by resetting F to 0). When a complete pass is done without swapping any items (F is still 0), the entries are in order.

The program then displays the sorted list of numbers and ends.

The key element of this sorting algorithm is the variable F, which is used for temporary storage of the swapped value. It controls the sort, in that its value will be 0 only when no items have been rearranged in the last pass through the list. To see how it functions, insert the "debugging" instruction

```
435    PRINT "AT END OF PASS F =";F
```

and run the program. At the end of each pass through the list, the value of F will be displayed. When it appears as 0, the sorted list will begin to appear on the screen.

Sorting is usually a long process, since many iterations are required before the list is ordered. The duration of a sort depends on the length of the list and how badly out of order the entries were to begin with. The longest sort occurs when the data are in complete reverse order. This is an example of a "CPU bound job"; the computer runs and runs and runs with no visible sign of activity. For that reason, line 310 issues the SORTING message to give the user reassurance that the computer hasn't stopped working.

The output of Figure 6.2 is in ascending order (low number to high number). You can reverse the process and produce a descending sort (high to low) by changing the relational operator in line 380 so that it reads

```
380    IF A(L1) >= A(L2) THEN GOTO 420
```

This program illustrates the manipulation of list entries. It's also a very useful piece of code to retain for inclusion in your programs. With slight modifications, lines 320–440 can be built into any program that requires the rearrangement of data into sorted order.

Minimum subscript—The highest subscript cannot exceed the size stipulated in a DIM statement, and the lowest cannot be less than zero. You *can*, however, have a zero subscript. Thus the range of subscripts for the list M$ in Figure 6.1(a) is 0 through 12, or in other words the DIM statement actually allocated a list of 13 entries, one more than the size specification. In this list, M$(0) is a valid entry.

There are some good and valid reasons for having a 0th entry. As we'll see when we get to Figure 6.3, the 0th entry comes in handy as a place to store the total (or some other computed value) of a numeric list.

In the list M$, however, the 0th entry simply takes up memory space without any purpose, since we don't use it. When you want to limit the minimum subscript to 1 for all lists and arrays in the program, you can place the instruction

```
OPTION BASE 1
```

at the start of the program (before the first DIM), and no list or array will have a Øth entry. Not all BASICs support this statement, but it is available in Microsoft BASIC.

Arrays and matrices

Lists and arrays differ in only one fundamental respect: a list has one dimension (length), whereas an array has two or more dimensions (length, width, depth). In fact, sometimes a list is called a one-dimensional array.

The simplest and most commonly used true array is of two dimensions in which data items can be thought of as being arranged in rows and columns. Mathematicians call this organization a *matrix*, a term sometimes used in programming too. The following is a two-dimensional array:

```
3 7 4
5 6 1
1 9 8
5 8 3
```

The dimensions of this array are four rows by three columns. If we call it by the variable name A1, we can allocate the space for it through the declaration

```
DIM A1(4, 3)
```

A1 is consequently a subscripted variable and any reference to it must include two subscripts indicating the row and column numbers, respectively, of the specific element. For instance,

```
PRINT A1(3, 2)
```

displays 9 (third row, second column of A1).

The individual elements in an array can be treated as separate, independent values, just as are entries in a list. Usually, however, some relationship exists among the elements in a given row and/or column. In this array, the third column of each row is the difference between the second column and the first. Thus we could change the array as follows:

```
300     LET A1(4, 2) = 7
310     LET A1(4, 3) = A1(4, 2) - A1(4, 1)
```

Row 4 will then read:

```
5 7 2
```

Two-dimensional arrays are often used in both business and scientific/ mathematical applications.

Figure 6.3(a) shows a business-type application, in which the test scores for a group of students are averaged to find their grades, and also the average achievement per test is calculated for the class as a whole.

As always, there are things to be learned from this sample program. Lines 150 and 160 set the dimensions vertically and horizontally for the grades array. Note that we use both a list and an array, and that—jumping ahead for a moment—in lines 500 and 520 the position of the student's name in the list corresponds numerically with the row for that student's

```
100 REM  **  PROGRAM 'GRADES'                                K. PORTER 1/8/83
110 REM  **  PRODUCES TEST SCORES AND GRADE AVERAGES FOR A GROUP OF STUDENTS
120 REM  **    AND ALSO AVERAGE SCORE ACHIEVED PER TEST FOR THE CLASS.
130 REM -----------------------------------------------------------------------
140 REM
150    LET N1 = 10                               :REM    NUMBER OF STUDENTS
160    LET T1 =  5                               :REM    NUMBER OF TESTS
170    DIM S$(N1)                                :REM    LIST OF NAMES
180    DIM G(N1, T1)                             :REM    GRADE ARRAY
185    LET I$ = "  ###.##"
190 REM
200 REM  **  LOAD LIST WITH NAMES, ARRAY WITH TEST SCORES
210    FOR R = 1 TO N1                           :REM    ROW INDEX
220      READ S$(R)                              :REM    STUDENT NAME
230      FOR C = 1 TO T1                         :REM    COLUMN INDEX
240        READ G(R, C)                          :REM    GRADES OF TESTS
250      NEXT C
260    NEXT R
270 REM
280 REM  **  COMPUTE AVERAGE GRADE PER STUDENT
290    FOR R = 1 TO N1
300      LET A = 0                               :REM    INITIALIZE TOTAL
310      FOR C = 1 TO T1
320        LET A = A + G(R, C)                   :REM    TOTAL STUDENT SCORES
330      NEXT C
340      LET G(R, 0) = A / T1                    :REM    AVERAGE FOR STUDENT
350    NEXT R
360 REM
370 REM  **  COMPUTE AVERAGE SCORE PER TEST
380    FOR C = 1 TO T1                           :REM    GO BY COLUMN
390      LET A = 0
400      FOR R = 1 TO N1
410        LET A = A + G(R, C)                   :REM    TOTAL TEST SCORES
420      NEXT R
430      LET G(0, C) = A / N1                    :REM    AVERAGE BY TEST
440    NEXT C
450 REM
```

```
460 REM  **  PRINT RESULTS BY STUDENT
470    PRINT "GRADE AVERAGES"
480    PRINT "--------------"
490    FOR R = 1 TO N1
500      PRINT S$(R); TAB(15);                :REM     STUDENT NAME
510      FOR C = 1 TO T1
520        PRINT USING I$; G(R, C);           :REM     SCORES
530      NEXT C
540      PRINT USING "     ###.#"; G(R, 0)    :REM     GRADE AVERAGE
550    NEXT R
560 REM
570 REM  **  PRINT AVERAGES BY TEST
580    PRINT
590    PRINT "  AVERAGES"; TAB(15);
600    FOR C = 1 TO T1
610      PRINT USING I$; G(0, C);
620    NEXT C
630    PRINT
640 REM
650 REM  **  RAW TEST DATA
1000    DATA   "BROWN, S.",     78,  89,  61,  74,  95
1010    DATA   "DAVISON, J.",   88,  78,  96, 100,  99
1020    DATA   "EDWARDS, B.",   66,  25,  95,  69,  88
1030    DATA   "GRAY, L.",      96,  95,  89,  99, 100
1040    DATA   "HARRIS, M.",    41,  22,  59,  70,  81
1050    DATA   "JENKINS, D.",   81,  84,  91,  73,  85
1060    DATA   "LARKIN, M.",    80,  77,  84,  83,  91
1070    DATA   "MORRIS, D.",    95,  96, 100, 100,  82
1080    DATA   "PARKER, K.",    87,  92,  89,  96,  75
1090    DATA   "SMITH, B.",    100,  74,  51,  95,  82
9999    END
```

(a)

```
GRADE AVERAGES
--------------
BROWN, S.       78.00   89.00   61.00   74.00   95.00      79.4
DAVISON, J.     88.00   78.00   96.00  100.00   99.00      92.2
EDWARDS, B.     66.00   25.00   95.00   69.00   88.00      68.6
GRAY, L.        96.00   95.00   89.00   99.00  100.00      95.8
HARRIS, M.      41.00   22.00   59.00   70.00   81.00      54.6
JENKINS, D.     81.00   84.00   91.00   73.00   85.00      82.8
LARKIN, M.      80.00   77.00   84.00   83.00   91.00      83.0
MORRIS, D.      95.00   96.00  100.00  100.00   82.00      94.6
PARKER, K.      87.00   92.00   89.00   96.00   75.00      87.8
SMITH, B.      100.00   74.00   51.00   95.00   82.00      80.4

  AVERAGES      81.20   73.20   81.50   85.90   87.80
```

(b)

Figure 6.3   (a) Program GRADES. (b) Sample run.

grades in the array. This is perhaps more clearly seen than explained: in the output, the student name is from the list and his or her grades are on the same row in the array.

Notice that we haven't specified OPTION BASE 1, which means each column and row in the grades array G has a Øth entry. These positions are used to store the average for each student (column Ø by row) and the average achievement by test (row Ø by column).

The five processing steps that comprise the work of the program are all essentially on the same model, consisting of a pair of nested loops. The sections beginning at lines 2ØØ, 28Ø, and 46Ø each step down row by row, in each row working across the columns from left to right with a nested loop that performs some operation. The section at line 37Ø works the array the other direction, scanning across column by column with a nested loop to total and average the rows.

This is a business-type application because it consists essentially of summarizing a relatively large amount of information with a relatively small amount of computation. On inspection you'll see that only four calculations are performed in the entire program (lines 32Ø, 34Ø, 41Ø, and 43Ø), and two of them are simply addition. The fact that the program deals with an academic setting doesn't diminish it as a business application from the programming perspective.

In the realm of scientific/mathematical programming, a relatively small amount of information is processed by a relatively large amount of computation. This is the basic difference between the two types of data processing. Figure 6.4 is a mathematical application using a two-dimensional array to calculate the statistical measurement of standard deviation.

```
100 REM  **  PROGRAM 'SDEV'                         K. PORTER 1/9/83
110 REM  **  COMPUTES STANDARD DEVIATION AND RANGE FOR A SET OF UP TO
120 REM  **     'M' OBSERVATIONS.
130 REM  **  SIGNIFICANT VARIABLES:
140 REM  **     NUMBER OF OBSERVATIONS                        N
150 REM  **     SUMS DEVELOPED IN COMPUTATIONS                S
160 REM  **     AVERAGE OF OBSERVATIONS (MU)                  A
170 REM  **     VARIANCE                                      V
180 REM  **     STANDARD DEVIATION                            D
190 REM  **     LOW RANGE                                     R1
200 REM  **     HIGH RANGE                                    R2
210 REM ------------------------------------------------------------------
220 REM
230      OPTION BASE 1
240      LET M = 25                           :REM     MAXIMUM OBSERVATIONS
250      DIM W (M, 3)                         :REM     WORKING ARRAY
260 REM
270 REM  **  GET THE OBSERVATIONS
```

```
280     PRINT "STANDARD DEVIATION, UP TO"; M;"OBSERVATIONS"
290     PRINT "----------------------------------------"
300     PRINT
310     FOR N = 1 TO M
320       INPUT "ENTER OBSERVATION (OR 9999 TO END INPUT)..."; W(N, 1)
330       IF W(N, 1) = 9999 THEN GOTO 360
340     NEXT N
350 REM
360 REM  **  COMPUTE AVERAGE OF OBSERVATIONS
370     LET N = N - 1                                 :REM     ADJUST NUMBER
380     LET S = 0
390     FOR L = 1 TO N
400       LET S = S + W(L, 1)                         :REM     SUM OF OBSERVATIONS
410     NEXT L
420     LET A = S / N                                 :REM     AVERAGE
430 REM
440 REM  **  COMPUTE DEVIATIONS OF EACH OBSERVATION
450     FOR L = 1 TO N
460       LET W(L, 2) = W(L, 1) - A
470     NEXT L
480 REM
490 REM  **  SQUARE THE DEVIATIONS
500     FOR L = 1 TO N
510       LET W(L, 3) = W(L, 2)^2
520     NEXT L
530 REM
540 REM  **  FIND THE VARIANCE BY SUMMING AND AVERAGING DEVIATIONS^2
550     LET S = 0
560     FOR L = 1 TO N
570       LET S = S + W(L, 3)
580     NEXT L
590     LET V = S / N
600 REM
610 REM  **  COMPUTE STANDARD DEVIATION
620     LET D = SQR (V)
630 REM
640 REM  **  CALCULATE RANGE (AVERAGE PLUS OR MINUS STD DEVIATION)
650     LET R1 = A - D
660     LET R2 = A + D
670 REM  **  DISPLAY RESULTS
680     PRINT
690     PRINT USING "AVERAGE                      ####.####"; A
700     PRINT
710     PRINT USING "STANDARD DEVIATION           ####.####"; D
720     PRINT
730     PRINT USING "RANGE FROM #####.## TO #####.##"; R1, R2
740     PRINT
750     END
```

Figure 6.4 Program SDEV.

Statistics is driven by a collection of raw numbers known as observations. These observations could be anything: the selling prices of cars, grades earned by students, the ages of employees in a company, stock dividends, or whatever. Anything measurable in a consistent way can form observations.

The observations are listed (column 1 in the array of Figure 6.4) and their total is divided by the number of observations to find their average. The deviation of each observation is found by subtracting the average from the observation (column 2 of the array). Each deviation is squared (column 3), and then the deviations are summed. The characteristic of variance, often used in statistics, is computed by dividing this sum by the number of observations. Standard deviation is the square root of variance.

It sounds like a lot of gibberish, but standard deviation is really pretty useful. If the observations are representative of all occurrences of their class, for example, the height of all males, then standard deviation provides a yardstick for predictions and evaluation; roughly 70 percent of all men will be of average height plus or minus the standard deviation, and about 95 percent will be of average height plus or minus twice the standard deviation. This information is useful to clothing manufacturers, auto designers, and people who figure out how high to make doors.

Multidimensional arrays are data organizations having more than two dimensions. Most BASICs permit up to seven dimensions per array. As in the case of lists and two-dimensional arrays, each dimension has to be declared via the DIM statement.

A three-dimensional array is useful for representing physical objects that have a spacial shape. The array can be thought of as having width, height, and depth (the X, Y, and Z axes in solid geometry). This third dimension—depth—consists of two or more planes, each with the same number of rows and columns. The subscripted variable C(5, 17, 4) refers to the fifth row, seventeenth column, of the fourth plane in the array C. This represents a point in space. Computer games, engineering applications such as computer-aided design, and holography (three-dimensional image projection) all rely on arrays of this kind.

Three-dimensional arrays are also handy when working with complex data. For example, a program that compiles team standings in a baseball league could use a three-dimensional array "P" with a row for each team, a column for each team played, and planes showing runs, hits, and errors on the part of the team in that game. To get the performance of Team 5 against Team 3, it would obtain runs from P(5, 3, 1), hits from P(5, 3, 2), and errors from P(5, 3, 3).

The characteristic of matrix inversion is applicable in this case. To find out how well Team 3 did in this game against Team 5, we would have only to reverse the row and column indices. Thus for Team 3 versus

Team 5, the runs are in P(3, 5, 1), the hits are at P(3, 5, 2), and the errors in P(3, 5, 3). (This kind of correlation can also be done in two-dimensional arrays.)

Because the mind tends to regard arrays in physical terms and there's no physical dimension beyond the third, it's convenient to think of multidimensional data as being in cubes with each cube consisting of so many rows, columns, and planes. A four-dimensional array is thus a stack of cubes one atop the other; a five-dimensional array is several such stacks side by side; a six-dimensional array several stacks high, wide, and deep. The seventh dimension is analogous to pallets of boxes in a warehouse.

To return to the baseball league example, you might use a cube (a three-dimensional array) to represent one season. The second season you would add a new cube and thus introduce a fourth dimension to the data. If you decided to keep track of two leagues—say, the National and American leagues—you would need the fifth dimension: a stack of cubes for each league.

Array characteristics—Arrays are a very efficient way of organizing data. Once the array is loaded, every element in it is instantly accessible, as though it had been placed into a variable all by itself. You can assign values to an element with a LET, INPUT, or READ, and you can use array elements in expressions, as the bounds for loop-control variables, and for any other purpose. You can even nest subscripts, for example,

```
LET R = J(V(N, 6), E(F,T))
```

The subscripts of array J are themselves subscripted variables, so that the row in J is determined by the value currently stored at V(N, 6) and the column in J is the value stored in E(F, T). It's not a good idea to take things to this extreme because of the complication it introduces into the program; the computer won't have any trouble figuring it out, but you sure will.

Arrays have the drawback that they gobble up memory like crazy. A single-precision numeric variable takes four bytes of computer memory. Therefore an array of 8 × 8 requires 256 bytes (8 × 8 × 4). When the dimensions are 8 × 8 × 8 for a cube, the array occupies 2048 bytes (256 bytes per plane times 8 planes). In four dimensions using two cubes [DIM A(8, 8, 8, 2)] the requirement doubles to 4096. If we now make it five-dimensional with DIM A(8, 8, 8, 2, 2)—two stacks of two cubes each—the space again doubles to 8192 bytes. The sixth dimension (two stacks wide and two deep) doubles this once more to 16,384 bytes. To add a seventh dimension of 4 quadruples the space to 65,536 bytes for a *single array*. This is the maximum total memory for most micros, leaving no room for the program or the operating system.

The problem is greatly compounded when you use string arrays. Most BASICs initially allocate 3 bytes for each string and then expand it as needed up to 255 bytes maximum per string. Consequently, the statement DIM A$(8, 8) for a two-dimensional string array immediately commits 192 bytes of memory and could grow to 16,320 bytes. The statement DIM A$(8, 8, 8) requires 1536 bytes right away and can expand to a whopping 130,560 bytes.

The intent here is not to scare you off from using arrays, which are both efficient and often necessary, but simply to caution you to dimension only as much array space as you actually need to process the data. And that, Friend, is why this chapter has stressed the use of symbolic constants to control arrays.

CHAPTER 7

STRINGS

> The ASCII code and hexadecimal. Character/numeric conversions: the CHR$ and ASC functions for character data, numerics and strings (the STR$ and VAL functions for grouped data). String comparison: sorts and searches. String manipulation: extracting strings, string searches, string insertion, string replacement.

A string in BASIC is a unit of alphabetic text. By and large BASIC is not a good language for writing word processing programs, but the reasons have more to do with speed than with capabilities. BASIC has a very powerful text-processing instruction set that can do almost anything to string data that anyone would ever want to do, but it does it slowly. If you want to write a true word processing program, take up a compiled language such as PASCAL (I recommend *Practical Programming in PASCAL*, by Yours Truly) or assembly language. If you want to do some text manipulation, BASIC has the ability to handle it.

BASIC receives strings in three ways: as literals, through assignment via LET or READ instructions—in which cases the string is built into the program itself—and through keyboard entry in response to the INPUT instruction.

When a string is specified as a literal, it must be enclosed in quotes, as in

```
PRINT "THIS IS A STRING"
```

The quote marks are not produced on the output as a result of this instruction; they merely delineate the start and end of the string (in computerese, a character such as the quotes that defines boundaries is called a *delimiter*). The same rule applies to a string assigned to a variable by a LET statement.

```
LET A$ = "THIS IS A STRING"
```

In a DATA statement a string doesn't have to be delimited by quotes, but for the sake of consistency it should be.

Quotes are *not* used in the keyboard entry of strings. This is a matter of consideration to the user, to whom it would seem unnatural to have to put quote marks around text items such as names and addresses. The INPUT instruction accepts a keyboard entry as a string from the first character until the ENTER key is struck. When text entries might logically include commas (names such as J.JONES, JR. or street addresses such as 123 3RD ST, NW) use the LINE INPUT instruction so that BASIC will treat the entire line as one string. Otherwise it will consider that the comma is a delimiter separating two different strings. This was discussed in Chapter 5.

A string variable is a data type in BASIC, and it is the only data type that absolutely must be identified. There are two ways to do this:

1. Declare a variable name as a string with the DEFSTR statement at the start of the program, or;
2. Attach the "$" tag as a suffix to the variable name whenever it's used in the program (for example, A1$).

The second is the convention used in this book, chiefly because all BASICs support it but not all have the DEFSTR statement.

String data are very different from numerics, and that's why the string type has to be identified. Numeric values are reformatted by BASIC into binary, but string data are left "as is" unless you manipulate them with some of the instructions discussed in this chapter. Numeric data always occupy two, four, or eight bytes of memory per value. A string can be of any length from zero to 255 bytes, and the length of the text assigned to a string variable can vary from one moment to the next during processing. Therefore, strings are an entirely separate class of data in BASIC, subject to virtually none of the same operations that we've grown accustomed to with numerics.

Although the actual alphabetic data in a string are unmodified by BASIC for purposes of internal representation, BASIC does change them by removing the quote marks. It also counts the characters in the string and keeps a record of its length. This length indicator never appears on output. It's just a note BASIC writes to itself to keep track of the number of characters in the string.

Usually, a program has to find out how long a string is before it works on it. BASIC provides a function called LEN(X$) to do this, in which (X$) is the name of a string variable. The variable name has to be enclosed in parentheses. The LEN function, as with SQR and INT discussed earlier, cannot be a target value in a LET statement; it *can* appear in an expression, and it can be used as a symbolic value. For example, in

```
520    LET B$ = "BALANCE"
 .      .
 .      .
 .      .
750    PRINT LEN(B$)
```

the PRINT in line 750 prints the number 7 (the character length of the string B$). Similarly, to set up a loop to scan the individual characters in string B$ you can code

```
840    FOR C = 1 TO LEN(B$)
```

and the loop will repeat once for each character.

A string variable to which nothing is currently assigned is called a *null string* or an *empty string.* Its length is zero. At program start-up time all strings are empty and only acquire contents through a LET, READ, or INPUT instruction. You can empty a string variable of its contents and restore it to null status with the instruction

```
LET B$ = ""
```

which resets the length indicator of B$ to zero.

Two or more strings are joined to form one through the process of *concatenation*, a fancy term meaning "to hook things end to end." When the elephants line up and each grabs the tail of the one ahead, that's concatenation. BASIC's concatenation operator is the plus sign, but this process should not be confused with addition. In arithmetic addition, the operands are superimposed one atop the other to develop their sum, whereas in concatenation the operands are connected end-to-end without any actual alteration of their contents. For example,

```
110    LET G1$ = "BOOK"
120    LET G2$ = "KEEPER"
130    PRINT G1$ + G2$
```

Line 130 prints the concatenated string BOOKKEEPER.

String variables and literals can be concatenated in the same instruction, and one of the operands in concatenation can also be the target variable, as in

```
200    LET N$ = "JANE"
210    LET N2$ = "DOE"
220    LET N$ = "NAME IS " + N$ + " " + N2$
230    PRINT N$
```

The last line prints the concatenated string

```
NAME IS JANE DOE
```

Note that in this case N2$ ("DOE") retains its original contents, but "JANE" is lost as an individual data item, since N$ was altered by being the target for the concatenation in line 220.

We could replace lines 220–230 with

```
220    PRINT "NAME IS " + N$ + " " + N2$
```

to produce the same output, and in that event N$ would remain unchanged as "JANE".

You have to take some pains in concatenation to provide for spacing. The literal "NAME IS " ends with a space, and one space is concatenated between N$ and N2$. Had we not included the spaces, BASIC would have jammed the string together to produce

```
NAME ISJANEDOE
```

Cancatenation joins strings in the order specified. To flip the names around and separate them with a comma we can code

```
220    LET N$ = N2$ + ", " + N$
```

```
100 REM  ** PROGRAM 'IOULIST'                    K. PORTER  1/10/83
110 REM  ** PRINTS A LIST OF EVERYBODY WHO OWES ME MONEY, AND HOW MUCH
120 REM  **     THEY OWE.
130 REM ----------------------------------------------------------------
140 REM
150       PRINT "IOU LIST"
160       PRINT "--------"
170       PRINT
180 REM
190 REM  ** LOOP TO PRODUCE REPORT
200       READ N$, D                          :REM     GET NAME, AMOUNT OF DEBT
210         IF LEN(N$) = 0 THEN GOTO 9999
220 REM
230 REM  ** BUILD BUFFER IMAGE
240         LET I$ = N$ + " OWES ME $$##.##"
250 REM
260 REM  ** PRINT OUTPUT LINE AND REPEAT TO END OF DATA
270         PRINT USING I$; D
280       GOTO 190
999 REM
1000    DATA "JOE DOAKS",        22.10
1010    DATA "SANDY SMITH",       2.15
1020    DATA "JIM BLANKENSHIP", 15
1030    DATA "JOHN DOE",           .75
9998    DATA "", 0
9999    END
```

Figure 7.1 Program IOULIST.

and then line 230 will print

DOE, JANE

Concatenation of strings can be used in all sorts of creative ways. One of them is shown in Figure 7.1, a program that prints an IOU list. Here the name of the debtor is concatenated in line 240 with a literal to form the buffer image for a PRINT USING instruction. Note, too, the use of the LEN function in line 210 to determine if end-of-data has been reached.

The ASCII Code and hexadecimal

Virtually without exception, all microcomputers use the American Standard Code for Information Interchange (ASCII, pronounced "askey") to represent string data internally and communicate with terminal devices. To understand ASCII or any other data-representation code you need to know something about binary.

Computers and related equipment operate on tiny electrical pulses that represent information. Eight of these pulses are sent side by side along parallel conductors whenever a character of information moves within the computer. The pulses can also be stored as charges of static electricity in memory or on a magnetic recording surface, such as a floppy disk.

A character of data obtains meaning through the pattern of its pulses. The presence of a pulse is indicated by the digit 1, its absence by a 0. When written down or stored electronically, a pattern of 1s and 0s conveys a unique meaning just as surely as the shape of a printed character conveys a unique significance. Therefore the pattern 01101101 means something entirely different than the pattern 10010110.

Streams of 1s and 0s confuse the eye and seem to have no discernible meaning, but this is a fundamental difference between machine and human perception. Computers deal well with pulses and poorly with shapes, whereas people find shapes easy to understand and pulses difficult. Consequently, there exists a direct one-for-one correlation between pulse patterns and written character shapes. A code such as ASCII simply standardizes this correlation so that the letter E is always represented as 01000101, no matter whose computer or terminal is involved.

Because an ASCII character can be either in motion over conductors or static in a memory device, its 1s and 0s are not always accurately portrayed as "pulses." The term applied to them is *bit*, short for binary digit. With every character consisting of eight of these things, ASCII is called an 8-bit code. Each 8-bit group, corresponding to a character, is called a *byte*.

Just as decimal numbers have place values depending on the position of a digit within the number, so do the bits within a byte have place values. In the decimal numbering system we have the digits 0 through 9, so any position within a number can be occupied by any of ten values. As a result, progressing from right to left the magnitude of each place value increases by ten times (units, tens, hundreds, thousands, etc.).

In binary, on the other hand, each digit (bit) position can only have one of two possible values, 0 or 1, and therefore the place values increase in magnitude by a factor of 2. The place values from right to left in an 8-bit binary number are 1, 2, 4, 8, 16, 32, 64, and 128.

The conversion from binary to decimal is tedious but relatively easy. You simply take each 1 and multiply it by its place value, then add up all the products. As an example, suppose we want to know the decimal equivalent of 01101001.

Place values →	128	64	32	16	8	4	2	1	
Byte →	0	1	1	0	1	0	0	1	
Decimal value →		64	+32		+8			+1	= 105

The binary number 01101001 is therefore equivalent to the decimal number 105.

The lowest byte is 00000000, equivalent to decimal 0; the highest is 11111111, which works out to 255. Thus an 8-bit code represents up to 256 letters, numbers, punctuation marks, and other graphic symbols, and for each symbol there is a corresponding numeric value. The letter "A" in ASCII is 01000001, which has a decimal value of 65. The letter "a" is 01100001, with a decimal equivalent of 97.

In fact there are not 256 graphic characters in any writing system, except a few in the Orient. In English we use about 90, including such oddball symbols as ^, {, and]. ASCII provides 96 graphic characters shown in Figure 7.2, plus 32 nonprinting control characters.

Binary	Decimal	Hex	Character
00001010	10	0A	LF
00001100	12	0C	FF
00001101	13	0D	CR
00100000	32	20	Space
00100001	33	21	!
00100010	34	22	"
00100011	35	23	#
00100100	36	24	$
00100101	37	25	%

00100110	38	26	&
00100111	39	27	/
00101000	40	28	(
00101001	41	29	)
00101010	42	2A	*
00101011	43	2B	+
00101100	44	2C	,
00101101	45	2D	–
00101110	46	2E	.
00101111	47	2F	/
00110000	48	30	0
00110001	49	31	1
00110010	50	32	2
00110011	51	33	3
00110100	52	34	4
00110101	53	35	5
00110110	54	36	6
00110111	55	37	7
00111000	56	38	8
00111001	57	39	9
00111010	58	3A	:
00111011	59	3B	;
00111100	60	3C	<
00111101	61	3D	=
00111110	62	3E	>
00111111	63	3F	?
01000000	64	40	@
01000001	65	41	A
01000010	66	42	B
01000011	67	43	C
01000100	68	44	D
01000101	69	45	E
01000110	70	46	F
01000111	71	47	G
01001000	72	48	H
01001001	73	49	I
01001010	74	4A	J
01001011	75	4B	K
01001100	76	4C	L
01001101	77	4D	M
01001110	78	4E	N
01001111	79	4F	O

(continued)

01010000	80	50	P
01010001	81	51	Q
01010010	82	52	R
01010011	83	53	S
01010100	84	54	T
01010101	85	55	U
01010110	86	56	V
01010111	87	57	W
01011000	88	58	X
01011001	89	59	Y
01011010	90	5A	Z
01011011	91	5B	[
01011100	92	5C	\
01011101	93	5D	]
01011110	94	5E	^
01011111	95	5F	_
01100000	96	60	`
01100001	97	61	a
01100010	98	62	b
01100011	99	63	c
01100100	100	64	d
01100101	101	65	e
01100110	102	66	f
01100111	103	67	g
01101000	104	68	h
01101001	105	69	i
01101010	106	6A	j
01101011	107	6B	k
01101100	108	6C	l
01101101	109	6D	m
01101110	110	6E	n
01101111	111	6F	o
01110000	112	70	p
01110001	113	71	q
01110010	114	72	r
01110011	115	73	s
01110100	116	74	t
01110101	117	75	u
01110110	118	76	v
01110111	119	77	w
01111000	120	78	x
01111001	121	79	y
01111010	122	7A	z
01111011	123	7B	{
01111100	124	7C		

01111101	125	7D	}
01111110	126	7E	~
01111111	127	7F	DEL

Figure 7.2 ASCII code chart.

This comes to 128 characters out of a possible 256. ASCII doesn't use the leftmost ("high order" or "most significant") bit of the byte to convey character information, so it is, in fact, a 7-bit code yielding 128 possible bit patterns. The high-order bit is reserved for a communications error-checking function called parity, which is not discussed in this book and does not affect the information carried in the other seven bits. (You should be aware, however, that some of the newer printers designed specifically for use with microcomputers obtain their extended character sets by the high-order bit being set to 1. There is no standard for these fancy features, which vary from one model to another, and this makes them special cases outside the realm of normal ASCII printing. The generation of special characters is discussed below in connection with the CHR$ function under the heading of character/numeric conversions.)

Globs of 1s and 0s boggle the eye, so the data-processing industry has developed a shorthand notation for binary called *hexadecimal*, or hex for short. Hex notation groups four bits into a half-byte called a "nibble" and represents each possible 4-bit pattern with a symbol. It takes two hex symbols to convey an 8-bit byte. These hex symbols are as follows:

Binary	*Hex*	*Binary*	*Hex*
0000	0	1000	8
0001	1	1001	9
0010	2	1010	A
0011	3	1011	B
0100	4	1100	C
0101	5	1101	D
0110	6	1110	E
0111	7	1111	F

The byte 01101101 (decimal 109) is written in hex as 6D, and represents the character "m." The hex number 57 could easily be confused with decimal 57, so an identifying convention is usually employed; hex 57 is written in Microsoft BASIC as &H57.

Few other BASICS provide for hex notation, and personally I've never found its absence to be a handicap. Decimal values with the CHR$ function are perfectly adequate; exactly the same character comes from PRINT &H57 and PRINT CHR$(87). No doubt, though, someone uses hex numbers in BASIC. At any rate, writers of some manuals for equipment such as printers irrationally persist in specifying hex characters as control codes even though few BASICs (and few nonprofessional programmers) have any idea what it is. For that reason, hex equivalents are included in Figure 7.2.

In ASCII the first 31 characters are terminal and communications control codes that do not generate printable characters. The purposes of most of these codes are far beyond the scope of an introduction to BASIC, and consequently the only ones included in the chart are:

Decimal	*Character*	*Purpose*
10	LF	Line feed—Advance to next line
12	FF	Form feed—Skip to top of next page
13	CR	Carriage return—Go to start of line

These are all print and/or display control codes essential to the operation of normal microcomputer-attached devices. The ENTER key on your keyboard generates a CR/LF sequence when you strike it. The PRINT instruction (not followed by a semicolon) automatically sends the same 2-byte sequence when executed, moving the cursor or print head to the start of the next line. The form-feed character is generated by CHR$(12) in a PRINT or LPRINT statement. This code universally applies to printers, causing the printer to eject the current page and skip directly to the top of the next; it also has the effect on some displays of clearing the screen. The generation of other ASCII and non-ASCII control codes is covered in the next section.

Character/numeric conversions

BASIC provides the two functions ASC and CHR$ to convert between ASCII characters and their numeric equivalents. As with all functions, the argument (the data item to be worked on or its symbolic name) must be in parentheses following the function name.

The ASC function returns the equivalent decimal value of one ASCII character. For instance,

```
PRINT ASC("T")
```

prints the number 84, which, as you see in Figure 7.2, is the decimal value of uppercase T. The instruction sequence

```
LET A$ = "T"
PRINT ASC(A$)
```

accomplishes the same thing, but uses a symbolic variable as the argument of the ASC function.

When you specify a string as the argument, ASC returns the decimal value of the first character only. Thus

```
PRINT ASC("THUNDERSTORM")
```

produces 84 only, regardless of how many characters follow.

The CHR$ function is the opposite of ASC; it generates the character associated with a specified decimal number. For example,

```
PRINT CHR$(84)
```

produces the letter T on the output device. Similarly,

```
LET L = 84
PRINT CHR$(L)
```

does the same thing using a variable as the argument.

The CHR$ function generates nonprintable control codes and extended non-ASCII printable characters. An example is the form-feed code. The statement

```
LPRINT CHR$(12)
```

causes the printer to eject the present page and skip to the top of the next. As another example, on my computer the cursor can be moved directly to a specific row and column on the screen by sending the ESC character (decimal 27), followed by uppercase Y, followed by the row number plus 32 and the column number plus 32. When R and C are variables containing the desired row and column numbers, respectively, the place-cursor instruction is written

```
PRINT CHR$(27); "Y"; CHR$(R + 32); CHR$(C + 32);
```

Since cursor addressing methods are not standardized among computers, yours probably takes a different sequence described in the machine's manual, but this will serve as a guide as well as being an example of the CHR$ function.

Some of the slick new printers produce special characters, such as Greek letters, exponents, and computer graphics figures, by accepting non-ASCII bytes with the high-order bit set to 1. The keyboard doesn't generate such characters, so you have to use the CHR$ function to create them. All decimal values between 128 and 255 turn on the high-order bit. If your printer produces a solid black square with the byte 10110110, you can generate this byte with CHR$(182). The printer manual will include a chart giving a cross-reference between extended character symbols and bit patterns. It might also furnish the decimal equivalents.

Figure 7.3(a) demonstrates the CHR$ function by displaying all printable ASCII characters and their decimal values.

```
100 REM  **  PROGRAM 'ASCII'                          K. PORTER  1/11/83
110 REM  **  DISPLAYS ALL PRINTABLE ASCII CHARACTERS AND THEIR DECIMAL
120 REM  **     EQUIVALENTS IN TABULAR FORMAT.
130 REM ------------------------------------------------------------------
140 REM
150     PRINT "ASCII CHARACTERS"
160     PRINT "----------------"
170 REM
180 REM  **  LOOP TO GENERATE CHARACTERS VIA CHR$ FUNCTION
190 REM  **     NOTE: TABULAR FORMAT OF 16 ROWS BY 6 COLUMNS.
200 REM  **             CHARACTER VALUE IS SUM OF OUTER AND INNER LOOP CNTRS.
210 REM  **             INNER LOOP STEPS BY 16'S ACROSS COLUMNS.
220     FOR L1 = 31 TO 46
230       FOR L2 = 1 TO 81 STEP 16
240         PRINT USING "!  ###    "; CHR$(L1 + L2), L1 + L2;
250       NEXT L2
260       PRINT
270     NEXT L1
280     END
```

(a)

```
ASCII CHARACTERS
----------------
   32   0  48   @  64   P  80   `  96   p 112
!  33   1  49   A  65   Q  81   a  97   q 113
"  34   2  50   B  66   R  82   b  98   r 114
#  35   3  51   C  67   S  83   c  99   s 115
$  36   4  52   D  68   T  84   d 100   t 116
%  37   5  53   E  69   U  85   e 101   u 117
&  38   6  54   F  70   V  86   f 102   v 118
'  39   7  55   G  71   W  87   g 103   w 119
(  40   8  56   H  72   X  88   h 104   x 120
)  41   9  57   I  73   Y  89   i 105   y 121
*  42   :  58   J  74   Z  90   j 106   z 122
+  43   ;  59   K  75   [  91   k 107   {  123
,  44   <  60   L  76   \  92   l 108   |  124
-  45   =  61   M  77   ]  93   m 109   }  125
.  46   >  62   N  78   ^  94   n 110   ~  126
/  47   ?  63   O  79   _  95   o 111      127
```

(b)

Figure 7.3 (a) Program ASCII. (b) Sample run.

Numerics and strings—The ASC and CHR$ functions work on one byte at a time, and all they do is govern the treatment of that byte as a number or a character without changing its format. Occasionally, however, we need to change a group of digits to or from string format. For that BASIC has the functions VAL and STR$.

VAL returns the numeric value of a number in a string, for example,

```
LET V$ = "1234.5"
LET N = VAL(V$)
```

The variable N containing 1234.5 can now be used in computations, which cannot be done on V$ since it's a string.

Now let's say we've done some calculations using N and we want to change the results back into a string V1$. The instruction to do this is

```
LET V1$ = STR$(N)
```

and *voila*! whatever number N represents is now also a string V1$.

You have to be careful with VAL to make sure nonnumeric characters don't appear in the string. Unpredictable results ensue if they do; Microsoft BASIC takes only the digits preceding the letter and issues no warning that something was fishy, while other BASICs crash the program or otherwise wreak havoc. You can't make a corresponding error going from numerics to a string with STR$, since an alphabetic can't creep into a numeric value.

The VAL and STR$ functions are seldom used, but they do occasionally come in handy.

String comparison

Strings—literals and/or variables—can be compared using the IF statement the same as numerics, and with the same relational operators (=, <>, >=, etc.).

When BASIC compares two strings, it goes character by character: the first two characters, then the second two, etc. On finding two unequal characters it acts on the relational operator as appropriate. If both strings are the same length and all characters are equal, the strings are equal. On the other hand, if S1$ has five characters and S2$ has seven, BASIC compares only five (the length of the shorter string), and if no differences are found, the shorter string is assumed to be ahead of S2$ in alphabetic order. Thus if S1$ is "JOHNS" and S2$ is "JOHNSON", S1$ is closer to A and S2$ is closer to Z.

Less than/greater than comparisons depend on the numeric equivalents of the ASCII characters comprising the two strings. The letter A comes before B because 65 is less than 66, the decimal values of those two letters. Thus, of the two names "SMITH" and "Smith," the all-uppercase SMITH is first inasmuch as the value of "M" is 77 and the value of "m" is 1Ø9.

This sequencing of strings based on decimal equivalents forces an "alphabetic order" on punctuation marks and other symbols as well as on letters, so that (you can follow this in Figure 7.2) + is lower than 3, which comes before =, which precedes R, which goes before [, all of which are followed by r. Since it's not truly alphabetic order, but rather a precedence based on the equivalent numeric values of characters, the data-processing industry calls this scheme *collating sequence*. The collating sequence of the major character groupings in ASCII is:

First—Digits in numeric order Ø through 9.
Next—Uppercase letters in alphabetic order A through Z.
Last—Lowercase letters in alphabetic order a through z.

The absolute collating sequence of all ASCII characters is indicated by their order in Figure 7.2.

By using the relational operators on string variables we can sort strings into collating sequence. The operation is essentially the same as the numeric sort done in Figure 6.2, except that the variables are strings. Figure 7.4 demonstrates a string sort. The only differences between this program and the SORTNUM program are that the variables are strings, and the end-of-sort condition is indicated by the length of F$.

When sorting or otherwise evaluating strings, you have to be careful to maintain consistency in the use of upper and lower case. SMITH and Smith are not the same or even close in collating sequence. If the list also includes the names SNYDER and Snyder, the sorted result will be

SMITH
SNYDER
Smith
Snyder

Therefore, every entry in a list to be sorted should be entircly in upper case, or every entry should be consistent in capitalization with lower case, to achieve sensible alphabetic order.

String comparisons can involve a variable and a literal. Maybe you're scanning a list for the part name WIDGET, in which case you can code

```
16Ø    FOR L = 1 TO 1ØØØ
17Ø      IF P$(L) = "WIDGET" THEN GOTO 25Ø
18Ø    NEXT L
19Ø    PRINT "NO WIDGET IN LIST"
```

This loop scans a list of 1000 part names. When it finds WIDGET, it transfers control to line 25Ø. If WIDGET is never found, line 19Ø issues a message to that effect.

```
100 REM  XX  PROGRAM 'SORTSTR'                              K. PORTER  1/5/83
110 REM  XX  ENTERS, SORTS, AND PRINTS A LIST OF UP TO 'N' STRINGS
120 REM -----------------------------------------------------------------
125 REM
130     LET N = 20                               :REM     LIST MAX LENGTH
140     DIM A$(N)                                :REM     LIST SPACE
150 REM
160 REM  XX  HEADER AND INSTRUCTIONS
170     PRINT "STRING SORT"
180     PRINT "-----------"
190     PRINT
200     PRINT "ENTER UP TO"; N; "STRINGS TO BE SORTED"
210     PRINT "   STOP INPUT BY ENTERING 0"
220     PRINT
230 REM
240 REM  XX  DATA ENTRY LOOP
250     FOR K = 1 TO N
260       INPUT A$(K)
270       IF A$(K) = "0" THEN GOTO 300           :REM     SORT ON 0 ENTRY
280     NEXT K
290 REM
300 REM  XX  SORT PREPARATION
310     PRINT "SORTING"
320     LET K = K - 1
330 REM
340 REM  XX SORT THE LIST INTO ASCENDING ORDER
350     LET F$ = ""                              :REM     RESET SWAP AREA
360       FOR L1 = 1 TO (K - 1)
370         FOR L2 = (L1 + 1) TO K
380           IF A$(L1) <= A$(L2) THEN GOTO 420  :REM   IF IN PROPER ORDER
390           LET F$     = A$(L1)                :REM     ELSE SWAP ITEMS
400           LET A$(L1) = A$(L2)
410           LET A$(L2) = F$
420         NEXT L2
430       NEXT L1
440     IF LEN(F$) <> 0 THEN GOTO 350            :REM     REPEAT UNTIL NO SWAPS
450 REM
460 REM  XX  PRINT SORTED LIST
470     PRINT "XXXXXXXXXXXXXXXXXXXXXXXXXXXXXXXXXXXXXXXXXXXXXXXXXXXXXXXXXXXXXXXX"
480     PRINT
490     PRINT "SORTED RESULTS:"
500     PRINT
510     FOR L1 = 1 TO K
520       PRINT A$(L1)
530     NEXT L1
540     END
```

Figure 7.4 Program SORTSTR.

String manipulation

Concatenation is by no means the only form of string manipulation. Strings can also be truncated, broken apart, extracted from inside larger strings, expanded by insertion, shortened by pulling out text, and searched. These activities are performed by the functions LEFT$, RIGHT$, and MID$. In addition, Microsoft BASIC has the search function INSTR that will be discussed here along with a way of replicating it in other BASICs. Taken together with LEN and other string functions, these instructions comprise a powerful set of text-processing capabilities.

Extracting strings—The LEFT$ and RIGHT$ functions extract a specified number of characters (a *substring*) from the left and right ends of a string, respectively. The extracted text has to be assigned to a variable via a LET statement (or alternately printed), and the operation does *not* modify the source string from which it was taken. As an example,

```
910    LET U$ = "THE QUICK BROWN FOX"
920    LET H$ = LEFT$(U$, 9)
```

Line 920 takes the leftmost nine characters from the string U$, and after these instructions:

```
U$ = "THE QUICK BROWN FOX"
H$ = "THE QUICK"
```

To break this string into two pieces we have to be more creative with the string manipulation functions, such as

```
910    LET U$  = "THE QUICK BROWN FOX"
920    LET L   =  LEN(U$)
930    LET H1$ =  LEFT$(U$, 9)
940    LET H2$ =  RIGHT$(U$, (L-9))
```

After these instructions have been executed:

```
U$  = "THE QUICK BROWN FOX"
H1$ = "THE QUICK"
H2$ = " BROWN FOX"
```

Note the use of LEN. This string has 19 characters, so after line 920, L = 19. In line 940 the length parameter of the RIGHT$ function is L=9, which is 10 in this case. Therefore, the right-hand ten characters are copied from U$ into H2$. We could have left line 920 out and written 940 as

```
940    LET H2$ = RIGHT$(U$, (LEN(U$) - 9))
```

to achieve the desired result, but that's harder to read.

This particular sequence of instructions always breaks U$ into two substrings, the first (H1$) nine characters long and the other (H2$) consisting of all *except* the first nine characters. Thus if we changed line 910 to read

```
910    LET U$ = "THE QUICK BROWN FOX JUMPED"
```

after line 940 the substrings would be

```
H1$ = "THE QUICK"
H2$ = " BROWN FOX JUMPED"
```

since the number of characters extracted by line 940 is variable depending on the length of the source string U$.

H2$ begins with a space character because the extraction done by RIGHT$ starts at the tenth position of the string, which happens to be a space. To leave the space out we'd extract one character less with RIGHT$(U$, (L−10)). The substring moved to H2$ would then begin with the eleventh character in U$.

Now suppose we have the same statements 920 through 940 as shown, but we changed the assignment of U$ to read

```
910    LET U$ = "NOW IS THE TIME FOR ALL GOOD MEN"
```

After executing through line 940, the extracted substrings are:

```
H1$ = "NOW IS TH"
H2$ = "E TIME FOR ALL GOOD MEN"
```

The break occurred in the middle of a word because the code has been structured to take the first nine characters for H1$ and the rest for H2$. Ways of making a program smarter than this will be covered presently.

If we change U$ to simply "NOW" the instructions won't work. Line 930 copies "NOW" into H1$, but line 940 calculates the length of the remaining string as 3 − 9 = −6, and then it issues the error message "Illegal function call in 940" and stops the program. BASIC gets mad if you try to copy a negative number of characters. It doesn't mind, however, if you copy fewer characters than specified when there aren't enough characters in the string to satisfy the length parameter, as in line 930.

The MID$ function gets inside a string. It's the most complex and versatile function in BASIC, requiring three arguments and capable not only of extracting text but also of inserting one string inside another, replacing text, and searching text for a specified group of characters. The form of this function is

```
MID$([string], [position], [length])
```

where [string] is a literal or variable, [position] is the place in the string where activity is to begin, and [length] is the number of characters involved.

To see how extraction using MID$ works, let's suppose T$ has been assigned the string "JOHN TRAVELS OFTEN" and we want to extract the word "TRAVELS". We can code

```
LET E$ = MID$(T$, 6, 7)
```

BASIC enters the string T$ at position 6 and copies seven characters to E$ as "TRAVELS". The source string T$ remains unchanged.

MID$ can be used in place of LEFT$ and RIGHT$. It does not have to access the source string in the middle. To extract "JOHN" from this string we can tell BASIC to

```
LET D$ = MID$(T$, 1, 4)
```

and the first four characters ("JOHN") are copied to D$. Similarly, to get "OFTEN" from T$ we can code

```
LET F$ = MID$(T$, 14, 5)
```

The position and length parameters can be variables and expressions. The statement above could be written

```
LET F$ = MID$(T$, (LEN(T$) - 4), 5)
```

and it would always copy the last five characters from T$ into F$, no matter what the length of T$.

Pursuing this line of reasoning a little further, the length of the last word usually varies from one string to another, so it needs to be represented by a variable that we'll call L3. To extract the final word from T$, we'd write

```
LET F$ = MID$(T$, ((LEN(T$) - L3) + 1), L3)
```

In this case L3, the length of the last word, is 5 and the length of T$ is 18. The position parameter is thus calculated as 18 − 5 + 1 = 14, which is the location of the first letter of the last word. (When computing the position by subtracting from the string length, always add 1; this is because the first character is at position 1 and not at position Ø.)

This statement suffers from the gobbledygook syndrome. The following improves its readibility while accomplishing the same purpose:

```
LET P = (LEN(T$) - L3) + 1   :REM  POSITION
LET F$ = MID$(T$, P, L3)     :REM  EXTRACT WORD
```

Obviously, the length of the last word (L3) has to be known before these statements are executed. In most cases a different approach is used; the position is determined by a string search and the length is figured from that, as discussed in the next section. The examples above are mainly for purposes of illustration.

Now let's suppose we've determined through a search that the string T$ ("JOHN TRAVELS OFTEN") contains two spaces at positions 5 (P1) and 13 (P2), and we want to extract the word between these spaces. To find the position of the first letter, we add 1 to P1. The length is the difference between P2 and the start of the word. This could be written as

```
LET E$ = MID$(T$, (P1+1), (P2 - (P1 + 1)))
```

A better way would be to write it in three instructions:

```
LET P = P1 + 1            :REM   START OF WORD
LET L = P2 - (P1 + 1)     :REM   LENGTH OF WORD
LET E$ = MID$(T$, P, L)   :REM   EXTRACT WORD
```

String searches—In string manipulations it's often necessary to search a line to determine the position of a specific character or substring (or if it's present at all). This is done using the MID$ function. Microsoft BASIC also provides the special function INSTR that searches strings more efficiently than MID$.

When we're going to break text into words, the logical character to search for is a space. The following loop finds the position of the first space in the string T$:

```
260   FOR P = 1 TO LEN(T$)
270     IF MID$(T$, P, 1) = " " THEN GOTO 350
280   NEXT P
```

Line 260 begins a loop whose control variable is successive positions within the string T$. Line 270 examines the character at position P to see if it's a space; if so, it jumps to line 350; otherwise the loop repeats for the next character position. If no space is ever found, the loop falls through to a "not-found" routine, since the string T$ does not contain the character sought.

At line 350 the character position P can be used to extract the first word from T$, as

```
350   LET E$ = LEFT$(T$, P-1)
```

Note that 1 is deducted from P in the length parameter to avoid copying the space at position P.

The proof of this pudding is in T$ = "JOHN TRAVELS OFTEN". Searching this string for the first space, the routine returns P = 5, the position of the space following JOHN. Since JOHN has four letters in his name, its length is P − 1.

If we want to break this string into separate words we can reuse the same search routine, but first we have to take out the extracted word. The value P can also be used for this:

LET T$ = RIGHT$(T$, (LEN(T$) – P))

Before this instruction is executed, T$ = "JOHN TRAVELS OFTEN". Afterwards, T$ = "TRAVELS OFTEN". Now we can loop back to line 260 and repeat the process, extracting the word TRAVELS.

The third time through, T$ = "OFTEN", so no space is found. This indicates that the line contains only one (final) word. The way this program keeps breaking words off the front of the string, sooner or later it will always arrive at the point where one word remains, so a special routine must be included in the program to handle the situation.

Figure 7.5(a) develops this algorithm. It's a simple text processor that breaks any entered string into its constituent words and lists them. It doesn't have much practical value, but it illustrates the string searching and manipulation facilities using standard BASIC functions.

Microsoft BASIC has the nifty function INSTR that replicates the search in lines 260–280. This function has the form

LET P = INSTR([start], [str1], [str2])

where P is a numeric variable, [start] is the character position where the search is to begin, [str1] is the string to search, and [str2] is the string or character to look for. The statement

LET P = INSTR(1, T$, " ")

can be read as "Starting at position 1, search string T$ for a space and put its position into the variable P."

```
100 REM  **  PROGRAM 'BREAKUP'                         K. PORTER  1/12/83
110 REM  **  BREAKS AN INPUT LINE INTO SEPARATE WORDS AND PRINTS EACH
120 REM  **     WORD IN ORDER.
130 REM ---------------------------------------------------------------
140 REM
150     PRINT "STRING BREAKUP"
160     PRINT "--------------"
170     PRINT
180     PRINT "TYPE A LINE (OR HIT 'ENTER' TO STOP)"
190     INPUT T$
200     PRINT
210 REM
220 REM  **  CHECK FOR END OF JOB
230     IF LEN(T$) = 0 THEN GOTO 9999
240 REM
```

```
250 REM  ** LOOP FOR EACH WORD IN INPUT STRING
260      FOR P = 1 TO LEN(T$)                          REM     SCAN FOR FIRST SPACE
270        IF MID$(T$, P, 1) = " " THEN GOTO 350
280      NEXT P
290 REM
300 REM  ** NO SPACE FOUND IN STRING (LAST WORD)
310      PRINT T$
320      PRINT                                         REM     PRINT WORD
330      GOTO 170                                      REM     REPEAT UNTIL T$ = ""
340 REM
350 REM  ** EXTRACT AND PRINT THE WORD
360      LET E$ = LEFT$(T$, P-1)
370      PRINT E$
380 REM
390 REM  ** REMOVE WORD FROM LINE
400      LET T$ = RIGHT$(T$, (LEN(T$)-P))
410      GOTO 250
9999     END
```

(a)

```
STRING BREAKUP
--------------

TYPE A LINE (OR HIT 'ENTER' TO STOP)
THE QUICK BROWN FOX JUMPED OVER THE LAZY DOG'S BACK

THE
QUICK
BROWN
FOX
JUMPED
OVER
THE
LAZY
DOG'S
BACK

TYPE A LINE (OR HIT 'ENTER' TO STOP)
THIS LINE APPEARS AS A COLUMN

THIS
LINE
APPEARS
AS
A
COLUMN
```

(b)

Figure 7.5 (a) Program BREAKUP. (b) Sample run.

If INSTR fails to find the string or character it's looking for, it returns a position of Ø.

The INSTR function lets us rewrite Figure 7.5(a) as shown in Figure 7.6. Note that now we have to check whether P = Ø and act on it (line 27Ø), but otherwise the program is simply shorter. It's a pity that the majority of BASICs lack this Microsoft enhancement.

```
100 REM  **  PROGRAM 'BREAKUP'                              K. PORTER  1/12/83
110 REM  **  BREAKS AN INPUT LINE INTO SEPARATE WORDS AND PRINTS EACH
120 REM  **     WORD IN ORDER.
130 REM ------------------------------------------------------------------
140 REM
150     PRINT "STRING BREAKUP"
160     PRINT "--------------"
170     PRINT
180     PRINT "TYPE A LINE (OR HIT 'ENTER' TO STOP)"
190     INPUT T$
200     PRINT
210 REM
220 REM  **  CHECK FOR END OF JOB
230     IF LEN(T$) = 0 THEN GOTO 9999
240 REM
250 REM  **  LOOP FOR EACH WORD IN INPUT STRING
260     LET P = INSTR(1, T$, " ")                REM     SCAN FOR FIRST SPACE
270     IF P = 0 THEN PRINT T$: GOTO 170
280 REM
290 REM  **  EXTRACT AND PRINT THE WORD
300     LET E$ = LEFT$(T$, P-1)
310     PRINT E$
320 REM
330 REM  **  REMOVE WORD FROM LINE
340     LET T$ = RIGHT$(T$, (LEN(T$)-P))
350     GOTO 250
9999    END
```

Figure 7.6 Program BREAKUP rewritten. This program only works with Microsoft BASIC. It demonstrates the use of the INSTR function for string searches.

Searches using either MID$ or INSTR can scan a string for substrings longer than one character. For example, we might want to find out whether the string T$ contains the character sequence "VEL" and if so, where it occurs. In data processing, to search text for a specific word or character sequence is called *parsing*. It's frequently used in command processors, such as the portion of the operating system that accepts and acts on your typed orders, and in language processors, such as the BASIC interpreter.

In parsing T$ for the substring VEL, BASIC compares VEL with the three characters starting at position 1 in T$, then with the three at position 2, etc., working across the string until either it finds a match or it arrives at the end of the string. If it finds a match, it stops comparing and returns the position of the V in VEL. The following parses T$ as described:

```
270     LET V$ = "VEL"
280     FOR P = 1 TO LEN(T$)
290       IF MID$(T$, P, LEN(V$))  = V$ THEN GOTO 320
300     NEXT P
310     LET P = 0        :REM      NOT FOUND
320     ....
```

```
100 REM  **  PROGRAM 'SEARCH'                             K. PORTER 1/13/83
110 REM  **  SEARCHES STRING T$ FOR SUBSTRING V$.  IF FOUND, SHOWS THE
120 REM  **     POSITION.  IF NOT, PRINTS A MESSAGE.
130 REM -----------------------------------------------------------------
140 REM
150     PRINT "STRING SEARCH"
160     PRINT "-------------"
170     PRINT
180 REM  **  GET INPUTS
190     PRINT "ENTER STRING TO BE SEARCHED"
200     LINE INPUT T$
210     PRINT
220     PRINT "ENTER SUBSTRING TO SEARCH FOR"
230     LINE INPUT V$
240     PRINT
250 REM
260 REM  **  SEARCH ROUTINE
270     FOR P = 1 TO LEN(T$)
280       IF MID$(T$, P, LEN(V$)) = V$ THEN GOTO 320
290     NEXT P
300     LET P = 0                                :REM    NO MATCH IN STRING
310 REM
320 REM  **  PRINT POSITION OF MATCH
330     IF P = 0 THEN GOTO 370
340     PRINT "MATCH FOUND AT POSITION"; P
350     GOTO 390
360 REM
370 REM  **  NO MATCH WAS FOUND
380     PRINT "MATCH NOT FOUND FOR "; V$
390    END
```

(a)

```
STRING SEARCH
-------------

ENTER STRING TO BE SEARCHED
Ask not what your country can do for you...

ENTER SUBSTRING TO SEARCH FOR
Kennedy

MATCH NOT FOUND FOR Kennedy
STRING SEARCH
-------------

ENTER STRING TO BE SEARCHED
Ask not what your country can do for you...

ENTER SUBSTRING TO SEARCH FOR
country

MATCH FOUND AT POSITION 19
```

(b)

Figure 7.7 (a) Program SEARCH. (b) Sample run.

The loop from lines 27Ø to 29Ø scans for a match. When it finds one, the position of the first matching character passes to line 32Ø. If there is no match, line 3ØØ sets the position as Ø. Line 32Ø can then act as appropriate, the value of P telling it whether or not the substring was found, and if so where it is in T$.

This is a generalized search routine that automatically adjusts itself; T$ can be any string, and you can use the routine to search T$ for any substring assigned to V$. Figure 7.7(a) incorporates this search routine.

The Microsoft INSTR function greatly simplifies this code, as the following equivalent routine illustrates:

```
27Ø    LET V$ = "VEL"
28Ø    LET P = INSTR(1, T$, V$)
29Ø    ....
```

As you can see, it takes only two lines instead of five to find the position where V$ begins within T$. Line 29Ø can then take appropriate action.

String insertion—Sometimes it's the objective of a search to find the point where a substring is to be inserted inside a longer string. An example of this is to expand the string "JOHN TRAVELS OFTEN" to read "JOHN TRAVELS TO EUROPE OFTEN". The procedure for doing this is:

1. Find the insertion point.
2. Break the string at that point using LEFT$ and RIGHT$.
3. Concatenate the LEFT$ portion, the new substring, and the RIGHT$ portion, in that order.

You have to be fussy about spaces when you do string insertions, since BASIC concatenates by joining the strings end-to-end.

Figure 7.8(a) illustrates string insertion. It requests the original string (prior to insertion), the text you want to insert into it, and the word after which it is to be placed. The program uses the generalized search routine to find the insertion point.

```
100 REM  ** PROGRAM 'INSERT'                          K. PORTER 1/13/83
110 REM  ** INSERTS SUBSTRING A$ INTO STRING T$ AFTER THE INDICATED WORD W$
130 REM ----------------------------------------------------------------
140 REM
150     PRINT "STRING INSERTION"
160     PRINT "----------------"
170     PRINT
180 REM
190 REM  ** GET THE INPUTS
200     PRINT "ENTER THE ORIGINAL STRING"
210     LINE INPUT T$
220     PRINT
230     PRINT "ENTER TEXT TO BE INSERTED"
240     LINE INPUT A$
250     PRINT
260     PRINT "INSERT AFTER WHICH WORD?"
270     LINE INPUT W$
280     PRINT
290 REM
300 REM  ** FIND INSERTION POINT
320     FOR P = 1 TO LEN(T$)
330       IF MID$(T$, P, LEN(W$)) = W$ THEN GOTO 400
340     NEXT P
350 REM
360 REM  ** INSERTION POINT NOT FOUND (ERROR ROUTINE)
370     PRINT W$; " NOT FOUND IN STRING"
380     GOTO 250                              :REM    TRY AGAIN
390 REM
400 REM  ** BREAK UP STRING AT INSERTION POINT
410     LET P   = P + LEN(W$)                 :REM    INSERT AFTER W$
420     LET T1$ = LEFT$ (T$, P)
430     LET T2$ = RIGHT$(T$, (LEN(T$)-P))
440 REM
450 REM  ** CONCATENATE FOR NEW STRING N$
460     LET N$ = T1$ + A$ + " " + T2$
```

(continued)

```
470 REM
480 REM  ** DISPLAY RESULTS
490      PRINT
500      PRINT "RESULTS"
510      PRINT "-------"
520      PRINT
530      PRINT "ORIGINAL STRING HAD"; LEN(T$); "CHARACTERS AND READ:"
540      PRINT T$
550      PRINT
560      PRINT "INSERTED "; A$; " AFTER THE WORD "; W$
570      PRINT
580      PRINT "RESULTING STRING HAS"; LEN(N$); "CHARACTERS AND READS:"
590      PRINT N$
9999     END
```
(a)

```
STRING INSERTION
----------------

ENTER THE ORIGINAL STRING
JOHN TRAVELS OFTEN

ENTER TEXT TO BE INSERTED
TO EUROPE

INSERT AFTER WHICH WORD?
TRAVELS


RESULTS
-------

ORIGINAL STRING HAD 18 CHARACTERS AND READ:
JOHN TRAVELS OFTEN

INSERTED TO EUROPE AFTER THE WORD TRAVELS

RESULTING STRING HAS 28 CHARACTERS AND READS:
JOHN TRAVELS TO EUROPE OFTEN
```
(b)

Figure 7.8 (a) Program INSERT. (b) Sample run.

The variable P indicates the *start* of the word after which insertion is to occur, so line 410 calculates where the word ends by adding its length to its starting position. The program then follows the procedure outlined above to break apart the string and reconnect it with the inserted text in place. Note that when the left portion is broken off in line 420 it takes with it the space where insertion occurs. In concatenation at line 460 this space will precede the inserted text, so we have to insert a space character (" ") between the new text and the right string. If we didn't, the resulting string N$ would read

JOHN TRAVELS TO EUROPEOFTEN

This program demonstrates a general approach that can be used to insert any text into any string at any point. Study it to see how to manipulate strings, and even more importantly how to make a program smart enough to adapt itself to infinitely variable circumstances within the scope of its purpose.

String replacement—String replacement can be done somewhat like insertion, in that you break off the pieces to be kept and concatenate them with the replacement text. This is the *only* way to replace a substring with text of a different length.

In Microsoft BASIC it's possible to replace text within a line using the MID$= function. This is an unusual kind of instruction that violates all the usual rules of BASIC; it's the only function that can appear to the left of the equals sign, where it does all its operations.

To see how it works let's take the well-worn phrase "JOHN TRAVELS OFTEN" (T$) and change it to read "JANE TRAVELS OFTEN". This is coded

```
MID$(T$, 1, 4) = "JANE"
```

The MID$= statement can be read "In string T$, starting at the first position replace four characters with the substring JANE." The resulting string T$ now says "JANE TRAVELS OFTEN".

In this usage of MID$, you can omit the length parameter and code the instruction

```
MID$(T$, 1) = "JANE"
```

and BASIC will replace the text starting at position 1 with as many characters as there are in the replacement specified to the right of the equals sign. On the other hand, you can code

```
MID$(T$, 1, 4) = "JANET"
```

and BASIC will take only four characters from the replacement string, thus replacing JOHN with JANE.

You cannot change the length of the target string (T$) with this function by replacing four characters with fewer or more than four (or however many). The instruction

```
MID$(T$, 1) = "JANET"
```

changes T$ to read "JANETTRAVELS OFTEN". Consequently, the MID$= function does not work in this form for text insertion.

As a final example in this chapter on string manipulation, let's say that given any string, we want to change all uppercase letters except the first to lower case.

To return to the ASCII chart in Figure 7.2, you'll note that the value difference between "A" and "a" is 97 − 65 = 32, so to change a letter from one case to the other we simply add or subtract 32. In this example, we want to go from upper to lower case, so we take the dccimal equivalent of the ASCII character and add 32, then change it back to character format. In Figure 7.9(a), line 300 does this. Very simple.

```
100 REM  **  PROGRAM "LOWRCASE"                                  K. PORTER 1/13/83
110 REM  **  CHANGES ALL LETTERS IN A STRING B$ EXCEPT THE FIRST TO LOWER
120 REM  **     CASE AND DISPLAYS THE RESULTS
130 REM -----------------------------------------------------------------------
140 REM
150      PRINT "UPPER CASE TO lower case"
160      PRINT "------------------------"
170      PRINT
180 REM
190 REM  **  GET THE INPUT
200      PRINT "ENTER A SENTENCE"
210      LINE INPUT B$
220      PRINT
230 REM
240 REM  **  CONVERT TO LOWER CASE STARTING AT POS 2 AND DISPLAY
250      FOR P = 2 TO LEN(B$)
260        LET A$ = MID$(B$, P, 1)               :REM   EXTRACT CHARACTER
270        LET A  = ASC(A$)                      :REM   CONVERT TO VALUE
280        IF A < 65 THEN GOTO 320               :REM   IGNORE NON-LETTERS
290        IF A > 90 THEN GOTO 320               :REM    AND LOWER CASE
300        LET A$ = CHR$(A + 32)                 :REM   CONVERT TO LOWER CASE
310        MID$(B$, P, 1) = A$                   :REM   REPLACE IN STRING
320      NEXT P
330      PRINT B$
9999     END
```
(a)

```
UPPER CASE TO lower case
------------------------


ENTER A SENTENCE
THERE ARE 365.25 DAYS IN A YEAR, SO LEAP YEAR ADJUSTS FOR THE FRACTION.

There are 365.25 days in a year, so leap year adjusts for the fraction.
```
(b)

Figure 7.9 (a) Program LOWRCASE. (b) Sample run.

Except that there's a problem we have to anticipate. If we convert *every* character by adding 32, then a space (value 32) becomes value 64, which is the @ sign. Similarly, a period becomes N and a comma turns into L. And if a character is already lower case, it will probably be converted to a nonexistent ASCII byte. Clearly this is bad news, so before we convert a character we'll have to check it to make sure it is, in fact, in upper case now.

Lines 280 and 290 do this by filtering out any characters whose values are less than that of "A" or greater than "Z." In other words, ineligible characters are left unchanged within the string, and only uppercase letters are converted to lower case.

This is a very practical, down-to-earth application of string manipulation by computer.

CHAPTER 8

SUBROUTINES AND FUNCTIONS

The nature of subroutines and functions. Subroutines: RETURN, GOSUB, nesting, structure, variables. Program modularization using subroutines. A modular program. Functions: built-in, user-defined, DEF FN, parameters and dummy arguments.

The nature of subroutines and functions

Before we go any farther, put the book down and go get a drink of water.

I've just told you to execute a subroutine. Probably you didn't really do it, but if you were a computer you would have interrupted your reading to get a drink, and then you would have resumed at the start of this paragraph. Let's pretend you did.

Between the first and second paragraphs no activity is actually specified, yet it has nonetheless occurred under a set of directions ("how to get a drink of water") located elsewhere. For a while you were busy executing instructions that don't appear between the paragraphs but that constitute part of their overall process. When you finished getting the drink of water you resumed at the point where you left off reading, having accomplished a necessary task according to directions only referred to and not spelled out at the point where they occurred.

Before we go any farther, put the book down and go get a drink of water.

You've now executed the subroutine again, following the same set of directions you did before. In fact they were exactly the same instructions, coded somewhere only once but executed from a different place. This time, however, you returned to this paragraph and not to the previous point of return. That's because the final instruction in the getting-a-drink subroutine says to resume at the point where you left off.

Now let's suppose this time I tell you to get a drink of juice. This process resembles getting a drink of water, but it varies in some respects; you have to pour from a container instead of a tap and your treatment of the "data"—the fluid consumed—differs, thus altering the procedure. Your getting-a-drink subroutine performs differently this time because I've changed a *parameter* from "water" to "juice." Nevertheless, the overall process is similar regardless of whether the parameter specifies water or juice, and the differences can be handled by IF statements in a common subroutine.

The purpose of this seemingly frivolous exercise is to illustrate the nature of subroutines and functions, "packaged tasks" outside the mainstream of events that can be called into operation from any point in the program. A given subroutine or function only has to be written once, and then it can be executed as many times and from as many places as necessary, simply by calling it and passing it some parameters. Subroutines and functions reduce program size and complexity by consolidating repetitive tasks. They're also useful for modularizing a program: isolating tasks defined by "one-liners" in a program plan.

In BASIC as in most programming languages there are two distinct classes of subroutines:

1. *Procedural subroutines* act on information passed to them and usually produce an effect external to themselves, such as writing a report line, positioning the cursor, rearranging and reformatting data.
2. *Functions* take one or more values called arguments, perform a calculation based on a prearranged equation, and return the results (computing the area of a circle given its diameter, or the number of TAB spaces necessary to center a string variable on the output).

In BASIC these two types of subroutines take very different forms as to both definition and usage, and so we'll treat them individually in this chapter. Henceforth the term subroutine will mean a procedural subroutine, as distinct from a function.

Subroutines

A subroutine is written in the same format as any other section of a BASIC program. The statements require line numbers that don't duplicate other line numbers in the program and that must be in ascending sequence. The instructions are the same, REMarks work the same, everything is the same.

Everything, that is, except that the last statement of a subroutine must be the instruction RETURN. Just as every loop has to have an exit, so does every subroutine, and RETURN is it. We can't use a GOTO to exit from a subroutine because GOTO requires a fixed line number; if the subroutine is called from four different points in the program, GOTO would only enable it to return to one of them. Instead, we want the subroutine to restore control to any point that called it. RETURN does that.

Obviously, then, we also need an instruction to call the subroutine. For that BASIC has the statement

```
GOSUB [line number]
```

where [line number] is the entry point of the subroutine to be executed. This entry point can be an executable statement or REMs, followed by the first executable instruction of the subroutine.

The latter is the convention we'll employ in this book, since in the spirit of program readability *you should always precede a subroutine with an explanation of what it does.*

The effect of the GOSUB/RETURN sequence is as follows. BASIC hums along executing statements, when suddenly it encounters

```
32Ø    GOSUB 2ØØØ
33Ø    PRINT A$
```

BASIC thinks of line 32Ø as being very similar to GOTO 2ØØØ, but before it performs the jump it notes down the fact that it encountered the GOSUB in line 32Ø. It then passes control to line 2ØØØ, the entry point of a subroutine, and begins executing the statements there. Sooner or later it comes across a RETURN instruction. Checking its notes, BASIC sees that the most recent GOSUB was issued in line 32Ø. It returns there and, finding no instruction subsequent to the GOSUB, it moves to line

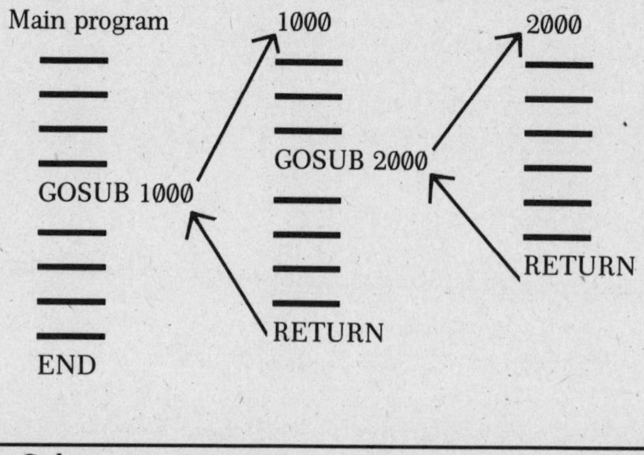

Figure 8.1 Subroutine nesting.

330 and resumes execution. Had line 320 contained a multiple statement, such as

```
320    GOSUB 2000: PRINT A$
```

BASIC, *after* returning from the subroutine, would have done the PRINT before moving to the next line.

As with loops, subroutines can be nested: the main program calls a subroutine, which calls another, which calls yet another, and so forth. Figure 8.1 shows this in a conceptual fashion. The main program executes until it encounters GOSUB 1000, and control then transfers to the subroutine at line 1000. That subroutine executes until it hits GOSUB 2000, a nested subroutine that then gains control. Somewhere beyond line 2000 a RETURN is found, and control reverts to the instruction following the most recent GOSUB, which is within subroutine 1000 (*not* the first GOSUB in the main program). Subroutine 1000 resumes execution until it comes to another RETURN, and this restores control to the main program. RETURN always refers to the most recent incomplete GOSUB.

If BASIC encounters a RETURN without having called a subroutine, it doesn't know where to return to, so it issues the message "Return without GOSUB" and halts. To keep this from happening, a certain amount of discipline is necessary in developing subroutines. First of all, BASIC has no way of knowing where a subroutine begins (a difference from other languages), so you have to make sure it doesn't wander into one. For example:

```
360         LET A = B * C
370         PRINT A, B
380         PRINT
390   REM
400   REM   ** SUBROUTINE TO COMPUTE THE...
 .
 .
 .
460         RETURN
```

This type of structure will inevitably lead to an error and a program crash. Lines 360–380 execute in order, and then BASIC barges into the subroutine at line 400. At line 460 RETURN has no place to go, since there was no GOSUB to establish a return address. To avoid this you have to insert a GOTO at line 385 that jumps around the subroutine. *Always make sure a subroutine can only be entered by a GOSUB.*

The second discipline is to *write subroutines that have only one entry point and one exit.* Generally these should be the first line and the last line of the subroutine, respectively. Most specifically, no subroutine should ever contain more than one RETURN. When multiple exits are required, use GOTOs to jump to a common RETURN at the end.

The following subroutine illustrates this principle. It controls the number of printed lines per page. When the page is full, it skips to the next page and prints a report heading (H$). The subroutine is called by GOSUB 1200 every time the main program or another subroutine does an LPRINT.

```
1200 REM  **  PAGE CONTROL SUBROUTINE
1210 REM  **  PRODUCES 54 LINES PER PAGE,
              THEN EJECTS PAGE AND
1220 REM  **  PRINTS HEADING H$ AT TOP NEXT, 4
              BLANK LINES.
1230 REM  **  USES VARIABLE C8 AS LINE COUNTER.
1240          LET C8 = C8 + 1
1250          IF C8 < 54 THEN GOTO 1300
1260            LPRINT CHR$(12)        :REM  EJECT PAGE
1270            LPRINT H$
1280            FOR C8 = 1 TO 4:  LPRINT: NEXT C8
1290            LET C8 = 0             :REM  RESET COUNT
1300            RETURN
```

As you see, the subroutine heading briefly explains its purpose. Lines 1240 and 1250 increment the line counter and, if the page isn't full, jump to the common exit at line 1300. When the page has filled, lines 1260 through 1280 skip to the top of the next one, print the heading, and space down four lines to begin the new page's text area. Line 1290 resets the line counter, and 1300 returns to the calling point.

Line 1250 could have been written

```
IF C8 < 54 THEN RETURN
```

but this would have violated the one-exit rule.

As another matter of subroutine discipline, note line 1230. It identifies C8 as the line counter, the implication being that C8 cannot be used for any other purpose. If the program contains a statement elsewhere such as

```
225     LET C8 = A * SQR(J)
```

the line counter will be changed and as a result the page control subroutine will malfunction. Unlike Pascal and other structured languages, BASIC doesn't have local and global variables, meaning that any variable can be accessed and modified anywhere in the program. Consequently, you must *make sure variables that a subroutine depends on are only modified by that subroutine.* The variable C8 is the case in point.

The exception has to do with parameters. A parameter is a piece of information passed to a subroutine to control its operation or to furnish data for it to work on. It must therefore be specified via a LET prior to calling the subroutine.

As an example, suppose that the report controlled by the paging subroutine has several sections, each with a different page heading. These headings are in a list R$, and the variable S keeps track of which section is currently being printed. We would then call this subroutine with

```
160     LET H$ = R$(S): GOSUB 1200
```

The LET passes H$ as a parameter to the subroutine, thus ensuring that when it starts a new page it prints the proper heading.

Furthermore we can use C8 as a parameter to force the subroutine to start a new page even if it's not at the end of the current one, which is desirable in passing from one section of the report to the next. At the point where S changes value, signifying a new section of the report, we issue the instructions

```
520     LET S = S + 1
530     LET H$ = R$(S): LET C8 = 99: GOSUB 1200
```

This assigns the new heading and sets the line counter to a value that triggers the subroutine's new-page operation.

A slightly different version of the page control subroutine is included in Figure 8.2(a), a program that produces an amortization schedule for a mortgage or other long-term loan. Before we examine that program, however, let's discuss. . . .

Program modularization using subroutines

The page control subroutine is a good example of a subroutine that might frequently be called from various points in the program. It's the sort of application where subroutines shine. Imagine what it would do to program length and complexity—to say nothing of tedium and errors—if we had to insert its half-dozen "worker" lines at each of 10 or 20 points!

Often, however, a subroutine is useful even when it's only called once. Such a subroutine enables you to isolate a specific operation from the rest of the program so that it's easy to find and doesn't get lost in the hubbub of other instructions.

Up to this point all our figures have been inline code, with the instructions taken more or less in sequential order. The one exception was Figure 4.8, the CALC program that demonstrated ON. . . GOTO. . . . We now embark upon a different philosophy of program organization called modularization.

In computerese a *module* is an integral part of a larger whole. You can think of a module as being analogous to one piece of a jigsaw puzzle; it

```
110 REM  **  PROGRAM 'AMORT'                            J. SMITH  1/18/83
120 REM  **  PRODUCES A LOAN AMORTIZATION SCHEDULE ON PAGE COPY, SHOWING
130 REM  **     PRINCIPAL AND INTEREST FOR EACH MONTH OVER LIFE OF LOAN.
140 REM  **  INPUTS:    P       PRINCIPAL AMOUNT OF LOAN
150 REM  **             I       INTEREST RATE
160 REM  **             N       NUMBER OF YEARS
170 REM  **  VARIABLES: B       CURRENT BALANCE
190 REM  **             M1      BASIC MONTHLY PAYMENT
200 REM  **             C1      MONTHLY INTEREST CHARGE
210 REM  **             A1      MONTHLY AMOUNT APPLIED TO PRINCIPAL
220 REM  **             P1      ACTUAL PAYMENT IN MONTH
230 REM  **             T       PAYMENT NUMBER
240 REM ------------------------------------------------------------------
250 REM
260 REM  **  DECLARE CONSTANTS, TYPES, ETC.
270      DEFDBL P, B
280      LET H$  = "LOAN AMORTIZATION SCHEDULE"
290      LET C1$ = "NO.      PAYMENT      INTEREST   PRINCIPAL   BAL. FWD."
300      LET C2$ = "---      -------      --------   ---------   ---------"
310      LET U$  = "###   $$#,###.##   $$#,###.## $$#,###.## $$##,###.##"
320 REM
330 REM  **  GET INPUTS
340      PRINT "LOAN AMORTIZATION"
350      PRINT "-----------------"
360      PRINT
370      INPUT "PRINCIPAL AMOUNT..."; P
380        IF P = 0 THEN GOTO 1250
390      INPUT "INTEREST RATE...   "; I
400        IF I > 1 THEN LET I = I / 100          :REM    ADJUST IF NECESSARY
410      INPUT "NUMBER OF YEARS... "; N
420 REM
430 REM  **  SET UP FOR RUN
440      LET N  = N * 12                  :REM    NO. OF PAYMENTS
450      LET I  = I / 12                  :REM    MONTHLY INTEREST RATE
460      GOSUB 700                        :REM    COMPUTE BASE MONTHLY PAYMENT
470      GOSUB 770                        :REM    PRINT LOAN PARTICULARS
480      GOSUB 1190                       :REM    COLUMN HEADINGS
490      LET C8 = 7                       :REM    INITIAL LINE COUNT
500      LET B  = P                       :REM    STARTING BALANCE IS PRINC.
510      LET T  = 1                       :REM    FIRST PAYMENT
520 REM
530 REM  ****    CONTROL SECTION    ****
540 REM
550 REM  **  LOOP FOR EACH PAYMENT
560      GOSUB 880                        :REM    COMPUTE MONTHLY ACTIVITY
570        GOSUB 1000                     :REM    PRINT REPORT LINE
580        LET T = T + 1                  :REM    NEXT PAYMENT NUMBER
590      IF B > 0 THEN GOTO 560           :REM    REPEAT UNTIL PAID OFF
600 REM
610 REM  ** END OF JOB
620      LPRINT CHR$(12)                  :REM    EJECT PAGE
```

```
630     GOTO 1250                          :REM    STOP
640 REM ---------------------------------------------------------------------
650 REM
660 REM         ******************
670 REM         *   SUBROUTINES  *
680 REM         ******************
690 REM
700 REM **  COMPUTE MONTHLY PAYMENT
710 REM **  USES I, N, P (BUT DOESN'T ALTER THEM)
720 REM **  RETURNS BASIC MONTHLY PAYMENT (M1)
730     LET M1 = P * (I / (1 - (1 + I)^(-N)))
735     LET M1 = INT((M1 * 100) + .5) / 100
740     RETURN
750 REM ----------
760 REM
770 REM **  PRINT LOAN PARTICULARS
780 REM **  ALTERS NO VALUES, PRINTS 7 LINES ON PAGE 1 OF REPORT
790     FOR C8 = 1 TO 5: LPRINT: NEXT C8
800     LPRINT H$: LPRINT
810     LPRINT USING "     PRINCIPAL AMOUNT            $$##,###.## "; P
820     LPRINT USING "     INTEREST RATE                      ##.##%"; I*1200
830     LPRINT USING "     NUMBER OF YEARS                    ##.## "; N/12
840     LPRINT: LPRINT
850     RETURN
860 REM ----------
870 REM
880 REM **  COMPUTE MONTHLY ACTIVITY ON DECLINING BALANCE
890 REM **  INPUTS ARE M1, I, B
900 REM **  OUTPUTS ARE C1, A1, P1
910 REM **  UPDATES B TO NEW BALANCE FORWARD AFTER THIS PAYMENT
920     LET C1 = INT(.5 + B * I * 100)/100
930     IF B < M1 THEN LET A1 = B: GOTO 950
940     LET A1 = M1 - C1                   :REM    APPLIED TO PRINCIPAL
950     LET B  = B  - A1                   :REM    UPDATE BALANCE
960     LET P1 = C1 + A1                   :REM    TOTAL PAYMENT IN MONTH
970     RETURN
980 REM ----------
990 REM
1000 REM **  PRINT MONTHLY ACTIVITY FOR CURRENT PAYMENT
1010     LPRINT USING U$; T, P1, C1, A1, B
1020     GOSUB 1060                              :REM    PAGE CONTROL
1030     RETURN
1040 REM ----------
1050 REM
1060 REM **  PAGE CONTROL
1070 REM **  PRODUCES 54 REPORT LINES PER PAGE, THEN EJECTS PAGE AND PRINTS
1080 REM **      PAGE HEADING AND COLUMN HEADINGS AT TOP OF NEXT.
1090 REM **  USES C8 AS LINE COUNTER
1100     IF C8 < 54 THEN GOTO 1160
```

(continued)

```
1110     LPRINT CHR$(12)                       :REM    PAGE EJECT
1120     LPRINT H$                             :REM    HEADING
1130     FOR C8 = 1 TO 4: LPRINT: NEXT C8      :REM    SPACE AT TOP
1140     LET C8 = 0                            :REM    RESET LINE COUNTER
1150     GOSUB 1190                            :REM    COLUMN HEADINGS
1160     RETURN
1170 REM ----------
1180 REM
1190 REM **  COLUMN HEADINGS ON REPORT
1200 REM **  THESE TWO LINES NOT COUNTED AGAINST PAGE LENGTH
1210     LPRINT C1$
1220     LPRINT C2$
1230     RETURN
1240 REM ----------
1250     END
```

(a)

LOAN AMORTIZATION SCHEDULE

PRINCIPAL AMOUNT	$2,000.00
INTEREST RATE	14.65%
NUMBER OF YEARS	2.00

NO.	PAYMENT	INTEREST	PRINCIPAL	BAL. FWD.
1	$96.64	$24.42	$72.22	$1,927.78
2	$96.64	$23.53	$73.11	$1,854.67
3	$96.64	$22.64	$74.00	$1,780.67
4	$96.64	$21.74	$74.90	$1,705.77
5	$96.64	$20.82	$75.82	$1,629.95
6	$96.64	$19.90	$76.74	$1,553.21
7	$96.64	$18.96	$77.68	$1,475.53
8	$96.64	$18.01	$78.63	$1,396.90
9	$96.64	$17.05	$79.59	$1,317.31
10	$96.64	$16.08	$80.56	$1,236.75
11	$96.64	$15.10	$81.54	$1,155.21
12	$96.64	$14.10	$82.54	$1,072.67
13	$96.64	$13.10	$83.54	$989.13
14	$96.64	$12.08	$84.56	$904.57
15	$96.64	$11.04	$85.60	$818.97
16	$96.64	$10.00	$86.64	$732.33
17	$96.64	$8.94	$87.70	$644.63
18	$96.64	$7.87	$88.77	$555.86
19	$96.64	$6.79	$89.85	$466.01
20	$96.64	$5.69	$90.95	$375.06
21	$96.64	$4.58	$92.06	$283.00

22	$96.64	$3.45	$93.19	$189.81	
23	$96.64	$2.32	$94.32	$95.49	
24	$96.66	$1.17	$95.49	$0.00	(b)

Figure 8.2 (a) Program AMORT. (b) Sample listing.

interlocks with all the others to form a complete picture. The overall strategy of modularization is to break a program into clear-cut units of activity. A "unit of activity" is a matter of individual judgement, but in general you should be able to define it in one written line in your program plan: "figure payment due" or "write a report line" or "work up monthly activity." Each module thus stands on its own within the larger context of the program.

Linking these modules together into a logical sequence is a control section consisting chiefly of GOSUBs with REMarks. This section clearly reveals the overall structure of a complex program, while the modules take care of details.

This design approach offers numerous advantages:

1. The operation of the program is summarized by the control section.
2. The control section's remarks read very much like the original program plan.
3. Everything pertaining to a specific activity is contained in one module, therefore easy to find and understand.
4. It's usually immediately obvious where an error or bug has occurred, and how to fix it.
5. Modifications and enhancements can be added without disrupting the structure or having to rewrite and redebug large parts of the program.

The only "down side" is that you have to plan the program a little more carefully before writing it. Even that small extra effort, however, more than pays for itself almost immediately; modular programs run right the first time much more often than those using inline design.

A modular program

When we left our friend John Smith, he was shopping for a loan to buy a car and some furniture. After much evaluation of alternatives—aided by his computer—John at length settled on a $10,000 second mortgage at 11.75% interest over 10 years. His monthly payment is $142.03.

With all this investing and borrowing, John's finances are becoming complicated. One thing that concerns him is the tax implication; he wants to make sure he deducts the correct interest for this loan. For that matter, it would be good to have printed records of all his loans, especially his home mortgage, showing how much he's paying out in interest and, in the event another ship comes in, how much he still owes at any time. What he needs is a program to produce loan amortization schedules.

Because loan amortization is pretty complex, John decides to use a modular design for his program. He'll call it AMORT, and his notes are shown in Figure 8.3.

Program: AMORT.BAS

Purpose: Print an amortization schedule for a loan of any amount at any interest rate over any period, for each month showing the payment number, total amount, amounts applied to interest and principal, and the balance forward. This report will cover every month over the life of the loan.

Inputs: Principal amount of loan (P)
Interest rate (I) (adjust as necessary)
Years (N)

Calculations:

1. Monthly payment (M1) with continuous compounding = (same as for LNPRICES)
2. In each month, interest charged on balance (C1) = Balance B × (Interest I / 12)
3. Monthly amount applied to principal A1 = Monthly payment M1 − Monthly interest C1
4. In final month, balance B will be less than basic monthly payment M1, so let A1 = B

General subroutines:

Page control—Limit output to 54 report lines per page. Top of each page except first, print a report heading, four blank lines, column headings.

Column headings—Separate for use alone on first page, otherwise called by page control on new page setup.

Procedure:

1. Get inputs (P, I, N)
2. Adjust interest to decimal value (<1)
3. Compute monthly payment (M1)
4. Print loan particulars top of first page, then column headings and set line counter C8.
5. Initialize balance B as principal P, payment # T as 1.
6. Control section (loop for each payment)

a. Compute monthly activity.
   (1) Interest charged on declining balance.
   (2) If balance is less than basic monthly payment, amount to principal is balance, skip to (4).
   (3) Amount applied to principal.
   (4) Update balance (B = B − A1).
   (5) Total payment for this month (C1 + A1).

b. Print report line (payment #, total payment, monthly interest charged, monthly principal, new balance).

c. Increment payment number.

d. Repeat until loan is paid off (B = Ø).

7. Eject last page and stop.

Figure 8.3 Notes for development of the AMORT program.

Program Example 8.2(a) lists the program John developed from these notes. It has five main parts: declarations, inputs, setup, control section, and subroutines, with each part clearly labeled.

The only thing remarkable about the declarations is his use of the DEFDBL instruction; the balance on a large debt such as a home mortgage could conceivably run to eight digits and will almost certainly have seven, so he's declared B as a double-precision number to avoid rounding on the printout. Note, too, that he placed the buffer image for his report lines (U$) directly under the column headings to ensure that all the fields line up right.

The use of modules begins in the setup section at line 46Ø, where he breaks out the computation of the base monthly payment and the top of the printed report. Line 49Ø sets a parameter for the page control subroutine to pick up on the first page only. It accounts for the loan particulars; from here on the subroutine will control the line counter.

Considering all it does, the control section is very brief. So short and self-explanatory, in fact, that it merits no discussion. The four instructions repeat until B = Ø at line 59Ø.

Now let's look at the subroutines. Note that John made a clear visual delineation between each pair with a short line of hyphens. Also, he explained each subroutine with some brief comments that, while not revealing every minor detail, provide enough information to understand their functions.

The final subroutine instruction we'll discuss is the ON...GOSUB.... This statement closely resembles ON...GOTO... discussed in Chapter 4, since for consecutive integer values of the control variable it branches to a line number in the corresponding position in a list. The difference is that ON...GOSUB... calls a subroutine starting at the line number rather than simply jumping there. At the end of each of the listed subroutines, the RETURN refers back to the statement following the ON...GOSUB....

Figure 8.4 is a rework of the CALC program (Figure 4.8) to demonstrate the ON...GOSUB... structure. The chief difference is that in Figure 8.4 the point of convergence for the alternatives follows the selection via ON...GOSUB..., since that's where the modules all return.

```
100 REM  ** PROGRAM 'CALC1'                          K. PORTER  1/21/83
110 REM  ** PERFORMS CALCULATOR FUNCTION ON ANY TWO NUMBERS.
120 REM  ** PROGRAM REPEATS UNTIL A ZERO IS ENTERED AS N1.
130 REM  ** VARIABLES:
140 REM  **             N1      FIRST INPUT
150 REM  **             N2      SECOND INPUT
160 REM  **             R       RESULT
170 REM  **             C       MENU CHOICE
180 REM ------------------------------------------------------------------
190 REM
200     PRINT "CALCULATOR:"
210     PRINT "-----------"
220 REM
230 REM  ** GET INPUTS, QUIT ON N1 = 0
240     PRINT
250     PRINT "FIRST NUMBER (0 TO QUIT)...";
260       INPUT N1
270     IF N1 = 0 THEN GOTO 1000
280     PRINT "SECOND NUMBER...";
290       INPUT N2
300 REM
310 REM  ** MENU
320     PRINT
330     PRINT "MENU:"
340     PRINT "-----"
350     PRINT
360     PRINT "1 ADDITION"
370     PRINT "2 SUBTRACTION"
380     PRINT "3 MULTIPLICATION"
390     PRINT "4 DIVISION"
400     PRINT
410 REM
420 REM  ** GET MENU SELECTION
430     PRINT "SELECT BY NUMBER...";
440       INPUT C
450 REM
460 REM  ** VALIDATE AND MAKE SELECTION
470     IF C < 1 THEN GOTO 1000                   :REM    QUIT
480     IF C > 4 THEN GOTO 420                    :REM    RANGE ERROR - REPEAT
490     ON C GOSUB 600, 700, 800, 900
495 REM
```

```
500 REM  ** PRINT RESULTS AND REPEAT
510      PRINT
520      PRINT "ANSWER = "; R
530      PRINT
540      GOTO 230
550 REM ----------
600 REM  ** ADDITION (MENU #1)
610      LET R = N1 + N2
620      RETURN
630 REM ----------
700 REM  ** SUBTRACTION (MENU #2)
710      LET R = N1 - N2
720      RETURN
730 REM ----------
800 REM  ** MULTIPLICATION (MENU #3)
810      LET R = N1 * N2
820      RETURN
830 REM ----------
900 REM  ** DIVISION (MENU #4)
910      LET R = N1 / N2
920      RETURN
950 REM ----------
1000 REM ** END OF PROGRAM
1010     END
```

Figure 8.4 Program CALC1.

Functions

In mathematics a *function* is a sort of numeric cause-and-effect relationship between two quantities, expressed in the general statement $y = f(x)$. What this means is that "given an equation whose variable is x and whose result is y, for any value of x there is a corresponding value of y." In other words, x determines the value of y. If the function's equation is $y = 2x$, then when $x = 1$ it produces $y = 2$, when $x = 2$, $y = 4$, etc. The result y derives in some predictable way from the value of x. Mathematicians say that x is the argument of the function, and that y is a function of x.

BASIC uses the same nomenclature and similar notation in mathematical functions. To specify $y = f(x)$ in BASIC we can write

LET Y = FNA(X)

If we have two different equations with an argument of X and a result Y, we can express the second function as

LET Y = FNB(X)

and, because the function name has changed ("A" to "B"), BASIC knows which equation we want it to use.

Higher mathematics gives names to functions, too. There are certain functions used so commonly and frequently that we don't even bother to wonder how they're computed, and whose names are part of the every-day vocabulary of students and professionals. Examples are square root, logarithm, sine, cosine, and tangent. Mathematically oriented occupations, such as economics and engineering, abound with functions. Tables of arguments and their corresponding functions are available everywhere; most pocket calculators produce transcendental functions at the push of a button. They are, in effect, the built-in functions of mathematics.

BASIC has them as built-in functions as well, and their names closely resemble the abbreviations used in math. We've already used three of the built-in functions: SQR, INT, and TAB. You'll recall that a function can't appear to the left of the equals sign in an assignment, and that its argument is enclosed in parentheses after the function name, as in LET Q = SQR(J + 3), where the square root of J + 3 is calculated and assigned to Q. All BASIC functions follow these rules, with the exception of a few string functions discussed in Chapter 7.

Built-in functions let you express complex values symbolically. You don't have to know how to compute the logarithm of R3, nor even what the present value of R3 or its logarithm are. All you have to do is use the function name to tell BASIC to compute it, as in LET L3 = LOG(R3).

In addition to the built-in functions discussed below, BASIC provides a means for setting up your own functions. These "user-defined functions" are a special kind of subroutine that can be called by a symbolic name included in an expression, rather than by a GOSUB. Even if you're not the slightest bit interested in the hyperbolic cosecants of an obtuse triangle (I'm not either), you'll find user-defined functions handy for such humdrum things as centering text on output and computing interest. The second part of our discussion of functions covers them.

Built-in functions come with BASIC, that is, they're predefined so all you have to do is include them in a statement and BASIC will return the function of the argument.

BASIC has many predefined functions, and not all of them are listed below. What are listed are the arithmetic functions pertaining to computations. Special functions, such as string manipulators, TAB, and file control operations are discussed at the appropriate points elsewhere in this book.

Also, Microsoft BASIC offers certain unique functions not generally available in other BASICs. They're identified by an asterisk after the argument. The argument itself is shown here as A; it could be any literal number, numeric variable, or computed expression. Here they are, with a brief description of each. Further discussion follows the list.

Function	*Purpose*
ABS(A)	Absolute value of A (convert A to positive if negative).
ATN(A)	Arctangent of A in radians.
CDBL(A)*	Convert A to double precision.
CINT(A)*	Convert A to nearest integer value.
COS(A)	Cosine of A in radians.
CSNG(A)*	Convert A to single precision.
EXP(A)	Return *e* (the base of a natural logarithm) to the power of A, where A ≤ 87.3365.
FIX(A)*	Truncate A. Similar to INT (but see below).
HEX$(A)*	Hexadecimal string equivalent to decimal number A.
INT(A)	Truncate A. Similar to FIX (but see below).
LOG(A)	Natural logarithm of A, where A > Ø.
OCT$(A)*	Octal string equivalent to decimal number A.
RND(A)	Random number between Ø and 1.
SGN(A)*	Sign of A. When A < Ø, SGN(A) = 1; when A = Ø, SGN(A) = Ø; when A > Ø, SGN(A) = −1.
SIN(A)	Sine of A in radians.
SQR(A)	Square root of A.
TAN(A)	Tangent of A in radians.

*Microsoft extended function.

Most of the Microsoft BASIC functions return single-precision values. The exceptions are string functions (e.g., HEX$) and those intended to force a change in the type of the data (e.g., CDBL, INT, CSNG).

The trigonometric functions ATN, COS, SIN, and TAN all work with radians and not with the more familiar degrees. In radians the measurement of angles is based on π and a full 36Ø degrees is 2π, or 6.28319. To convert from radians to degrees, divide radians by .Ø17453; from degrees to radians multiply degrees by the same factor. A more convenient conversion method is discussed in connection with user-defined functions. Appendix C describes how to use these basic trigonometric functions to derive further functions commonly used in higher math.

The INT and FIX functions are very similar in that both truncate the argument. FIX(28.2) and INT(28.2) both return the integer 28. The difference is in the way each deals with negative numbers. INT truncates to the next lower integer value regardless of the sign, so that INT(−28.2) returns −29. FIX truncates the absolute value and then restores the sign, so FIX(−28.2) returns −28. FIX is a Microsoft function not available in most other BASICs. If it's not on yours, you can replicate it as follows:

```
LET R = INT(X)
IF R < Ø THEN LET R = R + 1
```

RND picks the next number from a pseudorandom number generator, returning a single-precision value between Ø and 1. If you need a larger value, you can multiply it to achieve the desired range. For instance, RND * 1ØØ picks a number between Ø and 1ØØ.

As just shown (no, it wasn't a mistake) the RND function does not require an argument. If you do include an argument, RND(Ø) repeats the last number that was generated. An argument greater than Ø is the same as no argument.

The generator accessed by RND is not truly random. While the program runs, it produces an entirely random number series. However, each time the program is run the generator produces exactly the same sequence of random numbers. If you want to alter the sequence, you have to "reseed" the number generator with the instruction RANDOMIZE [expr], where [expr] is an integer between −32,768 and +32,768. The generator then uses [expr] as its base value in developing a sequence of random numbers. If you omit [expr] from the RANDOMIZE statement, BASIC interrupts execution and prompts you to enter a number in the indicated range. To achieve truly random numbers with RND, you have to reseed the generator with a different value every time the program runs.

Functions can be arguments of other functions, and the same rules of precedence apply as for nested factors, that is, the innermost level is resolved first. For example, INT(RND * 1Ø) returns a random integer number between Ø and 1Ø.

User-defined functions are those you create for use within a program. Like built-in functions, they take one or more arguments and return a calculated result.

The name of a user-defined function always begins with the letters FN and then follows the rules for BASIC variable naming. Thus FNR and FNR1 represent two different functions. If your BASIC supports long variable names, you can call a function FNCENTER, for example, if it computes the spacing necessary to center a string on the output.

To see how user-defined functions are used and set up, let's do just that: center a string on the output with the function FNC. In this case, the argument of the function is a string, since we have to use its length to determine how many spaces to tab in order to center it in an output width of 80 columns. If we have a string K1$ to center and print, we can write

```
PRINT TAB( FNC( K1$ )) K1$
```

and BASIC will print K1$ centered on the screen no matter what its length. Another way to code this would be

```
LET T = FNC(K1$)
PRINT TAB(T) K1$
```

which accomplishes exactly the same thing.

FNC(K1$) returns the number of spaces from the left edge of the screen to the point where K1$ is to begin. Assuming the screen has 80 columns, this is calculated as 80 minus the length of K1$, and then divided by two. For instance, if K1$ has 20 characters, it has to be tabbed over by (80 − 20) / 2 = 30 spaces.

Because BASIC doesn't intuitively know how to calculate FNC(K1$), the program has to define the function. Generally, definitions are located near the start of the program, in the "setup" section. Unlike a procedural subroutine that can be anywhere in the program, a function is a one-line subroutine that must be defined before it is called the first time. A function's equation is denoted with the DEF FN statement, for "define function." To define the centering function for *any* string, we can code

```
DEF FNC(X$) = (80 - LEN(X$)) / 2
```

To center a string A$, we use the same function as for K1$ by specifying FNC(A$), and BASIC will know how to compute the value; for a string B5$, the value is represented as FNC(B5$), etc.

In FNC(K1$), the argument is K1$. In the definition, however, the argument is called X$. Upon gaining control, the function plugs the argument you passed it into the argument in the definition. This function, then, substitutes K1$ for X$ at every point where X$ is specified. That way it knows that wherever you said X$ you really meant (this time) K1$. The next call for FNC(A$) tells BASIC to plug A$ into the *dummy argument* X$.

The variable X$, then, is not the same X$ that might appear somewhere in the body of the program. It's a string variable that exists only within the function as a symbol of the argument that's passed to it. Consequently, you could have a string variable X$ in the program and a dummy argument X$ in the function definition, and the two are entirely independent of each other. Change the value of one and the other is unaffected.

You can, however, name symbolic constants and variables in a function definition, and BASIC uses their current values. For example, suppose we declared the screen width as a constant and then used it in the centering function.

```
100    LET W = 80            :REM    SCREEN WIDTH
110    DEF FNC(X$) = (W − LEN(X$)) / 2
120    LET M$ = "M A I N   M E N U"
130    PRINT TAB(FNC(M$)) M$
```

This centers the string M$ the same as if we'd used 80 as a literal number instead of the constant W. Substitutions are only done on the dummy arguments of the function. Since no argument W is passed to FNC, BASIC uses the current value of W.

You can pass a numeric value to a function, too. In the last section we mentioned the need to convert between degrees and radians in dealing with BASIC's trigonometric functions SIN, COS, etc. A simple way to do this is with a pair of functions we'll call FNR and FND: FNR converts degrees to radians, FND radians to degrees. These functions are defined as follows:

```
DEF FND(R) = R / .017453
DEF FNR(D) = D * .017453
```

To find the sine of an angle A expressed in degrees, we can say

```
LET S = SIN( FNR( A ))
```

and BASIC will convert the degrees to radians before finding the sine of the angle.

A function can have more than one argument. As an example, to figure the monthly interest on a current balance we need to know the amount of the balance and the annual interest rate. The function is defined as

```
DEF FNM(A, E) = A * (E / 12)
```

This function is then called by passing it both arguments, for example, if the balance is B and interest is I,

```
LET M3 = FNM(B, I)
```

assigns the monthly interest charge to M3. In this case if the balance is $1764 and the annual interest is 0.15, FNM(1764, 0.15) returns the monthly interest charge of $22.05, since the function substitutes B for A and I for E.

When a function has multiple arguments, it's absolutely essential to ensure that they're stated in the proper order in the function call. If they get reversed, the function will return an incorrect result and you can waste a lot of time trying to figure out why the program keeps going bananas. Suppose that you've modified the text-centering function FNC so that the string length and the width of the output area have to be passed as arguments. This is defined as

```
DEF FNC(L, W) = (W - L) / 2
```

where L is the length of the string and W is the width of the output area. If the string is 22 characters long and the output area has 80 columns, FNC(22, 8Ø) returns 29, the number of TAB spaces needed to center the string. But if you mess up and specify the arguments in reverse order, the function returns −29, which causes TAB to place the string on the left margin of the line below the one where it should appear.

CHAPTER 9

ERROR HANDLING IN MICROSOFT BASIC

The ON ERROR statement: error handling routines. RESUME. The system variables ERR and ERL.

This chapter is intended exclusively for users of Microsoft BASIC, as its title implies. That's not to say that errors don't occur in other BASICs—most assuredly they do—but the methods for dealing with program bugs and circumstantial errors ("run time" errors) differ so widely from one BASIC to the next that there is virtually no consistency.

Microsoft BASIC and its variants have a special set of error-handling instructions to deal with conditions that arise during the running of programs. Such problems have to do with syntax errors (improperly formed instructions), missing statements (logic errors), data problems (mismatched types, overflow), machine limitations (out of memory), and file processing errors.

The ON ERROR statement

The foundation statement for error handling is

```
ON ERROR GOTO [line number]
```

where [line number] is the beginning of an error-handling routine. This statement can be inserted wherever appropriate in a program to set a *vector* (a target location) for BASIC to go to whenever an error occurs. The vector remains in effect until another ON ERROR GOTO... is executed. To cancel error handling you can issue the instruction

```
ON ERROR GOTO Ø
```

in which case any error will cause the program to halt with a message indicating the nature of the error and the line number where it occurred. The ON ERROR GOTO 0 automatically prevails in BASIC unless and until another vector is established.

For an example of the usage of this statement, let's consider the case of the ON... GOTO... and ON... GOSUB... statements. You'll recall that for each potential value of the control variable there has to be a corresponding line number to which execution is directed; if the control variable is 2, execution transfers to the second line number in the GOTO or GOSUB list. In the figures we filtered the control variable to prevent an out-of-range value from crashing the program. An alternative way would have been to code as follows:

```
300    ON ERROR GOTO 700
310    ON C GOTO 400, 500, 600
```

The statement at line 300 establishes a point to which control is handed when C (the control variable) is less than 1 or greater than 3. If the routines at 400, 500, and 600 all GOTO 650 upon completion, then at line 650 we could have the statement

```
650    ON ERROR GOTO 0
660    PRINT...
```

and line 650 would disable the error handler that takes care of range errors for the ON... GOTO... statement.

Similarly, in Figure 8.4 we had an ON...GOSUB...that acted on the menu selection. It could have been preceded by the ON ERROR as shown above (line 300). Each of the subroutines ends with a RETURN so, assuming the structure above, control would revert to line 320, where we could have

```
320    ON ERROR GOTO 0
330    PRINT...
```

to accomplish the same purpose as described: disabling the range error handler.

Resume

The structure of the error handler itself depends on the action we want to take in response to an error. To make the program halt we can simply print an error message followed by the instruction STOP, as in

```
700    PRINT "OUT-OF-RANGE VARIABLE"; C
710    STOP
```

If the menu selection was 7, the program would then display

```
OUT-OF-RANGE VARIABLE 7
Break in 710
```

In this case, however, we'd probably want to give the user another chance to enter an in-range selection, so we can print a message followed by a form of the RESUME instruction. Assuming the menu selection is made in line 210, we would code

```
700     PRINT "BAD CHOICE—TRY AGAIN"
710     RESUME 210
```

The RESUME instruction tells BASIC it's okay to continue running even though an error has occurred. Presumably the user will mend his or her ways upon receiving a scolding and make it right next time.

RESUME has several different forms depending on what you want to do about the error. If you code simply RESUME with nothing after it, BASIC attempts to continue running at the same point where the error occurred. Since the instruction has already caused an error, this usually accomplishes nothing except to send the program into a tizzy and an ultimate failure or an endless loop.

RESUME NEXT sends BASIC back to the instruction following the one that caused the error. In some cases, it might be acceptable to issue a warning message and resume processing (division by zero, for example, which returns "infinity" and might invalidate the results, but then again might not). If you want to know that an error has occurred but you don't want the program to stop as a result, use RESUME NEXT.

In most cases, however, you'll want the program to take definite action to overcome the problem: say, in a range error to obtain a new menu selection. For this, use RESUME [line number], or else display a diagnostic message followed by STOP.

The system variables ERR and ERL

Microsoft BASIC has two built-in variables to help an error handler determine what went wrong and where it happened. These are called ERR (error code) and ERL (error line), and they are accessible to the program. When an error occurs, ERL indicates the line number where it was detected. Thus, in the case of the ON...GOTO... above, the error handler at line 700 could read:

```
700     IF ERL = 310 THEN PRINT "BAD CHOICE—TRY
                  AGAIN": RESUME 210
710     IF ERL = 400 THEN PRINT "DIVISION BY ZERO":
                 STOP
```

The error handler then deals with two different problems depending on where they occurred; line 700 handles a range error in line 310 (the ON...GOTO...) by retrying from line 210, whereas line 710 stops the program because of bad data in line 400.

The ERR variable contains an integer indicating the nature of the error. These error codes are listed in Appendix B. Code 8 in ERR means a nonexistent line was referenced in an ON...GOTO..., while ERR = 11 indicates division by zero. Thus we could code the error handler at 700 as

```
700     IF ERR = 8 THEN PRINT "BAD CHOICE—TRY AGAIN":
                RESUME 210
710     IF ERR = 11 THEN PRINT "DIVISION BY ZERO": STOP
```

This has the same effect as the previous example.

Or does it? The previous example was limited to line numbers. Thus the handler acted on errors in specific lines rather than on general kinds of errors; if the range error occurred in a line other than 310, the handler was helpless. Similarly, if division by zero occurred in any line besides 400, the handler didn't know what to do about it.

Therefore, using the ERR code as the check value, we could place the statement ON ERROR GOTO 700 at the start of the program and then code various IF statements starting at line 700 to deal with broad categories of error conditions that might crop up anywhere in the program.

The ERL value can be used in diagnostic messages of this type. For example, if the program does division in many places, we can code an error-handling statement as

```
710     IF ERR  = 11 THEN PRINT
                  "DIVISION BY ZERO TOLERATED
                  IN"; ERL: RESUME NEXT
```

Then if an error occurs in line 940, this statement prints

```
DIVISION BY ZERO TOLERATED IN 940
```

and execution continues at the line following 940.

Microsoft BASIC also provides the instruction ERROR to let you develop your own error codes. Version 5.2 of BASIC-80 has codes 1–67 committed to system error messages, so it's advisable to assign error codes higher than 100 (preferably over 200 but less than 255) for your own use to avoid conflict with new codes assigned by Microsoft in future releases of the software.

To see how this instruction is used, let's suppose you need to limit a particular string A$ entered from the keyboard to 20 characters or less. To do this you can code:

```
190    ON ERROR GOTO 500
200    INPUT "WHAT IS A$"; A$
210    IF LEN(A$) > 20 THEN ERROR 250
220    LET...
 .      .
 .      .
 .      .
500    IF ERR = 250 THEN PRINT "STRING TOO
                   LONG": RESUME 200
```

Line 210 then evaluates the length of A$ and, if it's over 20, it sets an error code 250 and branches to the error handler at 500. It learns that the ERR code is 250 and displays the message, then sends control back to the INPUT at line 200 to try again.

As a practical matter, it's not advisable to try to anticipate and handle every potential error in a program. You should let a syntax error or a missing statement crash the program, since you don't want it to run with the problem. On the other hand, some situations cry out for rational error handling (such as the range problem with ON... GOTO... and unreasonable string lengths). For such keying mistakes and human errors, the ON ERROR instruction offers the potential for creating "friendly," tolerant programs. Also, as we'll find in the next chapters, it is a given that certain "errors" will occur in file processing and must be dealt with by the program using error handlers.

CHAPTER 10

SEQUENTIAL FILES

Random and sequential files. Overview of sequential files. File organization: records, fields, the end-of-file (EOF) marker. Sequential file instructions. Opening a sequential file: the "O" and "I" modes, reference numbers, concurrently open files. Closing files. Writing to a sequential file: the WRITE# and PRINT# instructions, a file writing example. Reading from a sequential file: IF EOF, LINE INPUT#. Copying a sequential file. Adding new data to the end of an existing file: KILL, NAME, error handling. Sequential file batch updates: file merging. Producing a report from a file: an example. File printing.

Up to this point nearly all the programs we've worked with have asked for data from the user and retained that data only long enough to compute results. The exceptions are programs containing DATA statements, in which input data are actually built into the program. Unfortunately DATA statements have no ability to store the results of processing for later reference, and when there are large amounts of input data that might vary from one run of the program to the next or from day to day, DATA statements are not very satisfactory.

Aside from their speed and relative ease of use, one of the things that makes computers powerful is their ability to accumulate and "remember" information that can later be recalled and reused or applied to new purposes. Such collections of information are called *files*, and BASIC has a number of facilities that make the reading and writing of files fairly simple and yet flexible.

Random and sequential files

BASIC supports two file organization techniques called sequential and random (or sometimes direct). Both have essentially the same purpose—to save and retrieve information—but they differ in the way this is done. In *sequential* organization information is written out in the order processed and read back in the same order as written: to find the 293rd item in a sequential file you have to read the preceding 292 items. In *random* organization, on the other hand, to read or write the 293rd item you go directly to it, bypassing the preceding information. Because these two approaches call for different computer actions and different programming methods, Microsoft BASIC has different instruction sets to accomplish them. In this chapter we'll deal with sequential files and in the next we'll cover random files.

Overview of sequential files

A sequential file isn't really much different from the DATA statements used in Figure 6.3, the GRADES program that computed average test scores for individual students and the average achievement by test. If you turn back to that sample program, you'll see the DATA statements starting at line 1000.

The primary difference between DATA statements and a file is that the file exists independently of the program. It has a name under which it is kept on disk. Thus we could have many such files—one per class, perhaps—and the data from any one of them can be processed simply by "connecting" the file to the program. This connection process is called an OPEN. The program then reads the data and acts on them. When it has finished, it closes the file, thereby "disconnecting" it from the program. This file can be read by many different programs since it exists independently.

The second difference between DATA statements and a file is that a file—unlike DATA statements—can be created and written automatically by a program. DATA statements are always keyed into the program by the programmer and can only be changed or added to by the same method. A file, on the other hand, is written by program instructions, and its contents can be modified, removed, and added to under program control. Files, therefore, greatly enhance the capability of the computer to retain and manage large collections of information.

Sequential files are most useful for batches of related information processed in groups, such as test scores for a class. They're easier to work with than random files, and entirely satisfactory when instant access to individual stored items isn't a requirement. They lend themselves to the repetitive processing of large amounts of information; for example, figuring grade averages for all students in the class, adding new test results to the files, evaluating individual pupil progress compared to classmates, assessing the relative difficulty of tests, and summarizing statistics. This is called *batch processing*, and computers do it extremely well with sequential files.

File organization

Every computer file has a name by which it is known to the system. This name is recorded on the directory of the diskette along with control information telling where the data are, how they're organized, etc. To create, write, or read a file, you must furnish its name and information about what you want to do. BASIC and the operating system then take care of the technical matters for you.

A file consists of some (variable) number of *records*, collections of associated items of information usually represented as one line on a printed report. In Figure 6.3 each DATA statement corresponds to a record:

```
1000    DATA    "BROWN, S."    78,  89,  61,  74,  95
```

is analogous to a record. In a file the line number and the DATA statement are omitted and the data are usually compressed, so this record would appear in a file as

```
"BROWN, S.",78,89,61,74,95
```

The other records would follow on sequential lines.

Individual items within a record are called *fields*. The record above contains six fields, the first alphabetic, the other five numeric. As in a DATA statement, the field delimiter is a comma and the string is surrounded by quote marks. When BASIC writes a record to a sequential file, it inserts these delimiters automatically. When it reads from a file, it identifies separate fields by the locations of commas. This is already familiar from earlier discussions concerning the INPUT and READ statements.

The end of a sequential file is identified by a byte called the end-of-file marker, or EOF. Under CP/M the EOF marker is the ct1-z character (ASCII 26), a character that does not occur anywhere in normal printed information. When a file is first created, the EOF marker is written at its start. Each time a new record is added to the file, the EOF marker moves to the end of the new record. It remains there when the file is closed (when the program terminates access to the file).

Later the same file is read by another program. As records are read, the system software watches for the EOF marker. It signals the BASIC program when it has found it, so that the program knows there's no more data to be read from the file and can then take appropriate action.

Sequential file instructions

Microsoft BASIC has the following instructions for handling sequential file operations:

OPEN	Creates a new file or establishes communication with an existing file.
WRITE#	Writes a record (preferred).
PRINT#	Writes freeform text to a file.
PRINT#, USING	Writes formatted output to a file.
INPUT#	Reads a data record.
LINE INPUT#	Reads a text record.
IF EOF	Tests for end of file.
CLOSE	Terminates access to file, saving it.
KILL	Deletes a file (contents *and* name).

Each of these statements has a particular place in the scheme of things and a set of syntax and usage rules, which are discussed in detail below.

Opening a sequential file

Before a program can access a file it must first establish communication with it. This is done via the OPEN statement.

When opening a sequential file you must always stipulate whether you want to read from the file or write to it. With sequential files you cannot perform both operations on the same file during the same "open." The indicator in the OPEN statement for input (reading) is "I" and for output (writing) is "O". This indicator is called the *mode*. The mode prevails from OPEN until the file is closed. It prevents you from writing to a file opened in the "I" mode or reading from a file opened as "O".

All file-handling statements refer to the file by a number following the symbol #. This number is assigned to the file by the OPEN statement. The instruction

```
OPEN "O", #1, "CLASS1.GRD"
```

means "open an output file to be referred to as #1, whose name is CLASS1.GRD." From this point on, the file is ready to accept output. This is the only time the file name is actually used in a program. All file writing instructions will refer to it as #1. If you have a second file open at the same time, it has to have a different reference number, presumably but not necessarily #2. The file name, by the way, can be a string variable with the name of the file assigned to it by a previous LET statement.

Microsoft BASIC will let you have three files open concurrently, and each file has to have a different reference number. If you want to open another file, you first have to close one of the open ones. When it's essential that you have more than three files open at one time, you have to start BASIC with the /F: option. For instance, to permit six open files concurrently, start BASIC with the command

```
BASIC/F:6
```

Most versions of the language package will allow up to 16 open files with reference numbers 1 through 16. A higher reference number than 16 is not permitted and causes an error. When you use the /F:n option to enable more than three files, each additional file (whether actually used or not) takes 306 bytes of memory. Thus this option shouldn't be exercised unless necessary.

The OPEN statement has different effects depending on circumstances. When you OPEN a file with mode "O" and no file presently exists on the disk with the name stated in the OPEN statement, BASIC creates a new file with that name and prepares to write data to it. Each time data are written, a byte indicating the end-of-file (the "EOF marker") is moved back to the end of the new entry. A new file has its EOF marker at the beginning of the space allocated to the file; in other words, the file is empty because no data precede the EOF marker. If the file named in the OPEN statement *does* already exist, BASIC moves the EOF marker to the start of the file and in this way erases all data that existed in the file prior to the OPEN. The message here is that you must make sure, before you open an existing file for output, that you no longer need its contents, because the moment OPEN executes, they are gone forever.

When the file is opened in mode "I" (to be read by the program), it must already exist, since obviously you can't read nonexistent data. An error results if the file does not exist for an OPEN "I". If the file does exist, the EOF marker stays where it is and the file can be read from start to finish, or from start to any point. When a file opened "I" is closed, it is exactly the same as it was at the time it was opened.

Closing files

Of all the file statements, CLOSE is the simplest. If you simply code the statement CLOSE, BASIC closes all open files. On the other hand, you might want to close file #2 and leave file #1 open for further processing, in which case you'd write

```
CLOSE #2
```

You can also close multiple selected files by listing their reference numbers separated by commas. To close files #1 and #3 but leave file #2 open, code

```
CLOSE #1, #3
```

If you forget to close files and the program ends normally (not as the result of an error), BASIC automatically closes them for you. This, however, is sloppy programming practice.

As a general rule, you should *always close a file as soon as you are finished with it*. Don't leave open files hanging, serene in the knowledge that BASIC will do your job for you. If the program crashes after you've written a lot of data to an output file, you lose all that data. Had you closed the file when you finished with it, you wouldn't have to rekey all that stuff and go through a bunch of grief and aggravation. The loss of data because of forgetting to close a file is a self-inflicted wound that deserves no sympathy.

The CLOSE instruction "disconnects" a file from the program, thus ending access to its contents. With output files, CLOSE ends access and also writes control information to the directory so that the file can be found the next time it's opened.

Writing to a sequential file

As you might have noticed in the list of sequential file instructions above, there are three different file write statements in Microsoft BASIC. Each of them has a purpose, and those purposes are summarized here. The #1 in these examples is for illustration of form only; it can be any open file number.

1. WRITE#1 is a general sequential file write. It's the instruction most often used to place a record in the file. It automatically inserts commas between fields and quotes around strings.
2. PRINT#1 is intended mostly for writing text to files the same way text is output via PRINT. It is, in fact, exactly the same as PRINT, except that it routes the output to a file. PRINT# can be used in lieu of the WRITE# statement, but if you have fields you have to tell it to insert commas as separators and to put quotes around strings.
3. PRINT#1,USING is equivalent to the PRINT USING statement, except that it places its output into a file. It is used to create report images on disk so that they can be printed later.

File writing example—Let's suppose you're the teacher of a class and you want to set up a file for tracking your students' test scores (this is a takeoff on Figure 6.3). It's the start of the term and no tests have yet been administered, but you want to establish the names of the students in the file and make space for the five tests you plan to give them.

The task is one of data entry. The program will prompt you for the name of each student, then write the name and five zeros to the file. When you have no more names to enter, you'll hit the ENTER key, instead of typing a name, to signify the end of the input data. Later, as tests are given, you'll use another program to fill in the zero field corresponding to the exam, so all you're doing with the five zeros right now is creating blanks for those future scores.

Because you have several classes and you want to set up a separate file for each one, the fact that the program also asks you for the file name proves to be a helpful feature. To minimize noncomputer recordkeeping, use easy-to-remember names: CLASS1.GRD for the first class, CLASS2.GRD for the second class of the day, etc. After you enter the file name, the program creates or reopens a file by that name for output.

```
100 REM  ** PROGRAM 'NAMENT'                      K. PORTER        1/23/83
110 REM  ** SETS UP A FILE OF STUDENT NAMES WITH ROOM FOR FIVE TEST SCORES.
120 REM  ** SCORE FIELDS ARE ZEROS TO BE FILLED IN LATER.
130 REM -----------------------------------------------------------------
140 REM
150      PRINT "STUDENT NAME INPUT"
160      PRINT "------------------"
170      PRINT
180 REM
190 REM  ** GET FILENAME
200      INPUT "FILENAME FOR THIS CLASS"; F$
210      PRINT
220 REM
230 REM  ** OPEN/CREATE FILE
240      OPEN "O", #1, F$
250 REM
260 REM  ** DATA ENTRY LOOP
270      LINE INPUT "STUDENT NAME ('ENTER' TO STOP)... "; N$
280        IF LEN(N$) = 0 THEN GOTO 320
290        WRITE#1, N$, 0, 0, 0, 0, 0
300      GOTO 270
310 REM
320 REM  ** CLOSE FILE AND QUIT
330      CLOSE
340      PRINT: PRINT "THANK YOU"
350      END
```

Figure 10.1 Program NAMENT.

Figure 10.1 is called NAMENT for "name entry." It opens the file in line 240 using the variable file name obtained at line 200, and then it enters the loop at 270–300. This loop uses LINE INPUT because the student names have commas in them. If you hit ENTER in response to a prompt, the length of the input string N$ will be zero, so the loop tests for that condition at 280. If it's not a 0 length, line 290 writes the name and five zero fields to the file and then repeats for the next name. When the length of N$ is 0, the loop exits to 320 and closes the file.

As you run this program, it might surprise you that disk activity doesn't occur after every WRITE# instruction. In fact, that's perfectly normal. BASIC has a file buffer that accumulates a fairly large amount of output data before it ships it to disk. As you put in a lot of names, the buffer empties periodically, starting disk activity at irregular intervals. This is normal in file processing. One of the things CLOSE does is to make sure any unwritten data in the buffer get moved into the file before closing it.

Reading from a sequential file

Data are read back out of a sequential file in the same order that they were written, which is, of course, why it's called a sequential file. To read a file, you have to open it in mode "I", meaning it's an *I*nput to the program. Otherwise the OPEN statement is the same as for an output file.

In the case of output, the OPEN statement either opens an existing file and resets the EOF marker to the start (deleting its previous contents) or else it creates a new file. With an input file, however, it only attempts to open a file that already exists under the specified name and if it can't find it, the OPEN fails with an error.

Therefore you should execute an ON ERROR statement before an OPEN in mode "I", so that your program knows what to do if it can't find the file. Circumstances dictate what is an appropriate action; in most cases, you'll probably issue a message and stop the program. Sometimes, though, especially in business programs, an OPEN will check for a file and pull in its data for processing if there is any, and simply keep running if there isn't. Chapter 9 gives some guidance on handling these circumstances.

Almost always, when we read in a sequential file we have no idea how many records it contains: could be none, three, or a million. Each time a file input is performed, the operating system checks for the EOF marker, and when it finds it, it sends a signal to the BASIC program. This signal is tested with the IF EOF instruction, which gives a line number to go to upon hitting the end of the file. The instructions there tell the program what to do, much like an error handler referenced by ON ERROR. And like ON ERROR, IF EOF is executed *before* the file input statement. For a file opened with reference number 3, this instruction is

IF EOF(3) THEN 2970

where 2970 is the line number of the instruction that gets control when the end of file is reached. To stop the program at the end of file #3 you can also code

IF EOF(3) THEN STOP

but it's better programming practice to jump to a CLOSE.

```
100 REM  ** PROGRAM 'FILEDUMP'                        K. PORTER 1/24/83
110 REM  ** THIS PROGRAM READS AND DISPLAYS THE CONTENTS OF ANY FILE.
120 REM ------------------------------------------------------------------------
130 REM
140      PRINT "FILE DUMPING PROGRAM"
150      PRINT "--------------------"
160      PRINT
170 REM
180 REM  ** GET FILENAME
190      INPUT "NAME OF FILE TO DUMP"; N$
200 REM
210 REM  ** OPEN THE FILE
220      ON ERROR GOTO 360                 :REM    IF FILE DOESN'T EXIST
230      OPEN "I", #1, N$
235      PRINT
240 REM
250 REM  ** LOOP TO READ AND DISPLAY FILE CONTENTS
260      IF EOF(1) THEN 310
270        LINE INPUT#1, X$
280        PRINT X$
290      GOTO 250
300 REM
310 REM  ** COME HERE ON END OF FILE
320      CLOSE
330      PRINT: PRINT "END OF FILE "; N$
340      GOTO 400
350 REM
360 REM  ** ERROR HANDLER IF FILE DOESN'T EXIST
370      PRINT: PRINT "NONEXISTENT FILE"
380      INPUT "TRY ANOTHER (Y/N)"; X$
390      IF X$ = "Y" THEN RESUME 180
400      END
```

Figure 10.2 Program FILEDUMP.

Figure 10.2 is a general-purpose program that displays the contents of any sequential file. It also demonstrates the main principles of file reading. The heart of this program is between lines 210 and 290. Line 220 points to the error handler at 360, which gives the user another crack at entering the name of an existing file. If the name N$ is valid, line 230 gives way to the loop at 250–290. This loop reads successive records from the file and displays them on the screen exactly as they appear in the file (LINE INPUT# handles the entire record as a single string). When the end of the file is reached, line 260 refers the program to the handler at 310, which closes the file and prints a "warm feeling" message to confirm that the entire file has been processed.

Copying a sequential file

When you have crucial data in a file, it's important to make and retain a backup copy for safekeeping, preferably on a different diskette. That way, if the primary file becomes damaged, you haven't lost data that might be irreplaceable. Also, as we'll see in the next section, you have to copy a file's contents to another file in order to change or add to the data.

Copying is a quick and simple operation that follows the following procedure:

1. Open the input file as #1.
2. Create the output file as #2.
3. Loop, reading a record from #1 with LINE INPUT#1, X$.
4. Write a record to #2 with PRINT#2, X$ and repeat.
5. At EOF(1), close the input file. If nothing further is to be done to #2, close it also.

Figure 10.3 is a file copy utility that makes a backup of any primary file, which is located in disk drive A, on another diskette in drive B. The names of the two files are identical, except that they're on different diskettes. If you don't have two drives or you're not running under CP/M, change the output file naming to conform with your configuration. On a one-drive computer, for instance, you might use string manipulations to change the file name suffix to .BAK, indicating a backup copy.

Note that the file write is done with PRINT# instead of WRITE#. The reason is that WRITE# puts quotes around strings, and since the entire record is treated as a string, it would surround it with quotes, even if the first field was a string and had its own quotes. Consequently, with WRITE# you could end up with two double quotes at the start of some records. PRINT#, on the other hand, writes the output to disk exactly as it is without first reformatting it.

You'll see that the program follows the procedure described above. It's a useful member of any program library.

```
100 REM  ** PROGRAM 'BACKUP'                      K. PORTER  1/23/83
110 REM  ** MAKES A BACKUP COPY OF THE NAMED FILE AND WRITES IT UNDER THE
120 REM  **     SAME NAME TO DRIVE 'B'.
130 REM ----------------------------------------------------------------------
140 REM
150     PRINT "FILE BACKUP"
160     PRINT "-----------"
170     PRINT
180 REM
190 REM  ** GET THE SOURCE FILE NAME
200     INPUT "NAME OF FILE TO BACK UP"; F1$
210 REM
220 REM  ** BUILD NAME OF OUTPUT FILE (SAME AS F1$, BUT ON DRIVE B)
230     LET F2$ = "B:" + F1$
240 REM
250 REM  ** OPEN THE FILES
260     ON ERROR GOTO 400
270     OPEN "I", #1, F1$
280     OPEN "O", #2, F2$
290 REM
300 REM  ** FILE COPY LOOP
310     IF EOF(1) THEN 360
320       LINE INPUT#1, X$
330       PRINT#2, X$
340     GOTO 300
350 REM
360 REM  ** CLOSE FILES
370     CLOSE
380     PRINT: PRINT "FILE COPIED": PRINT
390     GOTO 430
395 REM
400 REM  ** ERROR HANDLER
410     PRINT: PRINT "NO FILE NAMED "; F1$
420 REM
430 REM  ** SEE IF WANT TO COPY ANOTHER
440     INPUT "ANOTHER FILE (Y/N)"; X$
450     IF X$ = "Y" THEN GOTO 200
460     END
```

Figure 10.3 Program BACKUP.

Adding new data to the end of an existing file

When new records are to be added to a file, we get into something of a paradox. A file can be opened either in the "I" or the "O" mode. To write to a file it has to be in the output mode, but to find its end we have to read until EOF, and that's an "I" mode operation. What's a body to do?

Sequential files have been around since the inception of the computer, so it's hardly a new problem to the world at large even if it is to you. A procedural solution was long ago developed, and this is it:

1. Open the file to be added to as #1.
2. Create a new working file as #2.
3. Copy the contents of #1 to #2 with LINE INPUT#1 and PRINT#2 instructions.
4. At EOF(1), close file #1.
5. Write the new records into file #2.
6. Close #2.
7. Kill the original file #1.
8. Rename the new file #2 so it has the same name as the old file #1.

This procedure introduces two instructions we haven't used before, KILL and NAME.

The KILL statement has the form

KILL [filename]

where [filename] is either a literal or a string variable containing the name of a file that is *not* currently open. This instruction deletes the name of the file from the diskette directory, thereby terminating its existence and freeing the storage space it occupied. After a KILL, the named file is permanently erased and cannot be recovered.

NAME changes the name of a file. It has the form

NAME [oldfile] AS [newfile]

where [oldfile] is an existing closed file and [newfile] is a name that doesn't currently exist on the diskette. After the statement

NAME "WORKING.XXX" AS "CLASS9.GRD"

the file WORKING.XXX has the name CLASS9.GRD and can only be found under its new name. Three conditions must be satisfied to execute this instruction: the file can't be open, [oldfile] must be accessible under the name shown, and [newfile] can't conflict with the name of an existing file. The first two conditions are easily controlled by the program, but the third can be a problem. Thus, it's a good idea to set up a vector to an error handler via the ON ERROR instruction before doing a NAME.

For an example of adding data to an existing file, let's go back to the classroom application. Sometimes a new student moves to town in mid-term, and once in a while even a teacher makes a mistake and forgets to include somebody's name in a list. To add new name(s) to a class file, Figure 10.4 is needed.

```
100 REM  **  PROGRAM 'ADDNAMES'                      K. PORTER     1/23/83
110 REM  **  APPENDS NAME(S) TO END OF CLASS FILE ALONG WITH FIVE ZEROS FOR
120 REM  **     FUTURE TEST SCORES.
130 REM ------------------------------------------------------------------
140 REM
145     LET W$ = "WORKFILE.XXX"
150     PRINT "ADD NAME(S) TO CLASS FILE"
160     PRINT "-------------------------"
170     PRINT
180 REM
190 REM  **  GET CLASS FILE NAME
200     INPUT "FILENAME FOR THIS CLASS"; F$
210     PRINT
220 REM
230 REM  **  OPEN OLD CLASS FILE AS #1, WORKFILE AS #2
240     ON ERROR GOTO 600
250     OPEN "I", #1, F$
260     OPEN "O", #2, W$
270     PRINT "COPYING TO WORK FILE"
280 REM
290 REM  **  FILE COPY LOOP
300     IF EOF(1) THEN 350
310       LINE INPUT#1, X$
320       PRINT#2, X$
330     GOTO 290
340 REM
350 REM  **  CLOSE SOURCE FILE
360     PRINT "COPY COMPLETE": PRINT
370     CLOSE #1
380 REM
390 REM  **  GET ADDITIONS FROM KEYBOARD, WRITE TO FILE
400     LINE INPUT "NEW STUDENT NAME (HIT 'ENTER' TO END)..."; N$
410       IF LEN(N$) = 0 THEN GOTO 450
420       WRITE#2, N$, 0, 0, 0, 0, 0
430     GOTO 390
440 REM
450 REM  **  CLOSE WHEN NO MORE TO ADD
460     CLOSE #2
470 REM
480 REM  **  KILL OLD FILE, RENAME NEW ONE TO SAME NAME
490     KILL F$
500     ON ERROR GOTO 700
510     NAME W$ AS F$
520     PRINT: PRINT "ADDITIONS COMPLETE"
530     GOTO 999
540 REM
600 REM  **  ERROR HANDLER FOR TRYING TO OPEN NONEXISTENT FILE
610     PRINT "NO FILE NAMED "; F$
620     INPUT "TRY ANOTHER (Y/N)"; X$
```

(continued)

```
630     IF X$ = "Y" THEN GOTO 190
640     GOTO 999
650 REM
700 REM  ** ERROR HANDLER FOR RENAMING
710     IF ERR <> 53 THEN GOTO 740
720       PRINT "IN RENAMING, NO FILE NAMED "; W$
730       GOTO 780
740     IF ERR <> 58 THEN GOTO 770
750       PRINT "IN RENAMING, FILE "; F$; " ALREADY EXISTS"
760       GOTO 780
770     PRINT "ERROR CODE"; ERR; "AT LINE"; ERL
780       PRINT "PROGRAM HALTED -- ADDITIONS NOT MADE TO "; F$
790       STOP
999     END
```

Figure 10.4 Program ADDNAMES.

The program ADDNAMES follows the procedure outlined above. The procedure is contained in lines 230–530. In particular, note the use of symbolic file names F$ (the original file, entered by the user in line 200) and W$, the work file that ultimately becomes the new file F$. This technique—using symbolic rather than literal file names—ensures that the KILL in line 490 and the NAME in 510 won't be affected by typing errors. It also makes the error handler at 700 more complex than it needs to be, since certain of the errors it anticipates will never happen. The purpose at 700–790 is to show how an error handler can be constructed to deal with a multitude of circumstances.

Sequential file batch updates

Most applications using sequential files need to update the data from time to time, as, for instance, when a test is given and the students' scores are merged into the grades files.

The procedure for doing this is similar to the addition of new data, except that the individual records are modified as they pass through the program from the source file to the work file. This is the sequence of events:

1. Open the source (old) file as #1.
2. Open a work file as #2.
3. Read a record from #1.
4. Modify or add information.
5. Write the record to #2.
6. Repeat from 3 until EOF(1).
7. Close both files.
8. Kill the source file (old #1).
9. Rename the work file to the source file name.

```
100 REM  **  PROGRAM 'SCORENT'                        K. PORTER      1/23/83
110 REM  **  ADDS SCORES FOR ONE TEST (OF FIVE) TO STUDENT RECORDS.
120 REM -------------------------------------------------------------------
130 REM
135     OPTION BASE 1
140     DIM T(5)                                     :REM    SCORES LIST
150     LET W$ = "WORKFILE.XXX"
160 REM
170 REM  **  STARTUP QUESTIONNAIRE
180     PRINT "ADD TEST SCORES TO STUDENT RECORDS"
190     PRINT "----------------------------------"
200     PRINT
210     INPUT "FILENAME FOR THIS CLASS"; F$
220     PRINT
230     INPUT "SCORES FOR WHICH TEST NUMBER"; N
240       IF N > 5 THEN PRINT "TRY AGAIN": GOTO 230
250     PRINT
260 REM
270 REM  **  OPEN FILES
280     ON ERROR GOTO 540
290     OPEN "I", #1, F$
300     OPEN "O", #2, W$
310 REM
320 REM  **  LOOP TO READ, UPDATE, AND WRITE STUDENT RECORDS
330 REM      ---------------------------------------------
340 REM  **  READ NEXT RECORD
350     IF EOF(1) THEN 460
360       INPUT#1, N$, T(1), T(2), T(3), T(4), T(5)
370 REM
380 REM  **  GET THIS STUDENT'S SCORE
390       PRINT "SCORE FOR "; N$ TAB(30);
400       INPUT T(N)
410 REM
420 REM  **  WRITE TO WORKFILE
430       WRITE#2, N$, T(1), T(2), T(3), T(4), T(5)
440     GOTO 340
450 REM
460 REM  **  COME HERE ON EOF(1)
470     CLOSE
480     KILL F$
500     NAME W$ AS F$
510     PRINT "THIS CLASS COMPLETED"
520     GOTO 560
530 REM
540 REM  **  ERROR HANDLER FOR ATTEMPT TO OPEN NONEXISTENT FILE
550     PRINT "NO FILE NAMED "; F$
560     INPUT "ANOTHER (Y/N)"; N$
570     IF N$ = "Y" THEN GOTO 200
580     END
```

Figure 10.5 Program SCORENT.

Figure 10.5 shows one approach for updating the sequential files. This is an interactive update; for each student record the user is asked to enter the test score from the keyboard. The score is then recorded in the appropriate field in the record (its list index is known from the start-up question), and the updated record is written to file #2.

File merging is another approach to the same end-of-batch updates. Businesses in particular favor file merges: data are collected in a file for some period (e.g., daily invoices, weekly payroll changes) and then this file is run against the master file to make updates.

```
20 REM  **  PROGRAM 'CAPTURE'                      K. PORTER       1/25/83
30 REM  **  CAPTURES TEST SCORES AND ADDS THEM TO A BATCH UPDATE FILE.
40 REM  **     THIS FILE IS LATER USED TO UPDATE THE CLASS FILES BY
50 REM  **     RUNNING PROGRAM 'UPDATE'
60 REM  **  WRITES TWO TYPES OF RECORDS TO FILE 'UPFILE.BAT':
70 REM  **     1.  CONTROL RECORD (CLASS FILE NAME, -9, 0)
80 REM  **     2.  DATA RECORDS (STUDENT NAME, TEST #, SCORE)
90 REM  **  THREE-STAGE JOB:
100 REM  **     1.  COPY PRESENT UPFILE.BAT TO WORKFILE.
110 REM  **     2.  GET SCORES BY CLASS, ADD TO FILE.
120 REM  **     3.  BLOW AWAY OLD UPFILE, RENAME WORKFILE.
130 REM ------------------------------------------------------------------
140 REM
150      LET F9 =  0                              :REM    FLAG FOR NO U$
160      LET W$ = "WORKFILE.XXX"
170      LET U$ = "UPFILE.BAT"
180      PRINT "CAPTURE STUDENT TEST SCORES"
190      PRINT "---------------------------": PRINT
200 REM
210 REM  **  STAGE 1 - COPY OLD FILE OVER TO NEW
220 REM      -----------------------------------
230      OPEN "O", #2, W$                         :REM    NEW WORKFILE
240      ON ERROR GOTO 330
250      OPEN "I", #1, U$                         :REM    OLD UPDATE FILE
260      IF EOF(1) THEN 300                       :REM    COPY LOOP
270        LINE INPUT#1, X$
280        PRINT#2, X$
290      GOTO 260
300      CLOSE #1
310      GOTO 370                                 :REM    STAGE 2
320 REM
330 REM  **  IF NO UPDATE FILE SIMPLY CONTINUE
340      LET F9 = 9                               :REM    SET FLAG FOR NO U$
350      RESUME 370
360 REM
370 REM  **  STAGE 2 - CAPTURE TEST SCORES
380 REM      -----------------------------
```

```
390 REM  ** FIRST GET FILENAME FOR CLASS AND OPEN IT
400     PRINT "**********************************"
410     INPUT "FILENAME FOR CLASS"; F$
420     ON ERROR GOTO 460
430     OPEN "I", #1, F$
440     GOTO 500
450 REM
460 REM  ** ERROR IF CLASS FILE DOESN'T EXIST
470     PRINT "NO FILE NAMED "; F$
480     RESUME 680                          :REM    SEE IF WANT ANOTHER
490 REM
500 REM  ** WRITE CONTROL RECORD
510     WRITE#2, F$, -9, 0
520 REM
530 REM  ** GET TEST NUMBER
540     INPUT "TEST NUMBER"; T
550     IF T < 1 OR T > 5 THEN GOTO 540
560 REM
570 REM  ** LOOP TO CAPTURE, WRITE SCORES FOR EACH STUDENT
580     IF EOF(1) THEN 650
590       INPUT#1, N$, X, X, X, X, X
600       PRINT "SCORE FOR "; N$ TAB(30);
610       INPUT S
620       WRITE#2, N$, T, S
630     GOTO 580
640 REM
650 REM  ** AT END OF CLASS FILE
660     CLOSE #1
670     PRINT: PRINT "END OF THIS CLASS"
680     PRINT: INPUT "ANOTHER CLASS (Y/N)"; X$
690     IF X$ = "Y" THEN GOTO 400           :REM    REPEAT IF YES
700 REM
710 REM  ** STAGE 3 -- END OF JOB
720 REM     --------------------
730     CLOSE #2
740     IF F9 <> 0 THEN GOTO 760
750     KILL U$
760     NAME W$ AS U$
770     END
```

Figure 10.6 Program CAPTURE.

Applying this approach to our schoolroom case, we'll need two programs. The first (Figure 10.6) is a data-entry program that captures test scores and collects them in a file. The second (Figure 10.7) reads both the update file and the master file and merges their information into a new master file. The CAPTURE program (Figure 10.6) can be run as often as necessary to accumulate test scores. Whenever we get around to it, we can run the UPDATE program (Figure 10.7), and all the update information will be applied to the individual class files.

There are a couple of things to keep in mind about processing this way. First, the records have to be in the same order in both the update and master files. We've made sure of this in the way the CAPTURE program does interactive data entry.

The second thing is more a characteristic than a problem. The update file might collect information about many different classes in no particular order. Consequently, we have to include control information in the file to notify the UPDATE program when to switch from one class's master file to another, and which file to switch to. For that, the CAPTURE program writes a control record to the update file at the start of each class's scores (line 510). This record contains the name of the class file F$ and a −9 that serves as a dummy test number.

Should the update file and the class file get out of sync somehow during the running of UPDATE, the dummy test number −9 will attempt to access the −9th entry in the score list M. This will cause an error that halts the program, thus alerting the user that something is awry. It's not a very graceful way of flagging errors. We could write a handler to recover from it, but the object of the game here is to show how to merge files. An elaborate error handler would tend to obscure that purpose.

Whereas Figure 10.6 demonstrates how to strip data from one file to create another, Figure 10.7 shows how to work with multiple files, merging their data into a single output file. The nucleus of the file merge occurs between lines 350 and 420. The overall manipulation of files is at the start and end of the outer loop between lines 300 and 480.

```
100 REM  ** PROGRAM 'UPDATE'                        K. PORTER     1/25/83
110 REM  ** DOES BATCH UPDATES OF STUDENT TEST RECORDS BY APPLYING
120 REM  **    ACCUMULATED SCORES IN UPFILE.BAT TO CLASS FILES.
130 REM  ** HAS 3 FILES OPEN CONCURRENTLY:
140 REM  **    #1 IS UPFILE.BAT SOURCE FILE FOR UPDATES.
150 REM  **    #2 IS OLD CLASS FILE.
160 REM  **    #3 IS WORKFILE (NEW CLASS FILE).
170 REM ------------------------------------------------------------------
180 REM
190     LET U$ = "UPFILE.BAT"
200     LET W$ = "WORKFILE.XXX"
210     DIM M(5)                                 :REM    TEST SCORES LIST
220     PRINT "BATCH FILE UPDATES FOR TEST SCORES"
230     PRINT "----------------------------------"
240 REM
250 REM  ** OPEN UPDATE FILE
260     ON ERROR GOTO 550
270     OPEN "I", #1, U$
280     INPUT#1, F$, K, X                        :REM    FIRST CONTROL REC
290 REM
```

```
300 REM  ** LOOP FOR EACH CLASS IN UPDATE FILE (NAME GIVEN BY CONTROL REC)
310      IF EOF(1) THEN 500
320        ON ERROR GOTO 550
330        OPEN "I", #2, F$                          :REM   OLD CLASS FILE
340        OPEN "O", #3, W$                          :REM   NEW CLASS FILE
350 REM  ** NESTED LOOP FOR EACH STUDENT IN CLASS
360        IF EOF(1) THEN 440
370          INPUT#1, N1$, T, S
380          IF EOF(2) THEN 440
390          INPUT#2, N2$, M(1), M(2), M(3), M(4), M(5)
400          LET M(T) = S                            :REM   UPDATE TEST SCORE
410          WRITE#3, N2$, M(1), M(2), M(3), M(4), M(5)
420        GOTO 350
430 REM
440 REM  ** END OF THIS CLASS FILE
450        CLOSE #2, #3
460        KILL F$
470        NAME W$ AS F$
480      GOTO 300                                    :REM   REPEAT
490 REM
500 REM  ** FINISHED WITH UPDATE FILE (EOF(1))
510      CLOSE
520      KILL U$
530      GOTO 610
540 REM
550 REM  ** ERROR HANDLERS
560      IF ERL > 290 THEN GOTO 590
570      PRINT "** NO UPDATES WAITING TO BE DONE **"
580      GOTO 600
590      PRINT "** NO CLASS FILE NAMED "; F$;" **"
600      PRINT "   PROGRAM ENDED"
610      END
```

Figure 10.7 Program UPDATE.

The sequence of events should be apparent on inspection of the statements. Note that we read a record from the update file immediately on opening it (line 28Ø), since we know that the first record in that file contains the name of the class file to which the subsequent data pertains. That name (F$) is then used in line 33Ø to open the class file.

In the nested loop the update file still has priority as the one read first. We read a record from it and if it's the end of the file, we jump down to line 44Ø. Now see what happens: the program jumps back up to the start of the loop. At line 31Ø there's a test to find out whether we hit the end of the update file. If so, the show's over.

Most of the time, though, the input at lines 36Ø–37Ø will succeed. In 38Ø–39Ø we try to read the class file. When it works, the update and writing to the output file proceed normally and the loop repeats for the next pair of records. However, when the class file has been entirely read, line 380 sends control down to the "housekeeping" that begins at 440. More significantly, we know that the update file input at 370 has provided the name of the next class file and not the name of a student. This phasing of records is very important when you're merging data from two or more files.

This particular case has been structured to be fairly simple and easy to understand by ensuring a one-for-one correlation; for every student in the class there's a corresponding student record in the update file. Unfortunately, in most business-type applications of file merging it's not so straightforward, and programs usually update only some of the records in a file.

In this application, for instance, the test scores for all students are in the update, and even if a student didn't take the test he or she still gets a 0 score. Later when the student makes up the test we have to apply the score to the class file.

It would take a slightly different version of Figure 10.6 (CAPTURE) to create the update file. We could insert a new instruction

```
615     IF S = 0 THEN GOTO 630
```

that would only write makeup scores to the update file and disregard all others (any score entered as a 0, which is the score given to everyone who's already taken the test).

The change relevant to the discussion of matching records on a partial file update occurs in Figure 10.7. In this case, we could change the instructions in the loop as follows:

```
390       INPUT#2, N2$...etc.                (No change)
395       IF N1$ < > N2$ THEN GOTO 410
400       LET M(T) = S                       (No change)
410       WRITE#3, N2$...etc.                (No change)
415       IF N1$ < > N2$ THEN GOTO 380
420     GOTO 350                             (No change)
```

This has the effect of simply passing records that are not to be updated from the old class file to the new one. Only when the names read from the update and class files match do we update the student's score with line 400.

The catch in this approach is that the records have to be in similar order in both files. If the names are in alphabetic order in the class file and somchow the update file has them backwards (SMITH followed by JONES), the first name that matches is SMITH and then the program goes through the rest of the class file in the futile search for JONES, whose record has already been read getting to SMITH. As a result, poor Jones' score never gets updated and he's taken the makeup test in vain.

This particular situation will also stop the program with an error. When the class file has been passed and control goes back to the opens at 320–

340, the "control record" from the update file will show F$ as JONES and not the name of the next class file as it's supposed to. Consequently, BASIC will try to open a class file named JONES and the error handler will issue the disconcerting message

> ** NO CLASS FILE NAMED JONES **
> PROGRAM ENDED

That ought to tell you that something is screwed up.

The way these programs are structured this should never occur, but, of course, not all your programs will work the same way these do. The point is that, when working with sequential files, the proper sequencing of records is of the utmost importance. Before doing a file merge, most business applications sort both files on a particular field and then, during the update run, the program compares those fields as the modification above (lines 390–420) demonstrates. This ensures that the records in both files occur in the same order.

The next chapter suggests ways for dealing with data without regard for its order.

Producing a report from a file

The purpose of a file is to store variable information for later use. A program that pulls information from a file and converts it into a form useful to people is called a *report writer*. Very early in this book we pointed out that most of a computer's activity—and a programmer's job—has to do not with computations, but with I/O. A report writer is a prime example.

By and large a report writer does almost no calculations. It simply reads data from one or more files and formats it for output. That's enough work for one program, as Figure 10.8(a), one of the longest in this book, demonstrates.

```
110 REM  **  PROGRAM 'REPTCARD'                    K. PORTER     1/28/83
120 REM  **  PRODUCES TEST SCORES AND GRADE AVERAGES FOR A GROUP OF STUDENTS
130 REM  **     AND ALSO AVERAGE SCORE ACHIEVED PER TEST FOR THE CLASS.
140 REM  **  PROCESSES CLASS FILE FOR SELECTED CLASS.
150 REM ---------------------------------------------------------------------
160 REM
170      DIM G(5), T(5)                            :REM    INDIV GRADES, TOTALS
180      LET I1$ = "\             \"
190      LET I2$ = "  ###.#"
200      LET H$  = "NAME:                     1     2     3     4     5     A"
210      LET T$  = "TEST SCORES FOR "
```

(continued)

```
220 REM
230 REM  **  INPUT SECTION
240      PRINT "CLASS REPORT CARD"
250      PRINT "-----------------"  : PRINT
260      INPUT "FILE FOR CLASS "; F$: PRINT
270      IF LEN(F$) = 0 THEN STOP
280      PRINT "OUTPUT SELECTION MENU:"
290      PRINT "    1.  DISPLAY"
300      PRINT "    2.  PRINTER"
310      PRINT "    3.  FILE": PRINT
320      INPUT "      SELECTION..."; R: PRINT
330      IF (R < 1) OR (R > 3) THEN GOTO 280      :REM    RANGE CHECK
340      IF R <> 3 THEN GOTO 420                  :REM    GO IF NOT FILE
350        INPUT "OUTPUT FILENAME"; W$: PRINT
360      IF W$ <> F$ THEN GOTO 390                :REM    DUPLICATE NAME CHECK
370        PRINT "DUPLICATE -- PICK ANOTHER": GOTO 350
380 REM
390 REM  **  OPEN OUTPUT FILE ON MENU #3
400      OPEN "O", #2, W$
410 REM
420 REM  **  OPEN INPUT FILE
430      ON ERROR GOTO 1250                       :REM    IF NO SUCH FILE
440      OPEN "I", #1, F$
450      ON ERROR GOTO 0                          :REM    DISABLE ERROR HANDLER
460 REM
470 REM  **  INITIALIZE
480      FOR L = 1 TO 5: LET T(L) = 0: NEXT L     :REM    CLEAR TOTALS ARRAY
490      LET C = 0                                :REM    RESET STUDENT COUNT
500      ON R GOSUB 920, 970, 1020                :REM    REPORT HEADING
510 REM
520 REM  **  FILE PROCESSING LOOP
530 REM      --------------------
540      IF EOF(1) THEN 740
550        INPUT#1, N$, G(1), G(2), G(3), G(4), G(5)
560 REM
570 REM  **  AVERAGE GRADE PER STUDENT
580        LET A = 0
590        FOR L = 1 TO 5
600          LET A = A + G(L)                     :REM    TOTAL OF SCORES
610        NEXT L
620        LET A = A / 5                          :REM    AVERAGE GRADE
630 REM
640 REM  **  PRINT REPORT LINE TO SELECTED OUTPUT
650        ON R GOSUB 1080, 1130, 1180
660 REM
670 REM  **  ACCUMULATE SCORES BY TEST FOR CLASS, COUNT STUDENTS
680        FOR L = 1 TO 5
690          LET T(L) = T(L) + G(L)
700        NEXT L
710        LET C = C + 1
720      GOTO 520                                 :REM    REPEAT FOR CLASS
```

```
730 REM
740 REM  ** AT END OF FILE:
750 REM  ** CALCULATE AND PRINT AVERAGE SCORE PER TEST
760     IF C = 0 THEN PRINT "NO STUDENTS IN THIS CLASS": GOTO 870
770     LET A = 0
780     FOR L = 1 TO 5
790       LET G(L) = T(L) / C                        :REM    AVGE ALL STUDENTS
800       LET  A   = G(L) + A                        :REM    TOTAL ALL SCORES
810     NEXT L
820     LET A = A / 5                                :REM    AVERAGE ALL SCORES
830     LET N$ = " AVERAGE PER TEST"
840     ON R GOSUB 1080, 1130, 1180                  :REM    OUTPUT
850     IF R = 2 THEN LPRINT CHR$(12)                :REM    EJECT PAGE ON PRTR
860     CLOSE
870     PRINT "****************************"
880     GOTO 230                                     :REM    REPEAT FOR NEXT CLASS
890 REM ------------------------------------------------------------------------
900 REM
910 REM  ** REPORT HEADING SUBROUTINES
920 REM  ** DISPLAY
930     PRINT T$ + F$: PRINT
940     PRINT H$
950     RETURN
960 REM
970 REM  ** PRINTER
980     LPRINT T$ + F$: LPRINT
990     LPRINT H$
1000     RETURN
1010 REM
1020 REM  ** FILE
1030     PRINT#2, T$ + F$: PRINT#2, " "
1040     PRINT#2, H$
1050     RETURN
1060 REM
1070 REM  ** REPORT LINES FOR INDIVIDUAL STATEMENTS, CLASS AVERAGES
1080 REM ** DISPLAY
1090    PRINT USING I1$; N$;
1100    PRINT USING I2$; G(1), G(2), G(3), G(4), G(5), A
1110    RETURN
1120 REM
1130 REM  ** PRINTER
1140    LPRINT USING I1$; N$;
1150    LPRINT USING I2$; G(1), G(2), G(3), G(4), G(5), A
1160    RETURN
1170 REM
1180 REM  ** FILE
1190    PRINT#2, USING I1$; N$;
1200    PRINT#2, USING I2$; G(1), G(2), G(3), G(4), G(5), A
1210    RETURN
```

(continued)

```
1220 REM ------------------------------------
1230 REM
1240 REM **  ERROR HANDLER FOR NONEXISTENT CLASS FILE
1250     PRINT "NO SUCH CLASS FILE"
1260     IF R = 3 THEN CLOSE: KILL W$
1270     RESUME 870
```

(a)

```
CLASS REPORT CARD
-----------------

FILE FOR CLASS ?CLASS1.GRD

OUTPUT SELECTION MENU:
    1. DISPLAY
    2. PRINTER
    3. FILE

      SELECTION...? 2

TEST SCORES FOR CLASS1.GRD

NAME:                  1     2     3     4     5     A
BROWN, S.           78.0  89.0  61.0  74.0  95.0  79.4
DAVISON, J.         88.0  78.0  96.0 100.0  99.0  92.2
EDWARDS, B.         66.0  25.0  95.0  69.0  88.0  68.6
GRAY, L.            96.0  95.0  89.0  99.0 100.0  95.8
HARRIS, M.          41.0  22.0  59.0  70.0  81.0  54.6
JENKINS, D.         81.0  84.0  91.0  73.0  85.0  82.8
LARKIN, M.          80.0  77.0  84.0  83.0  91.0  83.0
MORRIS, D.          95.0  96.0 100.0 100.0  82.0  94.6
PARKER, K.          87.0  92.0  89.0  96.0  75.0  87.8
SMITH, B.          100.0  74.0  51.0  95.0  82.0  80.4
WATKINS, C.         85.0  87.0  66.0  89.0  91.0  83.6
 AVERAGE PER TEST   81.5  74.5  80.1  86.2  88.1  82.1
```

(b)

Figure 10.8 (a) Program REPTCARD. (b) Sample run. Note that scores have been added for tests 3 through 5.

This program produces report card data for any class by averaging the test scores per student, and also the average achievement per test and the average test score for all students taking all tests. It has rather more flexibility than most report writers in that it lets the user select any of three outputs for the report: the display, the printer, or a file containing the image of the report, which can be printed later in human-readable form (by Digital Research's DeSpool or one of the other spooled printing utilities).

Figure 10.9 shows the plan used to develop REPTCARD. Unlike most we've seen, this program plan contains no specifications for computation. The only calculations done by REPTCARD are addition and the averaging of lists. Everything else is I/O.

Purpose: Produce an end-of-term report for a class showing:

1. By student, scores for each of five tests taken, and grade average for all five tests (in rows).
2. By test, average achievement for the class and the average of all test scores in the class (by columns).

Input: Class file.

Outputs: (1) Display (2) Printer (3) Report image file

Procedure:

1. Get class filename.
2. Get output choice as above.
   If a file, get filename for output (reject duplicate of class file) and open.
3. Open input file.
4. Initialize
   a. Clear totals array.
   b. Reset student count.
   c. Output report heading.
5. File processing loop:
   a. Get next record from class file.
   b. Average grade for this student.
   c. Output report line for student.
   d. Accumulate scores for tests, count student.
   e. Repeat to EOF.
6. At EOF:
   a. Calculate average score per test.
   b. Output averages.
   c. Eject page if output to printer.
   d. Close all files.
7. Repeat from 1 for next class.

Figure 10.9 Program plan for REPTCARD.

Let's examine the program for some highlights. At line 280 there is a menu for selecting the output for the report, in which a variable R is loaded with a digit corresponding to the choice. If the user picks 3 for a file, he or she has to key in a file name, and REPTCARD then (at line

360) makes sure it's not the same as the name of the input class file. This doesn't protect an already-existing output file of the same name, but at least it prevents a conflict when the input file is opened at line 440.

The output selection (R) governs the destination of the report heading in line 500, where ON R GOSUB... sets up a vector for output to the display, printer, or file. It takes a different form of the PRINT instruction to accomplish each of these, and they're located in a subroutine area after the body of the program (lines 900+). Similarly, lines 650 and 840 use ON R GOSUB... to output report lines to the appropriate destination. These report lines use common subroutines for both student information and class achievement averages. The content is different, but the format is similar enough to make the subroutines common to both.

Line 710 counts the students in the class by incrementing a variable C for each record processed. Each student's scores are accumulated in the list T(X). After the last record (at EOF), the total scores by test are divided by the number of students to develop average achievement per exam, and those results are, in turn, averaged to find the average score for all tests taken.

Let's drop down to line 1100. The PRINT USING instruction prints a whole list of variables using the buffer image I2$. If you go back and check that image, you'll see that it specifies simply "###.#" and not six fields as the list in 1100 indicates. In a situation such as this, where the buffer is insufficient to contain all the variables in the list, BASIC keeps reusing the same image over and over until it has output the entire list. It does *not* start a new line on reuse of the image. Consequently, this instruction prints six formatted fields with two spaces separating each from its predecessor the same as if I2$ were set up as

"###.# ###.# ###.# ###.# ###.# ###.#"

This saves program space and complexity. The same technique is used in lines 1150 with LPRINT and 1200 with the file PRINT#.

The final thing to note about this program has to do with the form of file PRINT#s. In line 980, which outputs to the page printer, the instruction is LPRINT T$ + F$, but in printing to the file a comma is inserted in the instruction (PRINT#2, T$ + F$). This comma is a deviation from the normal usage of commas in PRINT statements, and is necessary to separate the file reference number from the list of output information. Therefore, in a PRINT# instruction the first comma does not cause a zone skip as it does in PRINTs to devices.

Similarly, in lines 1190 and 1200 the USING clause is set apart from the PRINT# by a comma, giving the statement

```
PRINT#2, USING I1$; N$;
```

This leads us to the general rule that *a file PRINT# must always be followed immediately by a comma* as part of the instruction, not as a spacing control character. A PRINT# to a sequential file is otherwise the same as a PRINT or LPRINT.

With, unfortunately, one other exception as well. When we want to create a blank line on output, we simply code PRINT, but a PRINT# with nothing after it is an error. It doesn't make much sense to me either, but that's the way it is. Thus, when you want to create an empty line in a file you have to send it one space character with the PRINT#, as shown in the second statement in line 1030 (PRINT#2, " ").

File printing

Figure 10.8(a) demonstrated one application where a report can be alternatively routed either to a normal output device or to a file. The file is an image of the printed report stored for later output.

The deferring of output in this manner is called *spooling*, and it's a fairly common practice in data processing. As you've no doubt observed, a printer is dreadfully slow in comparison to the computer. Unless you have a buffering device between your computer and the printer, the slow speed of the printer can tie up the computer for long periods, making it unusable. File operations are much faster, so spooling is a clever way of getting the work done. You can print later when the computer is idle.

The printing of stored-up reports is called *despooling*, a term that's hardly surprising. There are despoolers available, such as the Digital Research product that let you work at the computer while the printer is running. They work well, and if you have one you don't need the program we're about to discuss.

```
100 REM  **  PROGRAM 'LISTFILE'                K. PORTER  1/27/83
110 REM  **  LISTS ANY SEQUENTIAL FILE ON EITHER SCREEN OR PRINTER
120 REM -----------------------------------------------------------
130 REM
140      PRINT "GENERAL FILE LISTING PROGRAM"
150      PRINT "----------------------------": PRINT
160      INPUT "NAME OF FILE"; F$: PRINT
170      IF LEN(F$) = 0 THEN GOTO 9999
180      INPUT "ROUTE TO (1) SCREEN OR (2) PRINTER"; R
190      IF (R < 1) OR (R > 2) THEN GOTO 180
200 REM
210 REM  **  OPEN THE FILE
220      ON ERROR GOTO 390
230      OPEN "I", #1, F$
240      ON ERROR GOTO 0
250 REM
```

(continued)

```
260 REM  ** FILE OUTPUT LOOP
270      IF EOF(1) THEN 340
280        LINE INPUT#1, L$
290        ON R GOSUB 310, 320
300      GOTO 260
305 REM  ** OPTIONS
310      PRINT  L$: RETURN                    :REM    SCREEN OUTPUT
320      LPRINT L$: RETURN                    :REM    PRINTER OUTPUT
330 REM
340 REM  ** AT EOF...
350      IF R = 2 THEN LPRINT CHR$(12)        :REM    PAGE EJECT
360      CLOSE
370      GOTO 9999
380 REM
390 REM  ** ERROR IF NO FILE F$
400      PRINT "NO SUCH FILE"
9999     END
```

Figure 10.10 Program LISTFILE.

Figure 10.10 contains nothing new and it's unique among the programs listed in this book in that it has no lessons to offer. It's just a general sequential-file-listing program that lets you output either to the screen or to the printer, a sort of "poor man's despooler." It won't let you operate the keyboard while the printer is making page copy of your spooled files, but you can run it during slack times and thus make your sessions at the computer more productive. It's included here simply as a useful addition to your program library. Use it not only for despooling, but to make printouts of your most valuable data files. Floppy disks do occasionally fail.

A word of advice on managing spool files: Give them a suffix that identifies them as such, for example, .SPL. If the input file for a report is CLASS1.GRD, call the spool file CLASS1.SPL. That way you can issue the FILES command and readily spot the spool files awaiting printing, and usually you'll be able to figure out what's in the file. After you've printed it, kill it so that your disk doesn't get cluttered with a bunch of old dead reports and you lose track of what's been printed and what hasn't.

CHAPTER 11

RANDOM FILES

Sequential vs. random files. Random file statements. Opening and writing random files: "R" mode, FIELD, LSET/RSET, the MAKE and CONVERT functions, PUT, record number. Figuring record length. Reading random files: GET, finding the end-of-file. Arrayed variables: a trick for packing the FIELD. Reading and writing the same random file. A sophisticated interactive program. Sequential processing of random files. PRINT# to a random file. Indexing a random file with a sequential file. Housekeeping.

Sequential vs. random files

Sequential files lend themselves very well to repetitive processing, in which a similar action is performed on every record in the file. The batch update example and the print drivers in the last chapter demonstrated this classic data-processing usage of sequential files.

The problem with sequential files is that individual items of information are not readily accessible. To extract information from the thousandth record, you have to pass through the 999 preceding records just to find it. To update that record is even more cumbersome; then you have to copy 999 records into another file, update the one in question, copy the remaining records, then kill and rename files. A lot of work just to update one record. Sequential files aren't well suited for interactive computing.

While BASIC deals efficiently with sequential files, it's chiefly a language for interactive computing: conversing with the user by asking questions and immediately responding with processed results. This kind of computing needs a data organization that can dive into a file anywhere and grab the requisite information without sifting through masses of other data. It also needs the ability to update one record without passing through the rest of the file. Random organization does this, permitting a program to interact with the file just as it interacts with people.

The term "random" is misleading, suggesting that the file contents are thrown about helter-skelter. It's more accurate to think of random files in the sense of direct access. The program goes directly to the record in question, reading or writing it without regard for the other records in the file.

This is made possible by the blocking of records into units of a fixed length. Every record might occupy 100 bytes, so that the first record in the file starts at position 0, the second at position 100, the third at 200, etc. A record is then referred to by its sequence number. If we want record number 5, BASIC uses the record length to calculate the starting position of record 5 and then goes directly to it (in this example, record 5 starts at the 400th byte in the file and extends through the 499th).

If the data in a random record aren't long enough to use up the space that's been allocated for them, BASIC pads the unused space with filler characters to satisfy the length requirement. For instance, if the record length is 100 and the data take 75 bytes, BASIC puts 25 null characters at the end of the record to make it 100 bytes long. This makes it possible to have variable-length data within a fixed-length record. Thus, record 3 might hold 98 bytes of data, record 4 might have 31 bytes, record 5 75, etc., but all the records are physically 100 bytes long.

Random file statements

Unlike sequential files, random files can be written *and* read: no need to copy files to do an update. That way the program can read a record and show it to the user, and he or she can change it and write the new contents right back to the same place.

Because this is such a different way of processing files, Microsoft BASIC has an entirely different set of random file instructions (although, as we shall see later, some of the sequential instructions can be used in connection with random files). The random file statements and their functions are:

Statement	*Function*
OPEN	Opens or creates a random file.
FIELD	Defines the format of a random record.
GET	Reads a record from the file.
PUT	Writes a record into the file.
CLOSE	Closes the file.
LOC	Returns last record number accessed.

LSET	Puts a string at the left end of a field.
RSET	Puts a string at the right end of a field.
MKD$	Puts double-precision number into field.
MKI$	Puts integer number into field.
MKS$	Puts single-precision number into field.
CVD	Takes double-precision number from field.
CVI	Takes integer number from field.
CVS	Takes single-precision number from field.

Opening and writing random files

The OPEN statement for a random file resembles that for a sequential file, except that the mode is "R" and a record length parameter is added to it. To open a random file named XYZ.RND with a record length of 64 bytes as file #1, the statement is

```
OPEN "R", #1, "XYZ.RND", 64
```

This statement opens an existing file or creates a new one.

You can substitute symbolics for any of the parameters in the OPEN statement, as the following illustrates.

```
100   LET R9 = 64
110   LET R$ = "XYZ.RND"
120   OPEN "R", #1, R$, R9
```

This has the same effect as the first OPEN statement.

Never try to open a sequential file in the "R" mode or vice versa. The OPEN itself will work, but all you'll get is garbage and any writes to the file will screw it up beyond repair.

A sequential file is written entirely in ASCII so that it can be printed, edited, etc., exactly as it is. Random files are not; instead, in Microsoft BASIC, they're in binary format. As a result, a certain amount of preprocessing has to be done to data before writing it to a random file, and after reading it as well, in order to convert its format. That's the purpose of some of those strange instructions, such as MKI$, CVD, and LSET.

Before we get to them, however, let's talk about the FIELD statement. FIELD is, in a way, like the line image defined for a PRINT USING instruction. It describes the format of a buffer, except that in this case the buffer is an image of the random file record. FIELD symbolically describes how the record is organized, and for every random file you have open, you must have one (and only one) FIELD specification. This is usually given as soon as the random file is opened, and it cannot be changed while the file remains open. The FIELD statement associated with a given file has the same reference number as that file, so if you have a random file open as #5, the FIELD statement is called FIELD #5.

Because random files have binary numbers in them instead of ASCII digits, BASIC treats the numbers as strings. Random files can also contain true strings. Every field defined for a record by the FIELD statement is a string variable even if it's a number, and the maximum length of each field has to be specified.

Let's say we want to write a random file #2 that contains only names. The last name comes first and has a maximum length of 14 characters. The person's first name follows, with a maximum length of 10 characters. To set up the buffer for this, write:

```
FIELD #2, 14 AS N2$, 10 AS N1$
```

The last-name field in the record thus has the symbolic name N2$ and the first-name field is called N1$. You could read this statement as "the FIELDs for file #2 are 14 characters referred to as N2$ and 10 characters referred to as N1$."

Obviously there's a relationship between the length of the buffer as defined in the FIELD statement and the record length of the random file it refers to. Since this field buffer contains 14 + 10 = 24 characters, the minimum record length for file #2 is 24 bytes. It could be any number equal to or greater than 24; if it were 46, a record written to this file would contain 24 bytes of real data and 22 null characters to complete the 46 bytes. If, on the other hand, you opened the file with a record length of 20 bytes and then attempted to define the field buffer above, the program would fail with the message "Field overflow," meaning that the FIELD calls for more space than the record length allows. Thus a general rule is that *the FIELD statement defines a buffer whose length is equal to or less than the record length of the file it refers to.*

The field names N1$ and N2$ given in the FIELD statement should not be regarded as string variables, but instead as the names of data elements within the record. Don't manipulate them with string functions, use them in INPUT statements, or otherwise treat them as string variables, because you can run into all sorts of bizarre problems.

The specifications 14 AS N2$ is similar to the statement

```
LET N2$ = SPACE$(14)
```

in that it sets up an empty string area fourteen characters long. But whereas the SPACE$ function creates a variable out in memory somewhere, 14 AS N2$ establishes a fixed field at a specified point within the random file buffer.

Consequently, before you do a file write you have to load string variables into the record's fields. This is done with one of the two instructions LSET and RSET. LSET copies the string into the field so that it's to the extreme left end; RSET instead puts it into the right end of the target field. (These instructions were also discussed at the end of Chapter 7, on string handling operations.) The chart below illustrates the effects of LSET and RSET in a buffer field N2$ whose boundaries are indicated by the bar, where the variable A2$ is JONES.

```
                            |-------------|
LSET N2$ = A2$              JONES
RSET N2$ = A2$                      JONES
```

LSET copies the variable into the target area from left to right and fills the unused positions with null characters. If the variable is too long to fit (putting 18 characters into a field 14 characters long), LSET stops after the allocated space is filled, thus truncating the characters that won't fit at the right end. RSET does just the opposite, copying backwards from right to left. In the case above, the unused area at the left end of the target field is filled with nulls. However, if A2$ were 18 characters long, RSET would truncate the *first* four characters, yielding a rather strange result. Consequently, it's hard to imagine any time when you'd use RSET to copy a string into a file buffer.

In preparation for writing a record to file #2 using the FIELD statement for the names file, you have to load the record buffer with a pair of statements, such as

```
340    LSET N2$ = A2$
350    LSET N1$ = A1$
```

which places the strings currently assigned to A1$ and A2$ into the correct areas.

Numeric variables have to be placed into the file buffer as pseudostrings of binary numbers. Here the data type of the numeric comes into play. You may recall that single-precision, double-precision, and integer numbers have differing lengths. The length defines the amount of space necessary for a field of that type in the FIELD statement. These are shown in the chart below.

The "MAKE" functions prepare a numeric variable to be loaded into a string binary field. MKI$(X) handles an integer X, MKS$(X) prepares a single-precision variable X, and MKD$(X) a double-precision X. For each of these functions there's a corresponding opposite "CONVERT" function used to pull out and reformat numerics after a file input. They are, respectively, CVI, CVS, and CVD, and we'll discuss them presently.

Table 11.A shows, for each numeric type, the length requirement, the MAKE function, and the CONVERT function used in connection with random files.

Table 11.A

Type	Length	MAKE	CONVERT
Integer	2	MKI$	CVI
Single precision	4	MKS$	CVS
Double precision	8	MKD$	CVD

Now let's say we have a random file #3, each record of which contains a name in the first 18 positions, followed by a single-precision number. The buffer is defined as

```
FIELD #3, 18 AS N$, 4 AS D$
```

To load these fields prior to a file write we can code

```
570    LSET N$ = J$
580    LSET D$ = MKS$(D)
```

Line 580 makes the single-precision numeric variable D into a binary string and then copies it into the D$ field in the buffer.

The buffer is now ready to be written to file #3. This is done with the PUT instruction, which puts the buffer into the file at a specified record number. To put the buffer into record number 8, we'd write

```
PUT #3, 8
```

BASIC then calculates the position where the record belongs in the file and writes it there directly. If there were data in record 8, they're replaced by the new contents of the field buffer when the PUT has been executed. The record number can be a symbolic, that is,

```
630    INPUT "WRITE TO WHICH RECORD"; R1
640    PUT #3, R1
```

BASIC keeps track of the last record number accessed. This number can be obtained with the function LOC(f), where (f) is the reference number of the file. If you want your program to find out where it is in file #3, you can code

```
LET P = LOC(3)
```

and BASIC will load the variable P with the number of the last record in file #3 accessed with a GET or PUT.

It's often convenient to tie the record number to some numeric value associated with the data in the record. In a home checkbook system, for example, the record number could correspond to the check number. The data concerning check number 274 would then reside in record number 274. In a business inventory system the record number could be the part number (assuming no part numbers numerically greater than 32767). If you do this, you have to be prepared for some very large files. With a record length of 64, record number 274 begins 17,262 bytes into the file, and if that's the first record, all the preceding space will be empty. This can eat up a lot of floppy disk space.

When there's no correlation with some key data value on which to base a record number, you can index the random file with a sequential file. This is a rather sophisticated application that will be discussed toward the end of this chapter.

Let's bring this long discussion to a close with a short program example that demonstrates the creation and writing of a random file. Figure 11.1 reads the sequential file CLASS1.GRD from the last chapter and writes the records to a random file after formatting them.

```
100 REM  **  PROGRAM 'RCLASS'                          K. PORTER 1/31/83
110 REM  **  REFORMATS SEQUENTIAL FILE 'CLASS1.GRD' INTO A RANDOM FILE
120 REM  -------------------------------------------------------------
130 REM
140      LET R9 = 40                                   :REM    RECORD LENGTH
150      R$ = "CLASS1.RND"
160      S$ = "CLASS1.GRD"
170      RN = 1
180 REM
190 REM  **  OPEN FILES
200      OPEN "I", #1, S$
210      OPEN "R", #2, R$, R9
220      FIELD #2, 20 AS N$,4 AS T1$,4 AS T2$,4 AS T3$,4 AS T4$,4 AS T5$
230 REM
240 REM  **  LOOP TO READ, REFORMAT, WRITE RECORDS
250      IF EOF(1) THEN 390
260        INPUT#1, M$, T1, T2, T3, T4, T5
270        PRINT M$
280        LSET N$  = M$
290        LSET T1$ = MKS$(T1)
300        LSET T2$ = MKS$(T2)
310        LSET T3$ = MKS$(T3)
320        LSET T4$ = MKS$(T4)
330        LSET T5$ = MKS$(T5)
340        PUT #2, RN
350        PRINT "WROTE"; RN
360        RN = RN + 1
370      GOTO 240
380 REM
390 REM  **  CLOSE UP
400      CLOSE
410      END
```

Figure 11.1 Program RCLASS.

Figuring record length

By now it should be clear that record length is critical in random files. If you make the record too short, it won't hold all the data, but if it's too long, it wastes the limited space on a floppy disk. Therefore, in setting up a random file you have to calculate the record length carefully.

First list the data elements in a record and indicate the data types of the numerics: integer, single precision, double precision. For strings, try to anticipate the longest string that will be held in each field. To the left of the list of elements carry out the string lengths. Use Table 11.A to figure the length for each numeric element and place those in a column with the string lengths, and then total the lengths. This gives you the minimum record length for the file; that is, the sum of all string and numeric elements for a record. You'll need this information not only for computing record length, but for building the FIELD.

Reading random files

To read a random file record you first have to open the file and issue a FIELD statement. This process is absolutely identical to an open for a write, and if you've already opened the file for write, you can also read from it.

The read itself is done by the GET instruction, which has the same form as PUT. It specifies the file number and the record number, so the statement

```
GET #2, 76
```

directly reads record number 76 from the file opened as #2.

Just as PUT writes the buffer contents into the place in the file corresponding to the record number, so GET reads from the file and places the record into the buffer. Consequently, after a GET you have to pick the buffer apart. This is, in effect, the opposite from the buffer loading done prior to a PUT by LSETs.

Say we have a file open as #2 and the buffer definition

```
FIELD #2, 22 AS B$, 4 AS A1$, 2 AS A2$
```

To read record number 19 from this file we code

```
300     GET #2, 19
```

In this case, the field B$ is a string, A1$ is a single-precision number, and A2$ is an integer. We can break out the buffer contents after the GET as follows:

```
310     LET M$ = B$
320     LET F = CVS(A1$)
330     LET I% = CVI(A2$)
```

Line 310 moves the contents of buffer field B$ to a string variable M$. In line 320, CVS(A1$) converts the 4-byte binary string A1$ to a single-precision number and assigns it to the variable F. Line 320 converts a 2-byte string A2$ into an integer assigned to the typed variable I%.

This packing and unpacking of random file buffers is a nuisance, but it's not difficult. All you have to do is keep an eye on the FIELD statement and make sure you've pulled out all the fields you need before you begin to work on their contents. This is a good application for a subroutine, as we'll discuss shortly.

As an aside, you don't have to extract fields that you don't need from the buffer. Perhaps in some program that uses the file whose FIELD is shown above, you need only the integer value from any record and you don't care about the rest. The "standard" FIELD statement for the file is

```
FIELD #2, 22 AS B$, 4 AS A1$, 2 AS A2$
```

but in this case, since you care only about the last field in the record, you can define the buffer as

```
FIELD #2, 26 AS X$, 2 AS A2$
```

The leading field definition (26 AS X$) is a "dummy" that only serves to establish where in the buffer the desired field (A2$) begins. Then you can code

```
300     GET #2, R
310     LET I = CVI(A2$)
```

and you have the desired integer value from the Rth record.

This approach can be risky; for example, if you later enhance the program so that it uses the string portion of the record. Because X$ also includes a 4-byte single-precision binary number, the new instruction

```
LET J$ = X$
```

will bring along four characters of gibberish at the end of string J$. The only way to correct this problem is to revise the FIELD statement to reflect the actual format of the record.

Random files don't have an EOF mark as sequential files do, so the IF EOF check doesn't work. Say file #1 has 20 records and you execute the following sequence:

```
410     IF EOF(1) THEN 670
420     GET #1, 1247
```

Even though you're attempting to read the 1247th record from a file with only 20 records, line 410 doesn't tell you you're past the end of the file. Instead BASIC simply returns an empty record and continues blithely on. Consequently, if you want to check for end-of-file, you have to build an empty-record check. The following suggests one approach:

```
180    GET #2, R
190    LET F$ = B$
200    IF ASC(F$) = 0 THEN GOTO...
```

Line 200 checks for an empty record and takes action if it finds one. This only works when there is *always* a string in field B$ in a valid record, *and* when there are no holes in the file (a "hole" being an empty record 21 when record 22 contains valid data).

Figure 11.2 is a program to read and display any student's record from the random file created by Figure 11.1. Note that the OPEN sequence in this program (lines 250–260) is identical to that in Figure 11.1, except for the file number. The program is operated on the assumption that the user knows the record number of each student; he or she enters the desired record number at line 290. Line 310 fetches it and 330–390 pull the data from the record buffer in preparation for displaying it. An empty record message is displayed when, as a result of the check at 340, the name field is discovered to begin with a blank.

As an observation on programming technique, note how the input sequence is structured. Both the fetch/display loop and the error handler refer back to the record number query at line 290, so each time the user gets a record—or tries to—he or she is asked whether another is wanted. When the user replies "no" by entering 0, the program goes back to the file name query at line 200 to ask if he or she wants to access a different file. If the user types ENTER, the program stops. Notice, too, that before the query, any open file is closed. This is necessary on a repeat to avoid trying to open a new file #1 when one is already open under that reference number.

As mentioned before, you can't use random file handling instructions with a sequential file. The instructions themselves work, but the results are garbage. Run the FETCH program (Figure 11.2) and tell it to access the old sequential file CLASS1.GRD, then read some records and see what a mess comes up on the display.

In this instance, you can't cause any harm since the program only reads the file. However, if you write to a sequential file with random instructions, you'll damage the file beyond repair.

Arrayed variables

I'm going to let you in on a little trick having to do with arrayed numerics stored in a random record.

```
110 REM  ** PROGRAM 'FETCH'                        K. PORTER  2/1/83
120 REM  ** GETS ANY RECORD FROM A RANDOM FILE AND DISPLAYS IT
130 REM ------------------------------------------------------------
140 REM
150     DIM T(5)
160     LET R9 = 40
170 REM
180 REM  ** GET FILENAME
190     CLOSE
200     PRINT: INPUT "NAME OF FILE..."; R$
210     PRINT
220     IF LEN(R$) = 0 THEN GOTO 540
230 REM
240 REM  ** OPEN FILE
250     OPEN "R", #1, R$, R9
260     FIELD #1, 20 AS N$,4 AS T1$,4 AS T2$,4 AS T3$,4 AS T4$,4 AS T5$
270 REM
280 REM  ** LOOP FOR FETCHING, FORMATTING, DISPLAYING RECORDS
290     INPUT "RECORD NUMBER TO GET (0 IF NONE)..."; R
300       IF R = 0 THEN PRINT: GOTO 180
310       GET #1, R
320 REM
330       LET D$    = N$
340       IF ASC(D$) = 0 THEN GOTO 510
350       LET T(1)  = CVS(T1$)
360       LET T(2)  = CVS(T2$)
370       LET T(3)  = CVS(T3$)
380       LET T(4)  = CVS(T4$)
390       LET T(5)  = CVS(T5$)
400 REM
410 REM  ** DISPLAY
420       PRINT: PRINT "*** STUDENT RECORD ***": PRINT
430       PRINT "NAME:" SPC(5) D$
440       FOR L = 1 TO 5
450         PRINT USING "TEST NUMBER #    ###.#"; L, T(L)
460       NEXT L
470       PRINT: PRINT
480     GOTO 280
490 REM
500 REM  ** ERROR HANDLER
510     PRINT "RECORD NUMBER"; R; "IS EMPTY"
520     PRINT
530     GOTO 280
540     END
```

Figure 11.2 Program FETCH.

The FIELD statement for the student file is pretty long, a whole line in the program. That's because it contains six fields, one for the individual's name and five duplicate fields for the five test scores. Imagine how long it would be if we had 20 scores in the record. We can simplify the FIELD statement, however, by packing array T(X) into a single field in the record.

This scores list has five single-precision entries, and since single-precision takes 4 bytes each, the array needs a field 5 × 4 = 20 bytes long to hold it. Thus we first reconstruct the FIELD statement to read

```
FIELD #1, 20 AS N$, 20 AS T$
```

The N$ field still holds the name, but now the T$ field will hold all five test scores. The following fragment packs array T(X) into the field T$.

```
210    LET X$ = " "                 :REM    EMPTY STRING
220    FOR L = 1 TO 5               :REM    PACKING LOOP
230      LET X$ = X$ +MKS$(T(L))
240    NEXT L
250    LSET T$ = X$                 :REM    PUT IN BUFFER
260    PUT #1, R
```

On successive passes of the loop, line 230 keeps attaching the converted list entry T(L) to the end of string X$. After five iterations the whole list is packed into one 20-byte string, and line 250 writes it into the buffer field T$.

Because the maximum string length is 255 bytes, a loop of this kind can pack up to 63 single-precision numbers, 31 double-precision numbers, or 127 integers into a single FIELD entry.

Coming back out after a GET, we can also use string functions to unpack the field and load its elements into the list. The following fragment illustrates how.

```
200    GET #1, R
210    LET P = 1                             :REM  POINTER
220    LET X$ = T$
230    FOR L = 1 TO 5                        :REM  UNPACK LOOP
240      LET T(L) = CVS(MID$(X$, P, 4))
250      LET P = P + 4
260    NEXT L
```

The loop counter L keeps track of the current list entry, and P points to the current element position within the packed string X$. Line 240 extracts four bytes at position P from the string, converts them to a single-precision number, and stores the result in the current list entry T(L).

Reading and writing the same random file

Aside from instant access to information, the best feature of random files is the ability to read and write on the same OPEN. This allows a program to read a record, update it, and write it back out without touching the unaffected data.

A random file is opened for both reads and writes. The same FIELD statement is used for both, to ensure consistency in the record format. You have to write separate sections of the program (preferably subroutines) to load the file buffer before a PUT and to unload it after a GET. These separate file I/O sections are comparable to the routines for reading and writing two sequential files, except that only one actual random file is involved. The caveat is that you have to control the record number rather carefully to avoid accessing the wrong record.

A sophisticated interactive program

Figure 11.3 is a fairly sophisticated program that interacts with the user and with a random file. It introduces no new material, but instead brings together many of the BASIC programming elements discussed in various places throughout this book: maintainability, screen management, file operations, modular programming, readability, constants, functions, nested subroutines, and formatted output.

The overall purpose of this program is to enable the user to view and/or update student test scores interactively. It can correct existing test scores or enter new ones, with immediately visible results. Though somewhat limited, the program itself is representative of professional-quality interactive software.

Because it uses some simple screen control functions, you'll probably have to modify one or two statements to customize it to your display. Line 1060 establishes the character sequence to clear the screen and home the cursor in the upper left corner. Virtually all displays have this feature, but the control sequence to perform it varies from one machine to the next. On mine it's the form-feed character CHR$(12), so that's what's assigned to the string C$ here. On a Radio Shack computer, delete line 1060 altogether and anywhere that PRINT C$ appears in the program, replace it with CLS (the clear-screen instruction). If your display requires two or more control characters, use string concatenation to construct the sequence. For example, the Apple II clears the screen on ESC @, which is coded as

```
1060     LET C$ = CHR$(27) + CHR$(64)
```

Your computer manual will tell you what control characters you have to send to clear and home.

Another thing you might have to change is the screen width specification in line 1070. Most screens are 80 columns wide, but some are 64, some 72, some 40, and others something else. If you don't know, you'll have to look that up too, and change the constant W as necessary.

Now you're ready to enter the program. As you do it, note certain things about this program. First, lines 1100–1120 calculate certain control constants based on the value of N (the number of test scores). For this program to function with the current random file CLASS1.RND, N must equal 5. On that are based the length of the scores list (line 1130), the length of the packed field T$ in the file buffer (see line 1390 for the use of F1 in the FIELD statement), the record length R9 specified for the file, and most of the loop counters. In the future, should you decide to reformat the file and add another four test scores, you can implement that modification throughout this program simply by changing the value assigned to N in line 1100 to 9. This is what is meant by maintainability.

```
1010 REM  ** PROGRAM 'VUSCORE'                    K. PORTER 2/2/83
1020 REM  ** READS, DISPLAYS, UPDATES CLASS RANDOM FILES
1030 REM  ----------------------------------------------------------
1040 REM
1050 REM  ** SCREEN CONTROL (MODIFY AS APPROPRIATE FOR CRT)
1060    LET C$ = CHR$(12)              :REM   CLEAR SCREEN, HOME CURSOR
1070    LET W  = 80                    :REM   SCREEN WIDTH
1080 REM
1090 REM  ** OTHER CONSTANTS, DECLARATIONS, ETC.
1100    LET N  = 5                     :REM   NUMBER OF TEST SCORES
1110    LET F1 = N * 4                 :REM   NUMBER FIELD LENGTH
1120    LET R9 = F1 + 20               :REM   RECORD LENGTH
1130    DIM T(N)                       :REM   SCORES ARRAY
1140    LET H$ = "TEST        SCORE         AVGE"
1150    LET I$ = " ##         ###.#        ###.#"
1160    DEF FNC(X$) = INT((W - LEN(X$)) / 2)
1170 REM
1180 REM  ** GET FILENAME
1190    CLOSE
1200    PRINT C$                       :REM   CLEAR SCREEN
1210    PRINT "STUDENT RECORD REVIEW AND UPDATE"
1220    PRINT "--------------------------------": PRINT
1230    INPUT "NAME OF CLASS FILE..."; F$: PRINT
1240    IF LEN(F$) = 0 THEN GOTO 2280
1250    GOSUB 1360                     :REM   OPEN FILE
1260 REM
1270 REM  ** CONTROL SECTION
1280    GOSUB 1480                     :REM   GET RECORD
1290      IF R = 0 THEN GOTO 1190      :REM   GO IF NONE REQUESTED
```

```
1300      GOSUB 1710                    :REM    DISPLAY, UPDATE RECORD
1310      GOSUB 2080                    :REM    WRITE UPDATES IF ANY
1320    GOTO 1270                       :REM    REPEAT
1330 REM -------------------------------------------------------------
1340 REM            XXXX  SUBROUTINES FOLLOW  XXXX
1350 REM
1360 REM  XX  OPEN FILE F$ FOR RANDOM ACCESS
1370    ON ERROR GOTO 1430              :REM    IF NO SUCH FILE
1380    OPEN "R", #1, F$, R9
1390    FIELD #1, 20 AS N$, F1 AS T$
1400    ON ERROR GOTO 0                 :REM    DISABLE ERROR HANDLER
1410    RETURN
1420 REM
1430 REM  XX  ERROR IF NO SUCH FILE
1440    PRINT "NO FILE NAMED "; F$: PRINT
1450    RESUME 1230
1460 REM ----------
1470 REM
1480 REM  XX  GET RECORD
1490    PRINT: INPUT "RECORD NUMBER (0 FOR ANOTHER FILE)..."; R
1500    IF R = 0 THEN GOTO 1690
1510    GET #1, R
1520    IF ASC(N$) <> 0 THEN GOTO 1560  :REM    GO IF NOT EMPTY
1530    PRINT: PRINT "RECORD"; R; "IS EMPTY"
1540    GOTO 1480                       :REM    TRY AGAIN
1550 REM
1560 REM  XX  BREAK OUT DATA FROM RECORD
1570 REM  XX  NAME WITH BLANKS REMOVED
1580    LET S$ = N$
1590    LET P  = INSTR (1, S$, " ")     :REM    SCAN FOR BLANK
1600    IF  P  = 0 THEN GOTO 1630       :REM    GO IF NONE FOUND
1610    LET S$ = LEFT$(S$, P+1)         :REM      ELSE REMOVE BLANKS
1620 REM
1630 REM  XX  LOAD SCORES LIST FROM RECORD FIELD T$
1640    LET P = 1                       :REM    POSITION
1650    FOR L = 1 TO N                  :REM    UNPACKING LOOP
1660      LET T(L) = CVS( MID$( T$, P, 4))
1670      LET P = P + 4                 :REM    NEXT FIELD
1680    NEXT L
1690    RETURN
1700 REM ----------
1710 REM  XX  DISPLAY AND UPDATE RECORD
1720    LET S = 0                       :REM    RESET CHANGE SWITCH
1730    PRINT C$                        :REM    CLEAR SCREEN
1740    GOSUB 2210                      :REM    BAR ACROSS TOP OF SCREEN
1750    LET L$ = "X X TEST SCORES FOR " + S$ + " X X"
1760    LET P  = FNC(L$)                :REM    CENTER HEADING
1770    PRINT TAB(P) L$: PRINT: PRINT
1780    LET P  = FNC(H$)                :REM    CENTER COLUMN HEADS
1790    PRINT TAB(P) H$
```

(continued)

```
1800    LET A = 0
1810    FOR L = 1 TO N
1820      LET A = A + T(L)                :REM    CUMULATIVE SCORES
1830      PRINT TAB(P);                   :REM    CENTER
1840      PRINT USING I$; L, T(L), (A / L)
1850    NEXT L
1860    PRINT: GOSUB 2210: PRINT          :REM    BAR ACROSS BOTTOM
1870 REM
1880 REM  **  QUERY FOR CHANGES
1890    LET Q$ = "NUMBER OF TEST TO CHANGE (0 IF NONE)..."
1900    LET P  = FNC(Q$)
1910    PRINT TAB(P) Q$;
1920      INPUT C9
1930    IF C9 = 0 THEN GOTO 2040          :REM    EXIT IF NONE
1940    IF C9 > N THEN GOTO 1730          :REM    REPEAT IF RANGE ERROR
1950 REM
1960 REM  **  GET CHANGE AND REPEAT
1970    LET S  = 9                        :REM    SET CHANGE SWITCH
1980    LET Q$ = "NEW SCORE..."
1990    LET P  = FNC(Q$)
2000    PRINT TAB(P) Q$;
2010      INPUT T(C9)                     :REM    GET NEW SCORE
2020    GOTO 1730                         :REM    REPEAT
2030 REM
2040 REM  **  EXIT
2050    RETURN
2060 REM ----------
2070 REM
2080 REM  **  WRITE OUT RECORD IF UPDATED
2090    IF S = 0 THEN GOTO 2180           :REM    SKIP IF NOT CHANGED
2100 REM
2110 REM  **  PACK SCORES INTO RECORD (NAME UNCHANGED)
2120    LET Q$ = ""                       :REM    EMPTY STRING
2130    FOR L = 1 TO N                    :REM    PACKING LOOP
2140      LET Q$ = Q$ + MKS$(T(L))
2150    NEXT L
2160    LSET T$ = Q$
2170    PUT #1, R
2180    RETURN
2190 REM ----------
2200 REM
2210 REM  **  PUT BAR ACROSS SCREEN
2220    FOR L = 1 TO (W-1)
2230      PRINT "*";
2240    NEXT L
2250    PRINT
2260    RETURN
2270 REM ----------
2280    END
```

Figure 11.3 Program VUSCORE.

The function FNC(X$) defined at line 1160 provides centering of selected strings on the display, regardless of the width of the screen.

The file name entry starting at line 1180 is familiar by now, except that it calls a subroutine to open and FIELD the file for random access. That subroutine (line 1360) issues an error message if the file can't be found and lets the user retry. Otherwise, on a successful open, it returns to the control section.

The control section itself is a simple loop that reveals the overall program structure through remarks. It gets the record the user wants, displays it, obtains any updates, and writes the record back to the file if any changes have been made, and then it repeats for another record. When the user selects record 0 to indicate he or she is finished, line 1290 reverts to the file name query.

The "get-record" subroutine starting at line 1480 is smart. When the selected record number is 0, it bypasses everything and just returns so that line 1290 can exit the control loop. Also, if the indicated record turns out to be empty in line 1520, it tells the user and then prompts the selection of another. A successful GET is followed by the extraction of data from the record. Lines 1570–1610 might startle you a little: the unused portion of the student name field is filled with blank characters, and since we're going to center the name shortly, these instructions truncate the blanks so they don't count in the length of the string. The rest of the subroutine unpacks the scores and loads them into the list T(L).

The next subroutine (1710) is the real workhorse. Upon being entered, the subroutine sets the variable S at 0. This variable is a switch that only gets "flipped" if a record is updated by the user (line 1970). Later, the file write subroutine at 2080 knows whether a change was made to the record by sensing whether or not S is still 0. If it is, there's no need to write the record back out since it's unchanged, so the write subroutine just returns without taking action.

Now let's return to the display subroutine. Line 1750 concatenates the student's name into a literal that is then centered and displayed. Everything else on this display panel is centered also, using the FNC function.

The loop at 1810–1850 calculates the cumulative grade average for the student following each test and displays it along with the individual test scores, thus giving a running accounting of the student's grade average.

At line 1920 the user is given the opportunity to correct a test score by keying the test number and entering (at 2010) the new score. This same sequence can be used to post new scores. Any change to the existing data sets S to a nonzero value in line 1970, thus flipping the change switch as mentioned above. After each change, the updated record is displayed by repeating the subroutine, *except* for the resetting of the change switch. When the user enters a Ø change, the subroutine concludes.

When this program is used before all the tests have been taken, it still computes cumulative grade averages for all five (or "N") tests. For instance, if the class has taken three of the five exams, the display indicates Ø scores for tests 4 and 5, and the cumulative averages as though the student had completely "bombed out" those last two tests. We'll just have to give the user credit for knowing that all the exams haven't yet been given, and that the cumulative average as of the most recent test taken is the one that accurately reflects the grade average to date.

We could avoid this potential confusion by stopping the output of test results when a Ø score is encountered. That, however, would lead to a worse problem if the student missed one test and never made it up, but took subsequent exams; we wouldn't be able to find out what those scores are. Consequently, the averaging of achieved scores over more tests than have actually been taken can be regarded as a projection of the student's final grade average if he/she skips the remaining tests.

The final observation on Figure 11.3 concerns the subroutine at line 221Ø. The "bar" is a line of asterisks across the screen to the next-to-last column. Why not to the last? Because when you write a character into the rightmost position on the screen, the cursor "wraps" to the start of the next line automatically. Then when you execute the PRINT at line 225Ø, the cursor moves down yet another line. The wrap plus the PRINT would cause the cursor to drop two lines below the bar, rather than advancing only to the next line, so the last position is left blank.

Sequential processing of random files

Although the chief purpose of random files is to provide interactive nonsequential access to records, sometimes it's necessary to process a random file sequentially. An example drawn from the test scores case is a batch job at the end of the term to write reports showing all students' final grade averages.

There are many other instances where random files are either written or read in the same way as sequential files. Figure 11.1 demonstrated the creation of a random file in this way. You can do batch updates to a random file by merging in the contents of a sequential file (or another random file), as was shown in Figure 10.7. A random file can thus be used both for serial access and for interactive computing.

In sequential operations you simply increment the record number with each GET or PUT, as we did in Figure 11.1. Otherwise the OPEN "R", FIELD, and record processing are the same as for direct access. In effect, you're randomly accessing records that happen to be in numeric order. A random file opened at the start of a program can be sequentially read, sequentially written, and randomly read and written at different points in the same program without ever closing it.

The problem with sequentially reading a random file is that there's no EOF condition to check. Very seldom do you know how many records a file contains, so it's usually not possible to set up the program to read a fixed number of records with any assurance that you'll process them all.

One solution is to read and process random records sequentially until an empty record is encountered. The empty-record check thus replaces the IF EOF used with sequential files. This only works, however, when you're absolutely sure there are no empty records intermixed among valid ones. Because of the way random files are used, it often happens that a record somewhere in the file is blanked out (e.g., a student moves away during the school year), so this empty record would cause the program to ignore all subsequent records and thus return incomplete results.

The better solution is to find the highest numbered valid record in the file and then confine operations below it. The following fragment reads backwards, starting from an unrealistically high record number until a nonempty record is found. Using that record as the high-water mark, it then processes sequentially upward from the start of the file, ignoring any empty records. This assures that it processes every valid record in the file.

```
200        OPEN "R", #1, X$, 40
210        FIELD #1, 10 AS A$... etc.
220        FOR R = 500 TO 1 STEP -1
230          GET #1, R
240          IF ASC(A$) < > 0 THEN GOTO 270
250        NEXT R
260        PRINT "FILE IS EMPTY": GOTO 9999
270 REM      ** PROCESS FROM START OF FILE
280        LET H = R      :REM      HIGH-WATER MARK
290        FOR R = 1 TO H
300          GET #1, R
310          IF ASC(A$) = 0 THEN GOTO 380
.
.            (process the record)
.
380        NEXT R
```

For this routine to work, you have to know that the file never contains more than 500 records, and that the field A$ always has some content when the record is valid. You can modify this model to fit the circumstances, as will be done in Figure 11.4.

The backwards scan, incidentally, is a very rapid process. On my system it took about five seconds to scan back through 488 empty records and find the highest valid record (number 12).

PRINT# to a random file

Although you can't use random instructions with sequential files, you *can* use the sequential instructions PRINT# and PRINT# USING to write output lines into a random file.

You have to understand, however, that in this case (unlike with sequential files), PRINT# doesn't actually write the record to disk. It merely places the data into the file buffer, and then a PUT moves the buffer into the file. The following illustrates the use of PRINT# with a random file.

```
100        OPEN "R", #3, "SOME.FIL", 64
110        FIELD #3, 30 AS A$, 10 AS B$, 24 AS C$
120 REM      **   LOOP TO WRITE A RANDOM FILE
130        FOR E = 1 TO 20
.
.            (Build a line L$)
.
170          PRINT#3, L$
180          PUT #3, E
190        NEXT E
```

This loop writes 20 lines L$ to file #3. Note that the file reference number in the PRINT# must correspond to that in the FIELD instruction, so that BASIC knows in which buffer to place L$. The PRINT# is followed immediately by PUT to ensure transfer of the record to the disk file. The same procedure applies to the PRINT# USING statement.

In this case a line of up to 64 characters can be written to the buffer, since that's the file's record length. If you attempt to PRINT# a record longer than the buffer, the program will halt with the message "Field overflow." Note, too, that the field boundaries are ignored by the PRINT#. The buffer is divided into three areas, but PRINT# pays no attention and copies the line into the buffer from its left end, using as much space as it needs. In actual practice you'll probably never use PRINT# to load a buffer defined by a multiarea FIELD statement, such as that defined in line 110. It would be poor practice indeed to mix true random records and PRINT#ed records in the same file. Rather, you should specify the buffer for this case as

```
FIELD #3, 64 AS A$
```

The A$ variable name is never mentioned elsewhere and has no significance, except to satisfy the statement's syntax. The previous FIELD was included only for illustrative purposes.

The option discussed in the previous paragraph is seldom used, but it is handy in certain special circumstances. Random files that have been loaded with PRINT# or PRINT# USING statements are ASCII data and can thus be listed and processed as sequential files in which all records are of uniform length, regardless of the length of their data content. Some sorting packages require fixed-length records, so you can use this method to prepare files for sorts. Also, you can write formatted text lines (e.g., payment records, payroll changes, checks issued) to a file for random retrieval later.

The procedure for reading such a record is similar to that for accessing any other random record, except that in this case the entire buffer must be defined as a single field.

```
300     FIELD #2, 64 AS F$
310     GET #2, R
320     PRINT F$
```

These instructions directly read and print a 64-character record from a random file.

Indexing a random file with a sequential file

When a random file is organized by name, as the student files are, either the user has to know the record number for each student—unlikely—or else some other way of getting to the desired record must be available. The arbitrary assignment of student numbers is the sort of solution that has given computers a bad name in some quarters, and deservedly so. It's not a very "friendly" way of accessing data, that is, it's not people oriented.

A better way is to furnish an index to all the class files so that the user can browse and select the student by name, with the computer taking care of finding the record automatically.

It takes two programs to do this. The first is Figure 11.4, a batch program "MAKINDEX" that makes an index of all student records in a sequential file, listing them by name and showing their class file name and record number.

This program uses the sequential file processing methods discussed earlier. To use it, key in the name of each class random file as the program prompts you. The program passes through the file, stripping out the student names and adding them to a sequential file until you've processed all the random files. When all files have been scanned, hit ENTER in response to the prompt.

The last thing the program does is to display the number of entries in the sequential file INDEX.GRD. If you want the index to appear in alphabetic order, you'll have to write a sort program (Figure 7.4 provides a guide for sorting string data). The number of entries in the sequential index file is the size specification required for the string array you'll need for the sort. Your program should use LINE INPUT# to read in the records from the index file, close the file, sort the records, and then reopen the file for output and copy the sorted list back out. The result will be an alphabetical index of all students whose names appear in the class random files, cross-referenced to the appropriate random file name and record number.

Figure 11.5 uses this sequential index to access student records by selecting names. This program, although much shorter than Figure 11.3, is just as sophisticated in its own way and consequently, it merits detailed study.

```
100 REM  **  PROGRAM 'MAKINDX'                      K. PORTER  2/3/83
110 REM  **  CREATES SEQUENTIAL FILE 'INDEX.GRD' AS INDEX TO ALL CLASS
120 REM  **      TEST SCORE FILES BY STUDENT NAME.
130 REM  **  RECORD FORMAT IS:
140 REM  **               STUDENT NAME
150 REM  **               RANDOM FILE NAME FOR STUDENT'S CLASS
160 REM  **               RANDOM FILE RECORD FOR STUDENT
170 REM -----------------------------------------------------------------
180 REM
190     LET F$ = "INDEX.GRD"
200     LET C  = 0                          :REM    STUDENT COUNTER
210     LET L9 = 40                         :REM    RECORD LENGTH OF RND FILE
220     PRINT "STUDENT INDEX CREATION"
230     PRINT "----------------------": PRINT
240 REM
250 REM  **  CREATE NEW INDEX FILE
260     OPEN "O", #2, F$
270 REM
280 REM  **  LOOP FOR EACH RANDOM FILE TO BE INCLUDED
290     PRINT: INPUT "NAME OF FILE TO BE INDEXED..."; R$
300       IF LEN(R$) = 0 THEN GOTO 570
310       ON ERROR GOTO 620                 :REM    IF NO SUCH FILE
320       OPEN "R", #1, R$, L9
330       FIELD #1, 20 AS A$, 20 AS T$
340       ON ERROR GOTO 0                   :REM    DISABLE ERROR HANDLER
350 REM
360 REM  **  FIND END OF RANDOM FILE
370       FOR R = 50 TO 1 STEP -1
380         GET #1, R
390         IF ASC(A$) <> 0 THEN GOTO 430
400       NEXT R
410       PRINT "FILE IS EMPTY": PRINT: GOTO 530
420 REM
430 REM  **  STRIP NAMES FROM RANDOM FILE, COPY TO INDEX
```

```
440       LET H = R
450       FOR R = 1 TO H
460         GET #1, R
470         IF ASC(A$) = 0 THEN GOTO 510
480         LET N$ = A$
490         WRITE#2, N$, R$, R
500         LET C = C + 1                  :REM    COUNT STUDENT
510       NEXT R
520 REM
530 REM  ** CLOSE RANDOM FILE AND REPEAT FOR NEXT
540       CLOSE #1
550     GOTO 280                           :REM    END OF MAIN LOOP
560 REM
570 REM  ** END OF PROGRAM
580     CLOSE #2
590     PRINT "NUMBER OF ENTRIES IN INDEX ="; C
600     GOTO 650                           :REM    EXIT
610 REM
620 REM  ** ERROR HANDLER
630     PRINT: PRINT "NO FILE NAMED "; R$
640     RESUME 280
650     END
```

Figure 11.4   Program MAKINDEX.

As with Figure 11.3, this INDFETCH program has some screen control orientation. The clear/home control sequence for your display has to be placed into line 19Ø. Line 15Ø specifies a 24-line display; if yours has 16 lines or some other number, change the constant accordingly.

The array N$ and the corresponding list R are central to the indexing technique used in the program. The section from line 25Ø through line 43Ø lets you browse through the index in alphabetical order by name, a screen at a time. Each name is assigned a reference number. You select a name by keying its number, and if the desired name hasn't come up yet, you key Ø to advance the index screen by screen until you find the one you want.

Closer inspection reveals how this is done. Line 27Ø clears the N$ array and lines 28Ø–31Ø read in the next screenful of entries from the index file. The first entry in an array row receives the student name, the second the corresponding file name, and the related entry in list R obtains the record number for that student. When the screen has 24 lines, 22 entries are read; if 16 lines, 14 entries (i.e., two less than the number of lines).

Once a screenful is read, the name and the subscript for each student entry is displayed (lines 33Ø–39Ø). The file name and record number are of no interest to the user, so they're not shown on the display. The

```
100 REM  **  PROGRAM 'INDFETCH'                      K. PORTER 2/3/83
110 REM  **  USES SEQUENTIAL INDEX TO LOCATE AND RETRIEVE STUDENT RECORDS
120 REM  **     FROM ANY CLASS FILE.
130 REM ----------------------------------------------------------------
140 REM
150     LET L9 = 24                         :REM    NUMBER OF LINES ON SCREEN
160     DIM N$((L9 - 2), 2), R(L9 - 2)      :REM    NAME/FILE LIST, REC# LIST
170     LET I$ = "INDEX.GRD"                :REM    INDEX FILENAME
180     LET R9 = 40                         :REM    RND FILE RECORD LENGTH
190     LET C$ = CHR$(12)                   :REM    CLEAR SCREEN COMMAND
200 REM
210 REM  ** OPEN INDEX FILE
220     CLOSE
230     OPEN "I", #1, I$
240 REM
250 REM  **  READ IN ENOUGH INDEX ENTRIES AT A TIME TO FILL SCREEN
260     PRINT C$
270     FOR L = 1 TO (L9 - 2): LET N$(L,1) = "": LET N$(L,2) = "": NEXT L
280     FOR L = 1 TO (L9 - 2)
290       IF EOF(1) THEN 340
300         INPUT#1, N$(L, 1), N$(L,2), R(L)
310     NEXT L
320 REM
330 REM  **  LIST NAMES ON SCREEN WITH REFERENCE NUMBERS
340     LET H = L - 1                       :REM    ENTRIES READ
350     IF H = 0 THEN GOTO 210              :REM    GO IF NONE
360     FOR L = 1 TO H
370       PRINT TAB(10);
380       PRINT USING "##   &"; L, N$(L, 1)
390     NEXT L
400 REM
410 REM  **  SELECT
420     PRINT: INPUT "SELECT BY NUMBER (0 FOR NEXT SCREEN)..."; S
430     IF S = 0 THEN GOTO 250
440 REM
450 REM  **  OPEN THE RANDOM FILE FOR THE SELECTED STUDENT
460     CLOSE #1
470     LET F$ = N$(S, 2)                   :REM    FILENAME
480     OPEN "R", #1, F$, R9
490     FIELD #1, 20 AS Z$, 20 AS Y$
500 REM
510 REM  **  RETRIEVE THE STUDENT'S RECORD
520     LET A = R(S)                        :REM    RECORD NUMBER
530     GET #1, A                           :REM    GET IT
540 REM
550 REM  **  PICK OUT DATA AND DISPLAY IT
560     PRINT C$
570     PRINT "SCORES FOR STUDENT "; Z$: PRINT
580     LET P = 1
590     FOR L = 1 TO 5
```

```
600       LET X = CVS( MID$( Y$, P, 4))
610       PRINT USING "  TEST NUMBER #      ###.#"; L, X
620       LET P = P + 4
630     NEXT L
640     FOR L = 1 TO 4: PRINT: NEXT L
650 REM
660 REM  ** QUERY FOR ANOTHER
670     INPUT "VIEW ANOTHER STUDENT (Y/N)"; X$
680     IF X$ = "Y" THEN GOTO 210
690     END
```

Figure 11.5 Program INDFETCH.

selection is made in line 42Ø; if Ø, the next screen is brought up by repetition of the sequence.

When a student name has been selected, control moves on to the random file processor, starting at line 45Ø. First the index file is closed, and then the random file name corresponding to the student name is opened (lines 47Ø–49Ø). Lines 52Ø–53Ø use the student's record number from the R(S) list to fetch the record.

Because subscripted variables are used for the file name and record number, it's not necessary for the user to know or even care what file and record are accessed; he or she merely selects a name, and the program automatically knows how to find the record pertaining to that student, by means of a consistent subscript.

After the record has been retrieved, lines 55Ø–64Ø clear the screen and display the data. At line 66Ø the user can either halt the program by replying "N" to the query, or pull another record with a "Y" response. In the latter case, the entire process is repeated from the start of the alphabetic index.

A design of this sort lets you consolidate a single index to many files with automatic "user-friendly" access. The indexing routine (lines 21Ø–53Ø) can be adapted to any interactive program that requires direct access to large amounts of data.

Housekeeping

Because the use of random files tends to be dynamic, with frequent updates of individual records, additions, and deletions, a certain amount of housekeeping is usually necessary to keep the files compact and orderly.

When a file is likely to be added to, the program should begin by locating the high-water mark as discussed earlier. Each time you add a record, increment the high-water mark by one and write it to that record number.

A record can be deleted by doing an LSET of an empty string to each field in the buffer, then a PUT to the affected record number. The following fragment deletes record R.

```
310              FIELD #1, 12 AS A$, 12 AS B$
 .
 .
 .
520 REM            **DELETE RECORD
530              LSET A$ = STRING$( 12, 0)
540              LSET B$ = STRING$( 12, 0)
550              PUT #1, R
```

The effect of this sequence is to make a "hole" in the file by writing an empty record to replace the data in record R. The record therefore still exists physically as a unit of space in the file, but it contains no data, while presumably records R − 1 and R + 1 do still contain data.

If this happens very often, the file will eventually occupy more disk space than it has any right to, since in a file with fixed record lengths an empty record is the same size as a valid one. In time, a large percentage of the file space could be just "air," which is both inefficient and wasteful. Consequently, we need a maintenance program that compresses a random file by removing the dead spaces.

Figure 11.6 squeezes a class file by finding each empty space and moving the last valid record in the file into it, then emptying the last record space. This shrinks the file to minimum size by filling in the empty spaces with records brought forward from the end. It's strictly a batch job, requiring only that the name of the file be entered.

```
100 REM  ** PROGRAM 'SQUISH'                     K. PORTER  2/4/83
110 REM  ** COMPRESSES A RANDOM CLASS FILE BY REMOVING UNUSED RECORDS
120 REM ----------------------------------------------------------------
130 REM
140     LET R9 = 40                         :REM    RECORD LENGTH
150     PRINT "FILE COMPRESSION"
160     PRINT "----------------": PRINT
170 REM
180 REM  ** GET FILENAME AND OPEN
190     LET M = 0
200     LET R = 0
210     INPUT "NAME OF FILE TO COMPRESS..."; F$
220     IF LEN(F$) = 0 THEN GOTO 690
230     ON ERROR GOTO 660                   :REM    IF NO SUCH FILE
240     OPEN "R", #1, F$, R9
250     FIELD #1, R9 AS X$
260     ON ERROR GOTO 0                     :REM    TURN OFF ERROR HANDLER
270 REM
```

```
280 REM  **  FIND HIGH WATER MARK
290     FOR H = 100 TO 1 STEP -1
300       GET #1, H
310       IF ASC(X$) <> 0 THEN GOTO 360
320     NEXT H
330     PRINT: PRINT F$;" IS EMPTY": PRINT
340     GOTO 210
350 REM
360 REM  **  WORK FROM START OF FILE FINDING/REPLACING EMPTY RECORDS
370     LET H1 = H                          :REM    ORIGINAL HIGH RECORD #
380     LET R  = R + 1
385       IF R = H1 THEN GOTO 570         :REM    IF ALL RECORDS SCANNED
390       GET #1, R
400       IF ASC(X$) <> 0 THEN GOTO 380 :REM    NOT EMPTY
410 REM
420 REM  **  EMPTY RECORD FOUND
430 REM  **  MOVE UP LAST RECORD TO FILL THIS SPACE
440       GET #1, H
450       IF ASC(X$) <> 0 THEN GOTO 480
460       LET H = H - 1
470       IF H > R THEN GOTO 440 ELSE GOTO 570
480       PUT #1, R
490 REM
500 REM  ** CLEAR LAST RECORD, COUNT MOVE
510       LSET X$ = STRING$( R9, 0 )
520       PUT #1, H
530       LET M = M + 1                     :REM    COUNT MOVE
540       LET H = H - 1                     :REM    NEW LAST RECORD NUMBER
550     IF R < H THEN GOTO 380            :REM    REPEAT FOR ALL RECORDS
560 REM
570 REM  **  REPORT RESULTS
580     PRINT "INITIAL RECORD COUNT" TAB(25) H1
590     PRINT "RECORDS MOVED"        TAB(25) M
600     PRINT "FINAL RECORD COUNT"   TAB(25) H
610     PRINT
620     CLOSE
630     GOTO 180                            :REM    REPEAT FOR DIFFERENT FILE
640 REM ----------
650 REM
660 REM  **  ERROR HANDLER
670     PRINT "NO FILE NAMED "; F$: PRINT
680     RESUME 180
690     END
```

Figure 11.6 Program SQUISH.

After any change to a random file (addition, deletion, or compression), if the file is indexed, you have to rebuild the index with Figure 11.3 and, if desired, your sort program. If you fail to do this, your index will be either incomplete or incorrect or both, and it will not reflect the current structure of the data it accesses.

Random files, although more complex than sequential files, are obviously a great deal more flexible. For that reason they're central to nearly all the interactive personal computing for which BASIC is such an ideal programming language. This chapter has given only a glimpse of the tremendous potential of random files. Equipped with the understanding of programming in BASIC you've acquired, you should now be able to develop the computer programs you need for almost any information requirement that a personal computer can handle.

CHAPTER 12

ADVANCED TOPICS

> Global reinitialization. Program chaining and overlays. Direct access to memory addresses: POKE and PEEK. Logic operations. Machine-language subroutines: USR and CALL.

This discussion is intended for and thus addressed chiefly to experienced programmers who want to exploit advanced features of BASIC. The POKE/PEEK section applies to all BASICs operating on personal computers; the rest mainly to the Microsoft product.

Global reinitialization

MBASIC furnishes an instruction CLEAR that's useful for globally reinitializing a program currently in memory. This instruction should be considered armed and dangerous, and it should *never* appear anywhere except as the first executable statement of the program.

The effect of CLEAR is to reset all numeric variables to zero and all strings to null, and to delete all dimensioned arrays and lists. It also closes open files and releases buffers. CLEAR therefore restores the data work areas and control blocks to their condition at the time of loading a fresh copy of the program.

Two positional parameters can be passed to CLEAR, each preceded by a comma, to override the defaults. The first parameter sets the top memory address available to BASIC, thus defining the upper boundary of the program work area. Under CP/M, MBASIC uses the start of the BDOS jump vector in high memory (an address specified at location 6 in low core) as its default top. The purpose in passing an overriding address is usually to protect a machine-language subroutine loaded by the user just below the CP/M area and called by the BASIC program. As an example, if you had a subroutine starting at address 49152, you could protect it from overlay by issuing the statement

```
CLEAR ,49151
```

The second parameter overrides the 512-byte default stack size for MBASIC. It's difficult to imagine how any BASIC program, no matter how complex, could ever overflow a stack of this size. Besides, the programmer has no direct control over the utilization of the stack and therefore has no way of knowing whether 512 bytes is enough. Thus the only time this parameter might be helpful is when the program issues an "Out of memory" message. Try running it with a first instruction

```
CLEAR ,,756
```

If the program is truly out of memory, it will fail again a little sooner. If it's out of stack space instead, it will probably run to normal completion.

Program chaining and overlays

The Microsoft instruction CHAIN is used to link to external program modules. Its basic form is

```
CHAIN "PROGNAME"
```

where "PROGNAME" is the name of the program file to be loaded into memory from disk and executed.

When used in this form, CHAIN replaces the currently executing program. Once the load is complete, control automatically passes to the first executable instruction in the new module. At its conclusion this module can chain to yet another, or it can chain backwards to the original program that called it in, or it stops at end-of-job. The CHAIN statement is thus useful for breaking a program that is too large for the computer's memory into two or more sequentially executed job steps.

Although the CHAIN statement passes control to the first executable instruction of the newly loaded module, this action can be overridden by specifying a line number following the program name and separated from it by a comma. For example,

```
CHAIN "PROG1", 164Ø
```

loads the program PROG1 and begins executing it at line 164Ø.

When data in memory are shared by two chained programs, the variables have to be named identically and declared by a COMMON statement in both modules. The names of shared arrays are followed by empty parentheses in the COMMON statement, for example,

```
DIM A(12,5), B(12)
COMMON J1, C$, A()
```

This pair of instructions dimensions two arrays A and B, and declares as COMMON two other values plus array A. List B is not shared and thus is undeclared. The original program would include both statements; the program loaded by a CHAIN has only the COMMON statement, since the array is already dimensioned. The contents of these variables are available to the second module exactly as assigned by the first. All other variables are lost.

When the list of variables to be shared is quite long, it's easier to specify the ALL option in the CHAIN statement. This replaces a COMMON declaration and passes all variables from one module to another. Its form is

CHAIN "PROGNAME", ALL

The receiving module has access to all variables under the names given in the calling module, and data values are unchanged during the transition. When the ALL option encompasses arrays and lists, the receiving module cannot issue a DIM statement to size those arrays, since they already exist and their attributes are known to the receiving program just as though it had declared them itself.

The CHAIN statement has a number of other options that can be invoked by the interpreter, but that are unavailable to the Microsoft BASIC compiler. The first of these is MERGE, which is used in the form

CHAIN MERGE "PROGNAME"

The MERGE option correlates line numbers in the two modules. Each line brought in from the PROGNAME file replaces a line of the same number in the current program; lines with new numbers are merged in, and current lines without corresponding line numbers in the incoming file are left intact. This operation therefore treats lines from the file the same as the interpreter treats keyboard entry of lines with respect to a program already in memory.

The CHAIN MERGE almost always needs a line number so that BASIC knows where to pick up after the merge. If no line number is included in the statement, the first executable instruction in memory gains control as soon as the merge is complete.

The MERGE option makes it possible to establish an overlay structure for subroutines that are infrequently called. Say your base program has lines numbered through 900; you can then set up a group of external subprograms, each starting at line 1000, and use CHAIN MERGE statements in the main program to bring each one into the overlay area at appropriate time. These statements read

CHAIN MERGE "MODULE", 1000

where "MODULE" is the name of a subprogram. This statement always passes control to the module starting at line 1000.

A COMMON statement is needed to define variables shared between the main program and the overlay module, or you can use the ALL option.

The latter is usually better. The statement above with the ALL option is written

```
CHAIN MERGE "MODULE", 1000, ALL
```

An overlay module is *not* a subroutine, but rather a subprogram that must return to a specific place or else halt execution; it doesn't respond to a RETURN. Normally an overlay exit chains back to a specific line number in the main program. To free the space occupied by the subprogram and avoid the danger that irregularly incremented lines might corrupt the next module merged into this space, the subprogram should delete itself in the exit.

Let's suppose you have a program called LOANCALC that computes loan activities. This program occupies lines 100–7500. It has several overlay modules, all beginning at line 8000, one of which is called SETRATE and goes from line 8000 to line 9510. The main program calls in the overlay module with the statement

```
4360    CHAIN MERGE "SETRATE", 8000, ALL
4370  REM ** RETURN HERE FROM SETRATE
```

The module SETRATE is brought into memory and gains control with the transfer to line 8000. It shares all variables with the main program. After it completes its mission, SETRATE chains back to the main program's reentry point with the statement

```
9510    CHAIN MERGE "LOANCALC", 4370, ALL, DELETE
                 8000–9510
```

The DELETE statement is self-destructive in that it deactivates the subprogram in which it occurs. Note that it is the last clause of the CHAIN statement; when it has been executed, control moves to line 4370 as directed.

The Microsoft BASIC compiler does not support any of the CHAIN statement options. The only form of this statement with the compiler is CHAIN "PROGNAME". Variables are passed via the COMMON statement. That's not to say you can't use CHAIN with overlay subprograms; you simply can't create an overlay area above the body of the main program. Thus, a called-in overlay module has to return to the main program by CHAINing back to it.

Files are left open during the chaining operation, so that a file opened by the first module and never closed is open under the same reference number to the second module.

Direct access to memory addresses

All microcomputer-based dialects of BASIC are able to manipulate memory addresses directly through the PEEK function and the POKE statement.

Since an 8-bit byte can have any of 256 bit patterns, BASIC regards the contents of a memory location as an integer in the range Ø...255 (&HØ through &HFF in hex). PEEK thus extracts an integer and POKE writes an integer in that range.

Obviously you have to know the address you want to inspect or modify. This can be any address within the range of memory installed in the computer; the lowest address is Ø, the highest one less than the number of bytes available. A 64K memory holds 64 × 1Ø24 = 65,536 bytes, so the top memory address is 65535. In POKE and PEEK the address can be specified as a decimal number, a variable, or in hex notation.

As an example of usage, imagine a related group of programs to manage a law practice. Each morning the first thing the user is required to do is to run a program that captures today's date and prints a bring-up file. To ensure that this is done, the good-morning program ends by placing the arbitrary number 28 in the highest memory location in the machine (65535). All other programs then check this location when they start and if it doesn't contain 28 they refuse to run, instead issuing a message that tells the user to run the good-morning program.

The instruction to set the flag is

```
POKE 65535, 28
```

meaning "poke into location 65535 the bit pattern with the decimal value of 28."

The other programs check this location and decide whether or not to continue with the sequence

```
100    IF PEEK(65535) = 28 THEN GOTO 130
110       PRINT "ABORTED—RUN 'GOOD MORNING' FIRST"
120       STOP
130....
```

The function PEEK(65535) returns the contents of that address as an integer that's compared with the literal number 28. If they're equal, execution is allowed to continue at line 13Ø; if not, the program displays the message and stops.

You can also fetch the contents of an address and assign it to a variable, for example,

```
LET V = PEEK(49152)
```

PEEK and POKE can be combined with arithmetic and logic operations to manipulate memory addresses. In Chapter 5 we presented a method for resetting the CP/M IOBYTE to divert output from the display to the printer, thus avoiding use of LPRINT. The IOBYTE's two low-order bits are 01 (binary 1) for screen output and 10 (binary 2) for output to the list device. Therefore to redirect normal output to the printer you can add 1 to the value of the IOBYTE, which is located at address 3, as follows:

```
POKE 3, (PEEK(3) + 1)
```

This pulls out the current IOBYTE from address 3, adds 1, and puts it back in the same place. (*Note:* This might not work on all machines running under CP/M.)

To restore normal screen output, the IOBYTE's value is reduced by 1 with the statement

```
POKE 3, (PEEK(3) - 1)
```

Direct manipulation of memory addresses is a risky business that should be undertaken with extreme caution. It bypasses the carefully contrived storage management and defenses of software, exposing the entire integrity of the system to destruction by the unwary use of POKEs. Therefore, *be sure you know what you're doing before you use a POKE.*

Logic operations

Logic operations are sometimes used in exotic applications, such as data communications and industrial control, seldom in problem-solving. They act on the positionally corresponding bits of two bytes in various ways that resemble but differ from mathematical operations. In binary addition a carry is performed to the next higher order bit when two 1 bits are combined (1 + 1 = 0 with a carry of 1). Logic operations *never* carry, but rather confine their effects to a single bit position. Thus the resulting value of bit 4 after a logic operation is attributable to the settings of the two bits 4 in the operands. Note that although a logic operation works on positionally corresponding bits, it involves all the bits of both operand bytes.

As an example, suppose you want to isolate the lower four bits ("nibble") of a byte. This is sometimes done to convert ASCII digits into their corresponding binary values, and it's accomplished by turning off (resetting to zeros) the upper four bits with the logic operation AND.

The effect of logic operations is shown by a truth table. The truth table for AND is:

```
0  AND  0→0
0  AND  1→0
```

1 AND 0→0
1 AND 1→1

The symbol → is read as "yield," so "zero AND one yield zero."

To turn off the upper nibble of an ASCII digit, AND it with the bit pattern 00001111. The following shows this operation:

ASCII 6	0011 0110
AND	0000 1111
Result	0000 0110

If the ASCII digit 6 is a string variable D$, this instruction is written in BASIC as

```
LET V = ASC(D$) AND 15
```

The result is the binary value of the digit D$.

The AND operator can test to see whether a certain bit (or group of bits) in a byte is on or off. This is done with an IF statement; for example,

```
IF V AND 128 THEN...
```

tests the high-order bit of the variable V. If the bit is on, a TRUE condition is returned and the THEN clause is executed. On the other hand, if the leading bit of V is 0, the test returns FALSE and the instruction falls through to the next program line or an ELSE clause.

One of the logic operators is monadic (or unary), meaning that it takes only one operand. This is the NOT operator, which reverses all the bits as follows:

V = 0011 1001
NOT V = 1100 0110

This process is known as *complementing*, or in other words returning the exact binary opposite of the operand. All other logic operators are dyadic (take two operands).

In addition to AND, other patterns can be developed or tested via the operators OR, XOR, and EQV, all of which are more or less standard in programming languages. AND only sets a 1 bit when the two bits operated on are 1s, otherwise it sets a 0. OR returns a 1 bit any time that either or both the operand bits are 1, so the only time it returns a 0 is when both evaluated bits are zeros; that is, one or the other or both. XOR is "exclusive-OR," which means it returns a 1 only when one or the other operand bit is 1, but if both are 1 or both are 0, it sets a 0. EQV is the opposite of XOR, functionally the same as NOT XOR. The truth tables for these operators are:

OR	0	OR	0 → 0
	0	OR	1 → 1
	1	OR	0 → 1
	1	OR	1 → 1
XOR	0	XOR	0 → 0
	0	XOR	1 → 1
	1	XOR	0 → 1
	1	XOR	1 → 0
EQV	0	EQV	0 → 1
	0	EQV	1 → 0
	1	EQV	0 → 0
	1	EQV	1 → 1

In addition, Microsoft BASIC has the curious operator IMP, whose truth table is

IMP	0	IMP	0 → 1
	0	IMP	1 → 1
	1	IMP	0 → 0
	1	IMP	1 → 1

What makes this operator so strange is the one condition that returns a 0; the order of bits evaluated is significant. To the best of this writer's knowledge, Microsoft BASIC is the only programming language that offers such a logic operation.

Logic operations are often used in assembler and other system control languages, but they have little applicability in BASIC, a problem-solving language.

Machine-language subroutines

For the advanced programmer Microsoft BASIC furnishes a number of facilities for interfacing with machine-language subroutines. The details vary with the type of machine: in the following discussion an 8080/Z80 CPU type under CP/M is assumed, as is familiarity with 8080 assembly language. Our intent here is to give a general feel for machine-language interfacing rather than a comprehensive treatment of a rather complex subject. The Microsoft BASIC manual provides technical details that you'll need for developing assembly language subroutines.

BASIC resides in low core and builds its data work areas upward in free memory above the interpreter's program area. Your machine-language code must therefore start far enough above the interpreter to provide plenty of data work space for BASIC (a compiled BASIC program works on the same principle). Because BASIC assumes it owns all memory in the transient program area, it's advisable to protect your subroutine from being clobbered.

There are two ways to set an upward limit on BASIC's work space. The first is to start the program with the statement

    CLEAR, 49151

where 49152 is the address where your subroutine begins. This keeps BASIC from extending its data space beyond 49151; if more space is needed, the program goes down with an 'Out of memory' error. The upper limit of 49151 remains in effect during the execution of this program only. The other way to set an upper boundary is with the /M switch in the start-up command. If you start BASIC with the command

    BASIC /M:49151

the upper boundary will remain in effect as long as BASIC is active without a reboot or a SYSTEM command.

The machine-language subroutine can be loaded in one of two ways. Long subroutines written in assembly language should be linked and loaded into a .COM file. Prior to entering BASIC, key the name of the .COM file as a transient command. This will bring the subroutine into memory. Then go into BASIC and run your program, taking steps to protect it as described above.

In the case of short routines, you can hand assemble them and use POKEs in your BASIC program to place the codes in memory before the first call to the subroutine. This is best done by putting the codes associated with the machine-language instructions into DATA statements, then moving them to memory with a short READ/POKE loop in the program's self-initialization phase.

As an example of the use and interfacing of machine-language subroutines, we'll use a short module that converts a string of uppercase alphabetics to lower case. For the sake of brevity this subroutine is somewhat less selective than a "live" one ought to be because it doesn't verify that each character it converts is an uppercase letter. It only filters out space characters. Bear this in mind if you actually test it, and don't include digits or punctuation in your test data.

The subroutine itself is shown in Figure 12.1, the only non-BASIC program in this book. If you want to try it, use a general-purpose editor, such as the CP/M ED command, to enter the program, and save it in the file UC2LC.ASM. Assemble the program with the command

    ASM UC2LC

(*Note:* The files ASM.COM and LOAD.COM must be on your working disk to do this.) Finally, place the program into an executable .COM file by entering

LOAD UC2LC

You can ignore messages that pop up during execution of these commands, unless they indicate an error. Any errors will probably be the result of typos you made, or else you're trying to assemble 8080 code for a different CPU type. The flow of this subroutine will be discussed presently.

```
; PROGRAM 'UC2LC.ASM'                              K. PORTER 2/9/83
; 8080 ASSEMBLY LANGUAGE SUBROUTINE TO CONVERT UPPER CASE TO LOWER CASE.
; CALLED AS USR FUNCTION BY MICROSOFT BASIC.
; AT ENTRY, DE REGISTERS POINT TO STRING DESCRIPTOR.
;;
UC2LC   ORG     49152           ; START OF SUBROUTINE
        XCHG                    ; POINTER INTO HL REGISTERS FROM DE
        MOV     C,M             ; GET STRING LENGTH INTO C
        INX     H
        MOV     E,M             ; GET ADDRESS OF STRING INTO DE REGISTERS
        INX     H
        MOV     D,M
        XCHG                    ;    THEN PUT INTO HL REGISTERS
; LOOP TO CONVERT UPPER CASE TO LOWER CASE
LOOP    MOV     A,M             ; GET NEXT CHARACTER
        CPI     ' '             ; IS IT A SPACE?
        JZ      SKIP            ; SKIP IF SO
        ADI     32              ;      ELSE CONVERT TO LOWER CASE
        MOV     M,A             ;      AND PUT BACK INTO STRING
SKIP    INX     H               ; POINT TO NEXT CHARACTER
        DCR     C               ; COUNT
        JNZ     LOOP            ; REPEAT TO END OF STRING
        RET                     ;      THEN RETURN TO CALLER
```

Figure 12.1 Program UC2LC.ASM.

The first method of interfacing with a machine-language subroutine that we'll cover is the BASIC function USR, in which the subroutine is treated and called much the same as user-defined functions described in Chapter 8.

The existence of the subroutine must be made known to BASIC. This is done with a DEF statement similar to that for a function. For this subroutine we can code

DEF USRØ = 49152

USRØ is declared as the symbolic name of a subroutine that begins at address 49152. A second subroutine would be called USR1, a third USR2, etc., up through USR9, with their starting points declared by statements of this type. You can omit the digit if there's only one such subroutine, so in this particular case it would be okay to refer to UC2LC as simply USR. The designation USR is required for such a function.

Since UC2LC works on a string that can be anywhere in memory, the string's name has to be furnished as an argument of the USR function. To operate on the string D$, call the subroutine with USRØ(D$). The USR is functionally the same as any other function, so it must be included in an instruction, as in

```
LET Y$ = A$ + USRØ(B$)
```

This statement converts B$ to lower case, concatenates it after A$, and assigns the result to Y$.

Let's say we have an uppercase string S$, and we want to convert it to lower case and display the results on the screen. This is done by issuing the instruction

```
PRINT USRØ(S$)
```

Several things happen here. First, the address of S$ is placed in the DE register pair and BASIC, referring to the DEF USRØ statement, transfers control to its defined address (49152). The machine-language subroutine runs, converting the string. It returns to BASIC with the RET instruction, and BASIC then displays the reworked string S$.

To demonstrate this in action, enter the CP/M command level (by booting the computer, or from BASIC by entering the command SYSTEM). When A> appears on the screen, type UC2LC. The A> reappears after some disk activity. The machine-language program has now been loaded into memory at 49152. Now type BASIC. It loads and starts to run, but the code at 49152 remains intact.

With the OK prompt on the screen, enter the following:

```
100   CLEAR, 49151
110   DEF USR = 49152
120   INPUT A$
130   PRINT USR(A$)
140   GOTO 120
RUN
```

This simple program prompts you with a question mark. Type any uppercase text (no numbers or punctuation marks, please) and it prints the same text in lower case, then prompts again. You can stop it by pressing BREAK (or CTL-C).

Now let's investigate what's really happening. In line 13Ø the subroutine is called as a function with the argument A$. The call, however, doesn't furnish the actual address of the string A$. Instead it sets up the DE register pair to point to a "string descriptor," a control block in the BASIC symbol table, where A$ is described. The first byte of the string descriptor contains the length of A$, and its other two bytes give the starting address of the string.

Thus, when UC2LC gets control it "knows" the string descriptor address is in the DE register pair. Using this address, it gets the length into register C and the string location into the HL register pair. The loop in UC2LC fetches successive characters from the string and (except for spaces) converts them to lower case. For each character processed it bumps the string pointer in HL and decrements the count in C, repeating until the count reaches zero and the string is therefore entirely processed. It returns to BASIC with the RET instruction.

Because numeric variables don't have a string descriptor, processing them in a machine-language subroutine differs from this example. Consult the Microsoft BASIC manual for details of numeric types, implementations, and parameters in machine language.

The other method for using machine-language subroutines is through the CALL instruction. This statement is available in other BASICs as well as Microsoft. Its general form is

```
CALL [addr]
```

where [addr] is a numeric variable containing the address where the subroutine begins. When BASIC encounters this statement, it transfers control to the instruction at the named location. The subroutine then runs until it comes to a RET, returning the same way as a USR call.

Subroutines that are CALLed don't have to be declared via the DEF statement. They should be protected as discussed earlier. Note that the address of the subroutine in a CALL *has* to be a numeric variable; it cannot be specified directly in the CALL statement in Microsoft BASIC. This is not so in other BASICs.

The CALL statement above passes no parameters, that is, it gives the machine-language module no data to work on. Subroutines are occasionally called to perform non-data-related work (e.g., turning a remote device on or off), but ordinarily it's necessary to furnish them with further information, just as in the case of USR calls. Therefore, you can extend the CALL statement to include an argument list in parentheses. In the example of the subroutine to convert upper case to lower case, you'd call it with

```
LET A = 49152
CALL A (S$)
```

This statement has the same effect as USR(S$) in that it calls the subroutine at address A (= 49152) and passes it a pointer to the string descriptor for S$.

The CALL instruction, however, is more flexible than USR. A CALL can pass several parameters, whereas USR can pass only one. If you had another machine-language subroutine at address B that required three numeric arguments, you could call it with

```
CALL B (A, E, R)
```

The CALL instruction can pass any number of parameters this way.

The CALL statement sets up linkage to the machine-language subroutine differently than USR, which means that the subroutine must be specifically written to be called either by USR or CALL. CALL, like USR, furnishes pointers to numerics and string descriptors, but the register usage is not the same. In a CALL the first parameter is in the HL register pair, the second in DE, and the BC registers point to a list of the others in memory. Consequently, the subroutine has to know not only which kind of instruction called it, but how many arguments are being passed and their data types, and it has to act on these registers accordingly.

To modify the UC2LC subroutine for a CALL instead of USR, simply delete the first XCHG. Because the first (and only) parameter is already in the HL registers, the XCHG, which swaps DE and HL, isn't needed. Reassemble and load the UC2LC as before, then key its name as a command. After reentering BASIC, type in the following short program:

```
100    LET U = 49152
110    INPUT A$
120    CALL U (A$)
130    PRINT A$
140    GOTO 110
RUN
```

This program operates the same as the one demonstrating USR, and shows a simple implementation of the CALL instruction.

CHAPTER 13

DIALECTS OF BASIC

How BASICs differ. Radio Shack: Level II and Model II. Applesoft DOS BASIC. CBASIC and CB80.

How BASICs differ

In a broad sense all versions of BASIC are pretty much the same. You can look at a program in any dialect and immediately identify it as being written in BASIC. Assignment, functions, subroutines, string handling, calculations... all are about the same across the spectrum of BASICs. It's mostly details that differ, and that cause problems.

The one major discrepancy among BASIC dialects is in file handling. They all have some form of sequential and random files and some sort of OPEN statement, but the similarities end there. It's easy to believe that these differences have something to do with hardware and/or operating system, but that's not so. CBASIC and Microsoft BASIC both work under CP/M, but their file handling differs. Microsoft BASIC also works on the Apple II, and its file handling is the same there as it is under CP/M but very different from Applesoft DOS BASIC's. Obviously, it's not the environment, but rather the preference of the language designer, that drives the file handling techniques.

In the area of minor differences that make a program work fine under one BASIC but strangely under another are such as the RND function, LINE INPUT vs. INPUT LINE, the requirements for numbering program lines, support of long variable names, and other piddling but sometimes crucial details. There is also this insidious thing called extensions, which makes for instructions that appear in one BASIC but not in any other and whose purposes are almost impossible to discern (usually they turn out to be the key elements in whether or not a program works when moved to a different BASIC). And finally, there is the apparent aversion of those who publish BASIC programs to say which dialect they're written in.

The American National Standards Institute (ANSI) tried to make headway against this mishmash by adopting a minimal standard, saying that every BASIC has to include certain instructions with specific meanings. That was in 1978, and since then microcomputers have flourished and so have dialects of BASIC, some of which observe the ANSI standard when it's convenient. As of this writing, ANSI is attempting to formalize a much broader standard that will define the language once and for all. This is a laudable objective; unfortunately the proposed standard bears little resemblance to the actual BASICs in everyday use on a million computers. It's so sophisticated and incorporates so many enhancements that it seems predestined to be ignored. Had the ANSI effort been less ambitious and simply tried to reconcile the differences in existing BASICs, the vendors might be willing to listen, but probably no one is going to rebuild a successful BASIC product from the ground up just to make ANSI happy. The bottom line will no doubt be that the ANSI standard will become just another dialect of BASIC.

Given the proliferation of BASICs, there's no way to cover all of them in this brief treatment. Instead we'll discuss three major dialects, comparing highlights with Microsoft BASIC to get a feel for how dialects differ.

Appendix A contains a chart of the instructions and functions in each of the BASICs we'll discuss. This is a raw measure comparison that doesn't reflect nuances and syntax and options. It also omits graphics and color-related instructions available in Applesoft BASIC. The intent is not to show every single instruction in each of the four dialects but rather to show where they converge.

Radio Shack

Tandy actually offers a slightly different version of BASIC for each of their computer types, and all are variants of Microsoft BASIC, except for those on the color machine and the pocket computers. Level I BASIC is for nondisk machines (Models I and III), Level II is for those systems with disk drives, and Model II BASIC applies to the larger Models II, 12, and 16.

The Level II and Model II BASICs—yes, the designations are indeed confusing—closely parallel both each other and the general Microsoft BASIC discussed in this book. In fact, Tandy contracted with Microsoft to adapt its BASIC to their machines, so it's hardly surprising that Radio Shack BASIC is so close to the non-machine-specific version.

In adapting it, some changes were made. Some of these changes utilize hardware features unique to Radio Shack computers and are thus understandable and useful. Others are of a niggling and somewhat irrational nature and probably represent the flexing of someone's ego at the Tandy Corporation; there's no other apparent reason for them.

In the latter category, for example, is the BASIC prompt. In the general Microsoft BASIC it's "OK," but in Radio Shack BASIC it's "READY." Everything else concerning interaction with the interpreter is the same—EDIT commands, insertion/deletion, SAVE, RUN—only the prompt is different. Another example is in the NAME instruction, where "AS" has been changed to "TO." The following statements have the identical effect.

```
Microsoft      —  NAME A$ AS B$
Radio Shack    —  NAME A$ TO B$
```

Some instructions got left behind in the transfer. Radio Shack BASIC doesn't have the WHILE/WEND loop-control statements, while MBASIC does. Model II BASIC lacks (but Levels I and II do have) the POKE/PEEK instructions. There are other minor differences of this sort. Viewing them, one has to wonder why.

On the other hand, Radio Shack BASIC has a few instructions tied to the hardware, which a generalized product written for a diversified hardware market can't support. Notable among them is the PRINT@ statement, which places the cursor on a Radio Shack screen at a specified location and outputs from there. This is a good instruction and it's a shame a generalized BASIC can't be custom-configured (like the WordStar INSTALL feature) to support cursor addressing via PRINT@.

Unfortunately there's a discrepancy in PRINT@ between Level I/II and Model II BASIC. Level I/II is oriented toward small-screen (16 × 64) machines, where the display positions are sequentially numbered Ø . . . 1Ø23. To place the cursor at a given row/column you have to convert the coordinates into a print position. Row 3, column 7 is at position ((3 × 64) + 7) − 1 = 198, so to display the string T$ there you code

```
PRINT@ 198, T$
```

Model II BASIC is intended for full-screen (80 × 24) displays. On these machines the print positions are numbered Ø . . . 1919. The rub is that if you transfer a Level I/II program to a Model II and run it as is, the PRINT@ above places the cursor at row 2, column 39, instead of at row 3, column 7. Because the lines have different lengths (64 vs. 80) on the two classes of machines, position 198 occurs at different places on the displays.

The Model II PRINT@ has an optional alternate form for specifying the row and column directly, so you can code

```
PRINT@ (3,7), T$
```

and the cursor will be placed at the proper coordinates. Unfortunately, however, this form isn't available in Level I/II, so migration simply isn't graceful from one version of Radio Shack BASIC to the other, even though the code might look the same.

There are a few other hardware-dependent discrepancies as well. Model I and Model III have primitive graphics invoked by the SET and RESET instructions, which turn individual pixels (picture elements) on and off (using, it should be noted, a different coordinate system than row/column or print position). The upper level machines don't have pixels, relying instead on dot-matrix formation, and graphics are available only by purchasing an optional package, so Model II BASIC has no SET or RESET instructions. Meanwhile, standard Microsoft BASIC has a RESET *not* available in Radio Shack versions that reinitializes the disk controller, a function utterly unlike extinguishing a blip of light on a screen.

If you find this confusing, you're beginning to grasp the dimensions of the dialect problem. The upshot is that Level I/II, Model II, and Microsoft standard BASIC are all very similar, but not 100 percent compatible.

Applesoft DOS BASIC

BASIC is, as we've said, pretty much BASIC from one dialect to another. Most instructions from Microsoft BASIC work the same in Applesoft BASIC as far as computations, input, output, and control statements are concerned. The differences are fairly easy to deal with and can be translated without a great deal of expertise.

Applesoft, however, is implemented very differently from Microsoft BASIC, and file handling bears little resemblance to anything discussed in Chapters 10 and 11.

BASIC is the native language of Apple computers: Turn on the machine and you've got BASIC, because it's part of the system hardware (in ROM). It's divided into three levels called integer, floating point, and DOS (Disk Operating System). The first two are in ROM and you can switch from one to the other by typing INT or FP, commands whose intents are obvious. If you have disk drives, Apple DOS BASIC loads from the disk on power-up and automatically extends the ROM-based BASICs to include disk management through access to the operating system. You can only escape from BASIC by entering the MON command, which turns off the ROM interpreter and puts you into the monitor mode so that you converse directly with DOS.

As in Microsoft BASIC, Applesoft lets you execute statements in direct mode by omitting line numbers. These instructions are executed immediately as commands. If you precede statements with line numbers, they're stored as program instructions and can be run, saved, loaded, edited, etc., with commands slightly different from but equivalent to Microsoft's.

Applesoft is easy to use and fairly powerful, but it lacks a PRINT USING statement. Inasmuch as this is one of the most useful instructions in BASIC programming (and in any other application calling for good-looking output), its absence constitutes a distressing weakness.

On the other hand, Applesoft has numerous color- and graphics-oriented instructions (not included in Appendix A) that make for exquisite displays. The lack of PRINT USING but the inclusion of superb graphics perhaps reflects the early market thrust of Apple Computer toward home computing and games rather than toward professional/business applications. It must be said, though, that color graphics are finding a home in the business world, and they're well suited to statistics, charts, bar graphs, and the like, where different colors represent different measurable elements. It's just a shame there's no PRINT USING.

Applesoft also has a less disappointing but still disturbing characteristic called "tokenization." What this means is that what you see as you enter program lines is not what you get when you list the program later. Applesoft reformats lines automatically, taking out extra spaces and generally wreaking havoc with all precepts of program readability. You cannot, for instance, neatly line up remarks along the right side of the listing. You can type them that way, but Applesoft will shove them over to the end of the program instruction regardless, compressing the lines and creating a tight, barely legible mass of statements and text. Likewise, Applesoft won't let you indent loops. Tokenization thus makes Apple BASIC programs hard to read and there's nothing you can do about it.

Apple BASIC doesn't actually have any file handling statements of its own. Instead, the DOS acts on English-like command strings passed to it either from the keyboard or from an executing program. A command string is sent to DOS from a program by a PRINT, with a control-D [CHR$(4)] preceding the command text. To open a file called CLASS1, you code

```
PRINT CHR$(4) "OPEN CLASS1"
```

The PRINT dispatches the ensuing text to DOS for processing, and CHR$(4) tells DOS to execute the text rather than outputting it.

When you're ready to start writing records to the file, you issue the statement

```
PRINT CHR$(4) "WRITE CLASS1"
```

Subsequent to this instruction, all PRINTs write to the file instead of the display. Normal operation of PRINT is restored by

```
PRINT CHR$(4) "CLOSE CLASS1"
```

If you have several files open, you have to designate which file to print to by a preceding WRITE.

Similarly, a file called INFILE open for input is read by

PRINT CHR$(4) "READ INFILE"

and then all subsequent INPUT instructions read sequential records from it, until the file is closed or a different file is selected by another READ command.

Additions to sequential files are easier in Applesoft than in Microsoft BASIC. Instead of transferring records and adding and renaming and all that rigmarole, in Apple BASIC you simply open the file and issue an APPEND command. The DOS finds the end of the file and all PRINTs write to it from that point.

Random files are likewise easier to use in Applesoft. All files are in ASCII, so there's no need for the FIELD statement. The OPEN statement includes a record length; for example,

PRINT CHR$(4) "OPEN RFILE,L64"

where L64 indicates a record length of 64 bytes and its inclusion notifies DOS that this is a random file.

Two instructions are needed to read and write a record. The first tells DOS which operation and the record number, the second is an INPUT or PRINT to move the actual data between BASIC and DOS. For example, to read record #8:

```
210   PRINT CHR$(4) "READ RFILE,R8"
220   INPUT A1$, B, C2
```

Applesoft doesn't support long variable names (a minus), nor does it have single- and double-precision numerics (a plus). In floating-point BASIC, Applesoft has three data types: integer, floating point, and string. The range of values is 1×10^{-38} to 1×10^{38}. Decimal numbers can have up to nine digits.

By and large, with the exception of the two drawbacks mentioned earlier, Applesoft is a good language that demands less of the programmer than does Microsoft.

CBASIC and CB80

Digital Research, those same folks who gave us CP/M, sells a sophisticated product called CBASIC. This dialect is slanted toward professional programmers who develop software packages for sale.

CBASIC has two independent levels. The first is a semicompiler that translates source language statements into an "intermediate language level," that is, a bunch of gibberish, which is then interpreted by the run-time program CRUN.

For example, suppose you have a program called BUDGET. The source program is created by an editor and saved in a file with the name BUDGET.BAS. To semicompile it, you enter the command

```
CBASIC BUDGET
```

The output of the CBASIC semicompiler is another file called BUDGET.INT. When you want to run it, you type

```
CRUN BUDGET
```

CRUN is a separate program from CBASIC. It gets BUDGET.INT and converts the intermediate language into action. The .INT file cannot be listed, nor can it be changed except by recompiling, nor can it be executed except by CRUN. Therefore BUDGET.INT can be sold as a proprietary software product to anyone who owns the CRUN program, and the developer need have no fear that someone can steal the code and change it a little for resale.

The other level of CBASIC is a full, true compiler product named CB8Ø. CB8Ø takes a .BAS file and converts it (with an interim link step) into a machine-language program in a .COM file that can be run without the assistance of CRUN.

To a great extent this dual-level approach parallels the Microsoft BASIC interpreter and compiler products.

Although CBASIC instructions are pretty much the same as or equivalent to any other BASIC's, there is one very dramatic departure in CBASIC: no line numbers. You may use line numbers if you wish, but they are of no value and CBASIC ignores them. It assumes that instructions are to be taken in the order specified. (CBASIC, unlike the other dialects discussed here, has no build-in editor, so source language files are entered and modified by a separate text editor, such as the CP/M ED program.)

For GOTOs and GOSUBs, program sections and target statements are identified in CBASIC by labels. A label can be either a number or an alphanumeric identifier, so it's valid to write an instruction such as

```
GOSUB TAX.COMPUTATION
```

where TAX.COMPUTATION is the name of a subroutine. You can also use a number that looks like a line number but really isn't, for example,

```
GOSUB 9Ø15
```

Numeric labels can have decimal points, too, so that you can have a label such as 9Ø15.3 and it won't conflict with 9Ø15. There is no requirement to observe numeric progression in labels, with the result that label 9Ø15 can be followed by label 1ØØ. Labels are only reference points for transfer of control, and consequently few statements in a CBASIC program have anything resembling a line number. Until you get used to it, it looks funny.

Compared with Microsoft, CBASIC's facilities for calling machine-language subroutines are simpler but just as powerful. There is no USR function, but it's possible to define multiple-line functions and execute them with a CALL, and to call separate assembly language routines. CBASIC supports program chaining and, with the CB80 compiler, a true overlay structure that offers more flexibility than either the Microsoft interpreter or compiler. Its string handling lacks the MID$ = instruction and an INSTR function, both of which are unfortunate omissions, but string manipulations are very efficient in CBASIC. Floating-point numbers are double precision ("real" in CBASIC), and it also has an integer type.

File handling in CBASIC is rather easier than in MBASIC. Sequential files can be read and written on the same open, although this can be risky; when you write to a sequential file, the EOF marker is placed at the end of the newly written record. As a result, a misplaced write in the middle of a file deletes everything from there onward. On the other hand, to append to a file you read to EOF and then start writing to the same file, without copying over and renaming and so on.

Files can be either in ASCII (like Apple) or in binary (like MBASIC). READ# and PRINT# are the ASCII file I/O statements, with a record number included for random files as well as a record length in the OPEN statement, but lacking these parameters for sequential files. For binary files, GET and PUT are used; these functions are rather difficult to use in that they work on only one byte at a time. PRINT USING can write to either sequential or random ASCII files, although the format differs from that required by Microsoft BASIC.

In general, CBASIC is less convenient for program development than MBASIC, since a correction requires reopening the source file, making the change, and then recompiling. Compile times probably average five minutes, but I've had some take up to twenty. That can mean a lot of time fixing pesky bugs. On the other hand, CBASIC is a big, rich, powerful dialect of BASIC, well suited to the needs of professional programmers and in every way a respectable competitor for Microsoft BASIC.

APPENDIX A

CROSS-REFERENCE OF FOUR MAJOR BASIC DIALECTS

Instruction	CBASIC	Applesoft	Radio Shack	Microsoft
ABS(X)	X	X	X	X
AND	X	X	X	X
APPEND	.	X	.	.
ASC(X$)	X	X	X	X
ATN(X)	X	X	X	X
AUTO	.	.	X	X
BUFF	X	.	.	.
CALL	X	X	.	X
CATALOG	.	X	.	.
CDBL(X)	.	.	X	X
CHAIN	X	X	.	X
CHR$(X)	X	X	X	X
CINT(X)	.	.	X	X
CLEAR	.	X	X	X
CLOSE	X	X	X	X
CLS	.	.	X	.
COMMAND$	X	.	.	.
COMMON	X	.	.	X
CONCHAR%	X	.	.	.
CONSOLE	X	.	.	.
CONSTAT%	X	.	.	.
CONT	.	X	X	X
COS(X)	X	X	X	X
CREATE	X	.	.	.
CSNG(X)	.	.	X	X
CVD(X)	.	.	X	X
CVI(X)	.	.	X	X
CVS(X)	.	.	X	X
DATA	X	X	X	X
DATE$	.	.	X	.
DEF FN	X	X	X	X

Instruction	CBASIC	Applesoft	Radio Shack	Microsoft
DEF (type)	.	.	X	X
DELETE (file)	X	X	.	.
DELETE (lines)	.	X	X	X
DIM	X	X	X	X
EDIT	.	.	X	X
ELSE	X	.	X	X
END	X	X	X	X
EOF(X)	.	.	X	X
ERASE	.	.	X	X
ERL	.	.	X	X
ERR	X	.	X	X
ERRL	X	.	.	.
ERR$	.	.	X	.
ERROR	X	.	X	X
EQ	X	.	.	.
EQV	.	.	X	X
EXP(X)	X	X	X	X
EXTERNAL	X	.	.	.
FEND	X	.	.	.
FIELD	.	.	X	X
FILES	.	.	.	X
FIX(X)	.	.	X	X
FLOAT	X	.	.	.
FOR/NEXT	X	X	X	X
FRE	X	X	X	X
GE	X	.	.	.
GET	X	X	X	X
GO	X	.	.	.
GOSUB	X	X	X	X
GOTO	X	X	X	X
GT	X	.	.	.
HEX$(X)	.	.	X	X
IF END#	X	.	.	.
IF EOF(X)	.	.	X	X
IF/THEN	X	X	X	X
IMP	.	.	X	X
INIT	.	X	.	.
INITIALIZE	X	.	.	.
INKEY$	X	.	X	X
INP(X)	X	.	.	.
INPUT	X	X	X	X
INPUT#	.	.	X	X

Instruction	CBASIC	Applesoft	Radio Shack	Microsoft
INPUT$	.	.	X	X
INPUT LINE	X	.	.	.
INSTR	.	.	X	X
INT(X)	X	X	X	X
INTEGER	X	.	.	.
KILL	.	.	X	X
LE	X	.	.	.
LEFT$(X$)	X	X	X	X
LEN(X$)	X	X	X	X
LET	X	X	X	X
LINE INPUT	.	.	X	X
LINE INPUT#	.	.	X	X
LIST	.	X	X	X
LLIST	.	.	X	X
LOAD	.	X	X	X
LOC	.	.	X	X
LOCK	X	X	.	.
LOF(X)	.	.	X	X
LOG(X)	X	X	X	X
LOMEM	.	X	.	.
LPOS	.	.	.	X
LPRINT	.	.	X	X
LPRINT USING	.	.	X	X
LPRINTER	X	.	.	.
LSET	.	.	X	X
LT	X	.	.	.
MATCH	X	.	.	.
MEM	.	.	X	.
MERGE	.	.	X	X
MFRE	X	.	.	.
MID$	X	X	X	X
MID$=	.	.	X	X
MKD$	.	.	X	X
MKI$	.	.	X	X
MKS$	.	.	X	X
MOD	X	X	X	X
NAME	.	.	X	X
NE	X	.	.	.
NEW	.	X	X	X
NOT	X	X	X	X
NULL	.	.	.	X
OCT$	.	.	X	X

Instruction	CBASIC	Applesoft	Radio Shack	Microsoft
ON ERROR GOTO	X	X	X	X
ON/GOSUB	X	X	X	X
ON/GOTO	X	X	X	X
OPEN	X	X	X	X
OPTION BASE	.	.	.	X
OR	X	X	X	X
OUT(X)	X	.	X	X
PEEK(X)	X	X	.	X
POKE	X	X	.	X
POS	X	X	X	X
POSITION (file)	.	X	.	.
PRINT	X	X	X	X
PRINT USING	X	.	X	X
PRINT#	.	.	X	X
PRINT# USING	.	.	X	X
PRINT @ (pos)	.	.	X	.
PUT	X	.	X	X
RANDOM	.	.	X	.
RANDOMIZE	X	.	.	X
READ (data)	X	X	X	X
READ (file)	X	X	.	.
REAL	X	.	.	.
RECL	X	.	.	.
REM	X	X	X	X
RENAME	X	X	.	.
RENUM	.	.	X	X
RESET	.	.	.	X
RESTORE	X	X	X	X
RESUME	.	X	X	X
RETURN	X	X	X	X
RIGHT$(X$)	X	X	X	X
RND	X	X	X	X
ROW	.	.	X	.
RSET	.	.	X	X
RUN	.	X	X	X
SADD(X$)	X	.	.	.
SAVE	.	X	X	X
SGN(X)	X	X	X	X
SIN(X)	X	X	X	X
SIZE(X$)	X	.	.	.
SPACE$(X)	.	.	X	X
SPC(X)	.	X	X	X

Instruction	CBASIC	Applesoft	Radio Shack	Microsoft
SQR(X)	X	X	X	X
STEP	X	X	X	X
STOP	X	X	X	X
STR$(X)	X	X	X	X
STRING$	X	.	X	X
SWAP	.	.	X	X
SYSTEM	.	.	X	X
TAB(X)	X	X	X	X
TAN(X)	X	X	X	X
TIME$	.	.	X	.
UCASE$(X$)	X	.	.	.
UNLOCK	X	X	.	.
USR(X)	.	X	X	X
VAL(X$)	X	X	X	X
VARPTR(X)	X	.	X	X
VERIFY	.	X	X	.
WAIT	.	X	.	X
WHILE/WEND	X	.	.	X
WIDTH	X	.	.	X
WRITE	.	.	.	X
WRITE (file)	.	X	.	X
XOR	X	.	X	X

APPENDIX B

MICROSOFT BASIC ERROR CODES, MESSAGES, AND EXPLANATIONS

When Microsoft BASIC detects an error condition, it loads a system variable called ERR with an integer code indicating the nature of the error. The program can trap the error by issuing the instruction ON ERROR GOTO [line number], where [line number] is the start of a user-written error handler. This error handler can then access the error code by utilizing ERR as a program variable. The condition can be overridden and execution continued with appropriate action followed by the RESUME instruction.

When there is no user-written error handler, Microsoft BASIC suspends execution on detecting an error condition and issues a standard message keyed to the value in ERR. Following are the error codes and their corresponding standard messages, along with explanations of the probable causes.

ERR	*Text*
1	NEXT without FOR In a FOR/NEXT loop, a NEXT statement was issued without a preceding FOR, or the variable cited in the NEXT does not match the variable in the most recent FOR. Loops can't overlap each other.
2	Syntax error The statement is improperly formed and BASIC cannot figure out what's wrong with it. Look for misspelled instructions, unmatched left and right parentheses, missing punctuation or operators.
3	RETURN without GOSUB A subroutine was entered improperly (without being called by a GOSUB). Check to make sure the preceding instructions jumped around the subroutine.

4 Out of data
A READ instruction is attempting to read past the end of data in DATA statements. To prevent this error, set an end-of-data value and test for it after each READ so that the program knows when there is no more data.

5 Illegal function call
Something is wrong with the way the function call is set up. Check to make sure the number of arguments agrees with those required for the function. Also, check that none are zeros or null strings, and that the data types of the arguments are appropriate (not trying to pass a numeric for a string, etc.).

6 Overflow
The program has computed a value too large to be represented in BASIC.

7 Out of memory
The amount of data being processed and the program size together have consumed all the available memory in the computer. This error also occurs when there are too many unresolved GOSUBs and FOR/NEXT loops. See the discussion of CLEAR in Chapter 12 for suggestions.

8 Undefined line
A GOTO, GOSUB, or other line-oriented instruction has attempted to reference a nonexistent line number.

9 Subscript out of range
The subscript is greater than the dimensioned size of the array or list. Also occurs when an incorrect number of subscripts is specified (e.g., two subscripts for a one-dimensional list).

1Ø Redimensioned array
A DIM statement is attempting to dimension an array that has already been dimensioned. To redimension an array, first issue an ERASE statement. Also, if the first use of a variable includes a subscript, BASIC automatically gives that variable a dimension of 1Ø; a subsequent DIM for the variable causes this error to occur.

11 Division by zero
The divisor is a zero; division by zero is a mathematical impossibility. This error also occurs in attempting to raise zero to a negative power. Division by zero doesn't halt the program, but the results are dubious.

12 Illegal direct
Some statements in BASIC cannot be used in direct mode.

This error message only appears when such a statement is keyed as a BASIC command (without a line number).

13 Type mismatch
The statement is attempting to mix strings and numerics, as in addition of a number to a string. Also, a function that expects a numeric is given a string argument or vice versa.

14 Out of string space
BASIC has used up all memory available for string data. This is similar to the out of memory condition (error 7).

15 String too long
The maximum string length in BASIC is 255 characters. The string in the offending instruction is longer than that.

16 String formula too complex
Too many string functions have been placed into a single statement. Break the statement into several steps.

17 Can't continue
The program has halted due to an error that prevents it from resuming, or during a break in execution a statement was modified and you tried to resume.

18 Undefined user function
A USR (subroutine) function has been called without first being defined by the DEF USR statement.

19 No RESUME
An error handler is attempting to resume execution by a GOTO rather than by a RESUME, thereby not canceling the error condition. Substitute RESUME [line number] for GOTO [line number] and try it again.

20 RESUME without error
A RESUME statement has been encountered when there was no error in the program, so now there is one. Take it out.

21 Unprintable error
Although it seems that BASIC is furious with you, this message simply means that there is no standard error message to diagnose the problem.

22 Missing operand
An instruction has specified a mathematical or logical operation with only one operand, for example, LET A = B +. This is usually the result of a typo.

23 Line buffer overflow
There are too many characters in the input line.

26 FOR without NEXT
BASIC never found a NEXT statement to match the FOR, so the loop is incomplete.

29 WHILE without WEND
Similar to FOR without NEXT (error 26).

30 WEND without WHILE
A WEND statement has attempted to terminate a loop that was never started with a WHILE.

50 Field overflow
The total number of bytes in a FIELD statement is greater than the record length declared for the file, or the program is trying to write more data into the field buffer than it is built to contain.

51 Internal error
You have discovered a bug in Microsoft BASIC. This problem should be reported to Microsoft. They might ask you for a copy of your program so they can replicate the failure.

52 Bad file number
The program has attempted to access a file reference number that hasn't been assigned in an OPEN statement. Also, if you attempt to open more than three files without starting BASIC with the /F option, this error will occur.

53 File not found
Your program is trying to LOAD, KILL, OPEN, or reNAME a file that doesn't exist under the specified name.

54 Bad file mode
You're trying to use random file instructions with a file opened "I" or "O", or to write to a file opened "I" or vice versa, or the OPEN statement has a mode specification other than I, O, or R. Check the OPEN statement.

55 File already open
An attempt is being made to open a file for output that's already open "O", or to kill a file that's still open.

57 Disk I/O error
A read or write to disk failed. This is most often due to a faulty diskette; run a surface analysis program to test the diskette. It also occurs because of hardware problems.

58 File already exists
A NAME instruction is trying to give a file a name that is

already in use on the diskette. Duplicate file names are not permitted on the same storage medium.

61 Disk full
The program is trying to write more data to a diskette that is completely filled.

62 Input past end
The end of the file has been reached (or the file is empty) and the program is attempting to read from it. The IF EOF statement should be used to avoid this error.

63 Bad record number
The record number given for a random file record is either less than 1 or greater than 32767.

64 Bad file name
The file name specified in an OPEN, LOAD, SAVE, KILL, or RUN instruction violates the rules for naming files.

66 Direct statement in file
A BASIC program loaded from disk contains a line without a line number. The LOAD stops on finding a direct statement, and the only way to inspect the program file is with a file dump utility (e.g., Figure 10.10).

67 Too many files
The diskette directory is full and an attempt is being made to save or create another file on the diskette.

APPENDIX C

EXTENDED TRIGONOMETRIC FUNCTIONS

The built-in BASIC trigonometric functions can be combined to calculate extended functions used in higher mathematics.

Note that all trig functions in BASIC use radians rather than degrees. The following are conversion factors:

Radians to degrees	rad / .Ø17453
Degrees to radians	deg * .Ø17453

The following are extended function definitions that can be used in BASIC programs exactly as shown, when the BASIC in use supports long variable names. Note that the symbol A is used here as a dummy argument. The name of each function is followed by its defijnition using standard built-in functions.

Secant
```
DEF FNSEC(A)        = 1 / COS(A)
```
Cosecant
```
DEF FNCSC(A)        = 1 / SIN(A)
```
Cotangent
```
DEF FNCOT(A         = 1 / TAN(A)
```
Inverse sine
```
DEF FNARCSIN(A)     = ATN(A / SQR(-A * A + 1))
```
Inverse cosine
```
DEF FNARCCOS(A)     = -ATN(A / SQR(-A * A + 1)) + 1.57Ø8
```
Inverse secant
```
DEF FNARCSEC(A)     = ATN(A / SQR(A * A - 1)) +
                      SGN(SGN(A)-1) * 1.57Ø8
```
Inverse cosecant
```
DEF FNARCCSC(A)     = ATN(A / SQR(A * A - 1)) +
                      (SGN(X)-1) * 1.57Ø8
```
Inverse cotangent
```
DEF FNARCCOT(A)     = ATN(A) + 1.57Ø8
```
Hyperbolic sine
```
DEF FNSINH(A)       = EXP(A) - EXP(-A)) / 2
```

Hyperbolic cosine
DEF FNCOSH(A) = (EXP(A) + EXP(−A)) / 2

Hyperbolic tangent
DEF FNTANH(A) = ((EXP(−A) / EXP(A) + EXP(−A)) * 2) + 1

Hyperbolic secant
DEF FNSECH(A) = 2 / (EXP(A) + EXP(−A))

Hyperbolic cosecant
DEF FNCSCH(A) = 2 / (EXP(A) − EXP(−A))

Hyperbolic contangent
DEF FNCOTH(A) = (EXP(−A) / (EXP(A) − EXP(−A)) * 2) + 1

Inverse hyperbolic sine
DEF FNARCSINH(A) = LOG(A + SQR(A * A + 1))

Inverse hyperbolic cosine
DEF FNARCCOSH(A) = LOG(A + SQR(A * A − 1))

Inverse hyperbolic tangent
DEF FNARCTANH(A) = LOG((1 + A) / (1 − A)) / 2

Inverse hyperbolic secant
DEF FNARCSECH(A) = LOG((SQR(−A * A + 1) + 1) / A)

Inverse hyperbolic cosecant
DEF FNARCCSCH(A) = LOG((SGN(A) * SQR(A * A + 1) / A)

Inverse hyperbolic cotangent
DEF FNARCCOTH(A) = LOG((A + 1) / (A − 1)) / 2

INDEX